100 Years

. 100 Works of Art

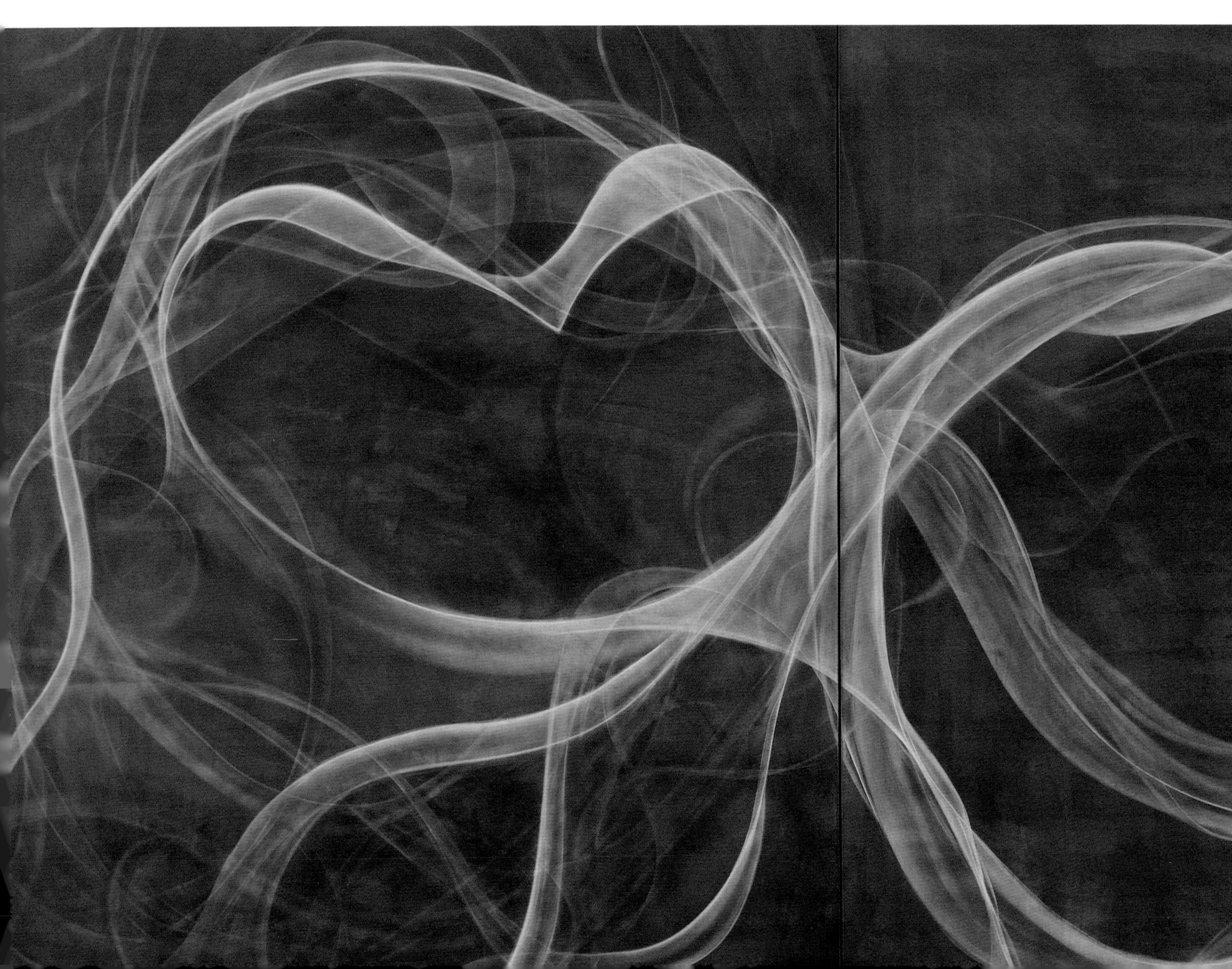

100 Years **.** 100 Works of Art

Introduction to the Collection of the Grand Rapids Art Museum

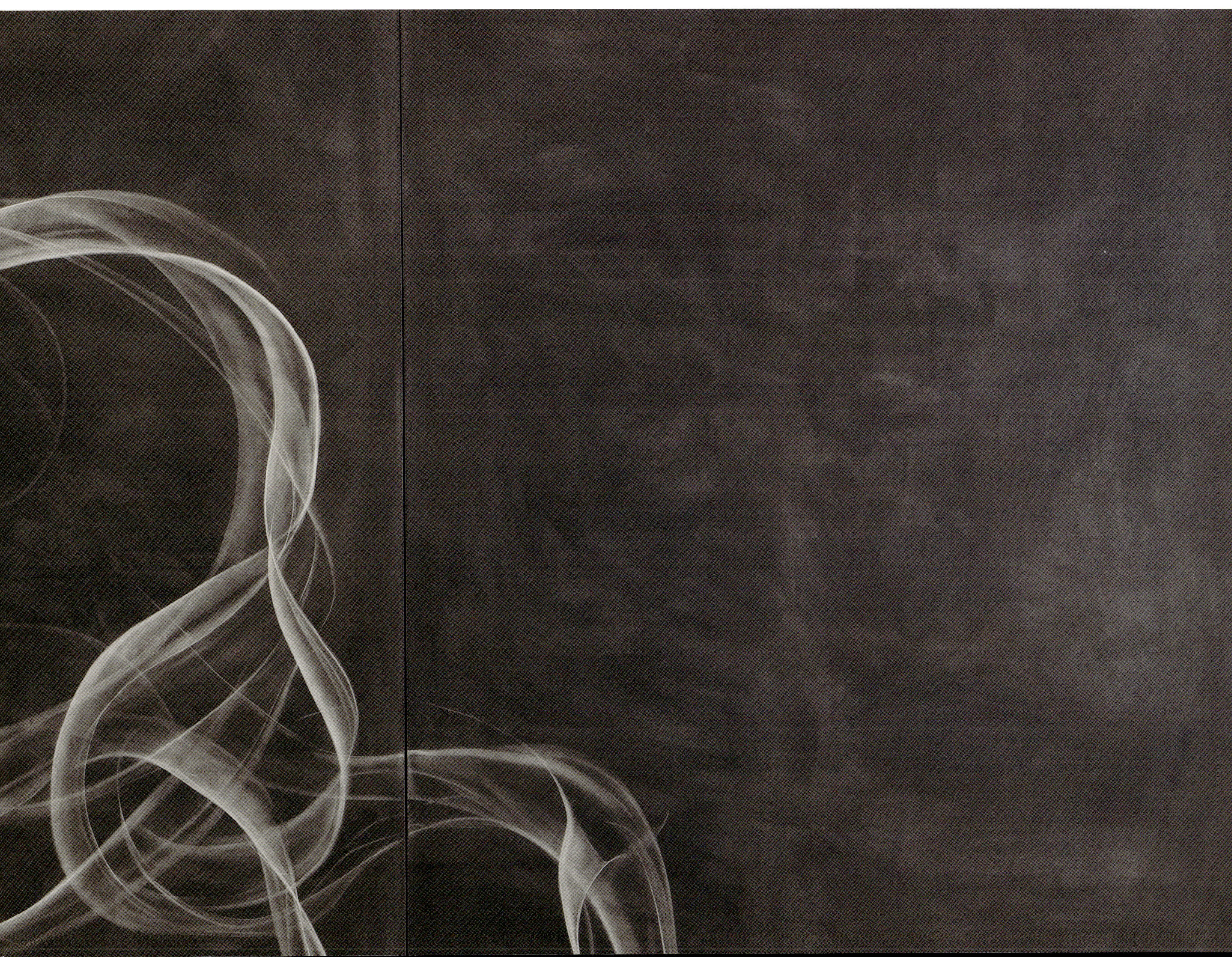

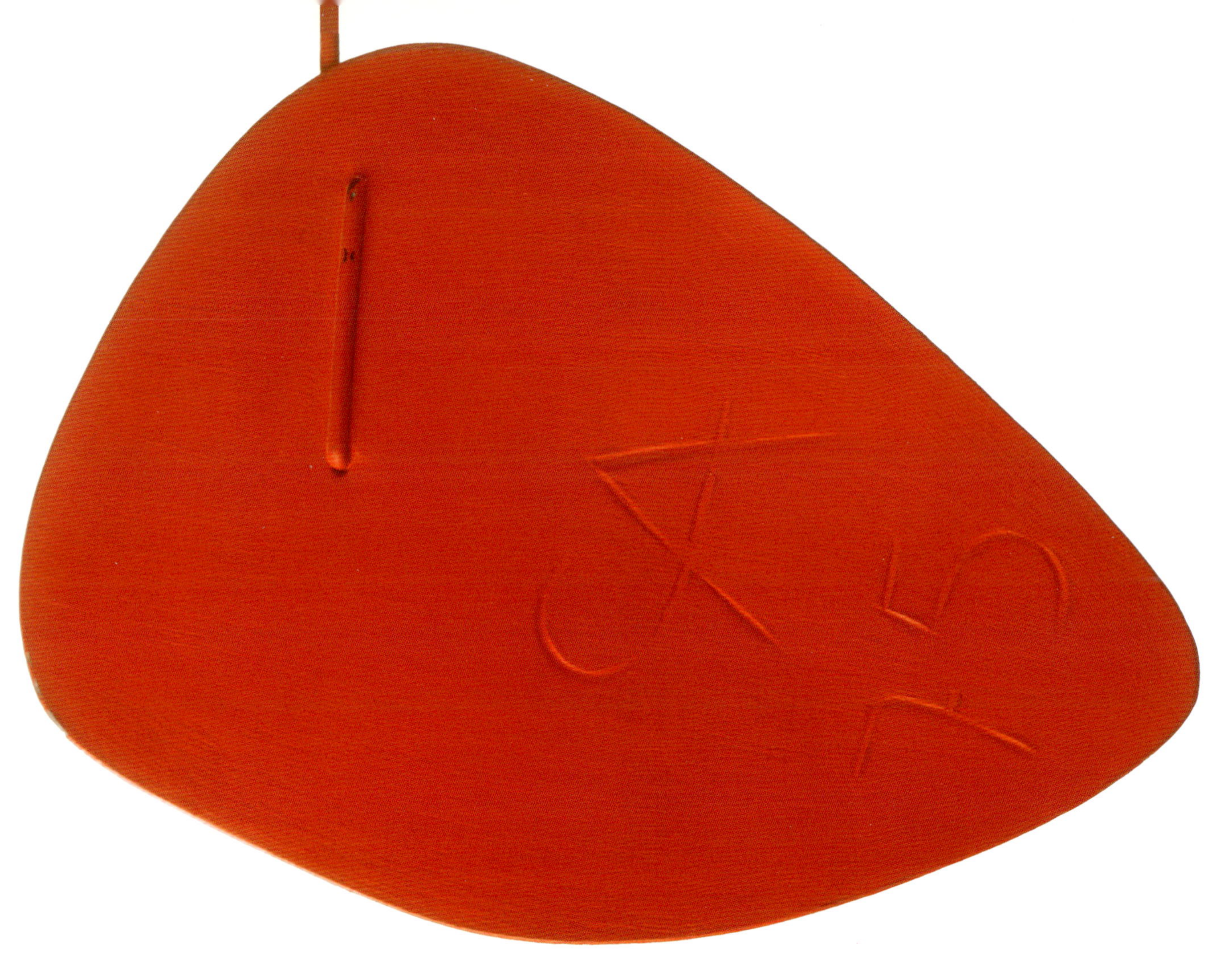

CONTENTS

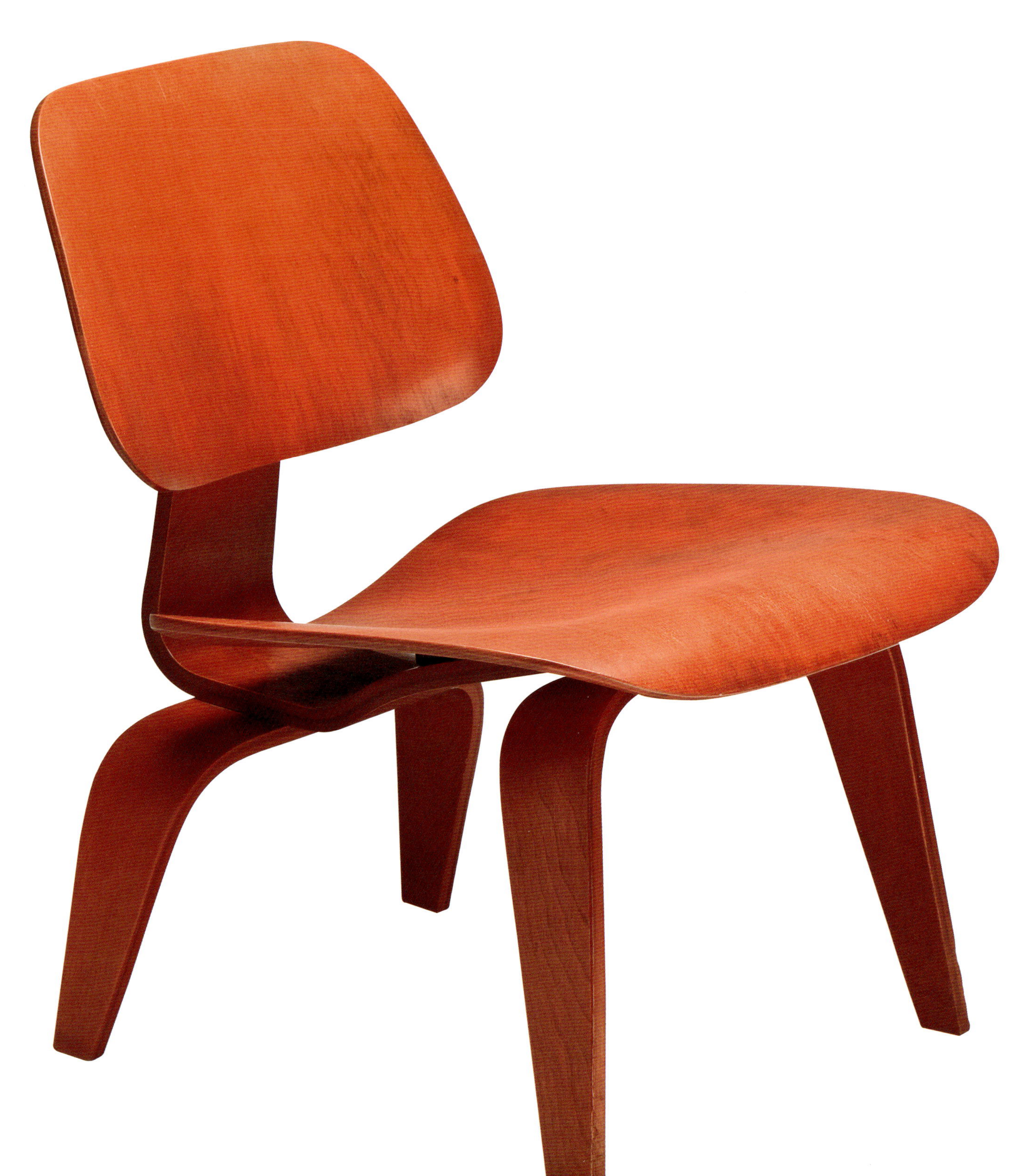

  A Centennial is cause for celebration and the Grand Rapids Art Museum has enlivened 2010, our one hundredth anniversary, with a yearlong sequence of special exhibitions, programs, events, and cultural partnerships. This publication, featuring one hundred of the finest works of art in the permanent collection, presents the Museum's most treasured resources. Thousands of Museum members, visitors, and cultural tourists have visited our beautiful new facility since it opened in 2007 to experience these works first hand and to learn more about the artists who created them. Fulfilling its stated mission, The Grand Rapids Art Museum provides "a gathering place where people of all ages and backgrounds can enrich their lives through interaction with authentic works of art that nourish and delight the mind and spirit." The Museum is now positioned as an anchor arts institution in the Midwest and looks forward to its next one hundred years. This book provides an unprecedented record of images and information about the meaning and aesthetic value of the collection as we begin a new century of community engagement and education at the Grand Rapids Art Museum.

I wish first to express deepest appreciation to all the Centennial Donors whose names are listed here. They have generously supported this year's fine accomplishments and this excellent publication. They invigorate the Museum and empower it to touch the lives of so many. I also extend sincere thanks to all of the donors of art throughout the Museum's hundred-year history, who have gifted cherished personal possessions of art to a larger and appreciative audience.

Our gifted authors Richard H. Axsom, Senior Curator, with Jon Carfagno, Education Director, and Cindy Buckner, Associate Curator, have shared their talents and insights in the texts that follow. Ed Marquand, Creative Director, Jeff Wincapaw, Design Director, and Brynn Warriner, Managing Editor of Marquand Books, photographer Dirk Bakker, and Richard H. Axsom, project director, have crafted a wonderful book. Staff members Alexander Paschka, Garrett Brooks, Dan Van De Steeg, and Erwin Erkfitz worked on artistic planning and preparation. More than half of the works of art included here were acquired during the tenure of Celeste Adams, who served as Museum Director from 1997 to 2010. Her constant effort and vision enriched and elevated the Museum collection and many of her insights are revealed in these pages.

On behalf of the Board of Trustees, I hope that you enjoy this Centennial Book and that it draws you into the Museum to befriend and enjoy our remarkable collection of art.

Scott Wierda, President
Board of Trustees

 The new and nationally acclaimed Grand Rapids Art Museum celebrates its centennial year in 2010. As the world's first green art museum, receiving its LEED Gold certification in 2008, the new museum provides a serene and innovative setting for special exhibitions and for works of art from a permanent collection one hundred years in the making. The museum experience is direct and reflective, both aesthetic and intellectual. The presentation of art in the special setting of a museum enhances an aesthetic response and fosters a desire to gain knowledge and an understanding of art. The aesthetic experience arises from our personal responses to works of art. The word "aesthetic" comes from the Greek and means "sense perception." A work of art concentrates perception, producing vivid feelings in the viewer. It is visceral and immediate, simulating life's moments in heightened form—be they joyful, anxious, sad, or tranquil. This type of reaction gives us a sharpened awareness of being in the world, and our relationship to it.

The aesthetic experience at the Grand Rapids Art Museum is prompted and enhanced by the simplicity and elegance of the museum's design. At the entrance, in the Wege Pavilion, Ellsworth Kelly's monumental *Blue White* (2006) declares the beauty of color wedded to geometry. The galleries play in concert with works of art, drawing the museum into a harmonious whole. Skylight lanterns atop the Wege, DeVos, and Keeler permanent collection galleries permit abundant natural light to enter classically proportioned spaces. The windows throughout the building also allow vistas of city skylines and street life. An enclosed open-air courtyard and reflecting pool bring nature into the building's interior. On the outside of the building, Maya Lin's *Ecliptic* (2001) is an extension of the museum's magnificent entrance façade. As an urban oasis of rolling grass mounds, water features, and Michigan birches, it announces democratic access to art within the museum's walls.

The visitor's overall experience of the exterior and interior spaces of the museum is conducive to an aesthetic contemplation of art. To appreciate a work of art most fully, concentration is imperative. A viewer must have the opportunity to be absorbed into works of art. The Grand Rapids Art Museum provides this environment.

In preparation for the move to this beautiful new facility, works by many prominent artists were added to the permanent collection in order to teach its areas of strength in a more comprehensive manner. These recent acquisitions allow the museum visitor to trace a wider survey of the history of western art from the year 1500 C.E. to the present in prints, and from the nineteenth, twentieth, and twenty-first centuries through a variety of media, including painting, sculpture, drawings, photographs, design, and modern craft.

The Education Department, a cornerstone of the new museum's identity, interprets the collection to facilitate aesthetic and learning experiences. Housed in the Meijer Education Center, museum educators plan programs and create materials that promote a lifetime of learning for people of all backgrounds. The dynamic engagement of audiences was an integral component of lead benefactor Peter M. Wege's vision for the new Grand Rapids Art Museum. In an address commemorating the start of construction on this landmark building, he said, "My wish is that true art in all its forms should lift the

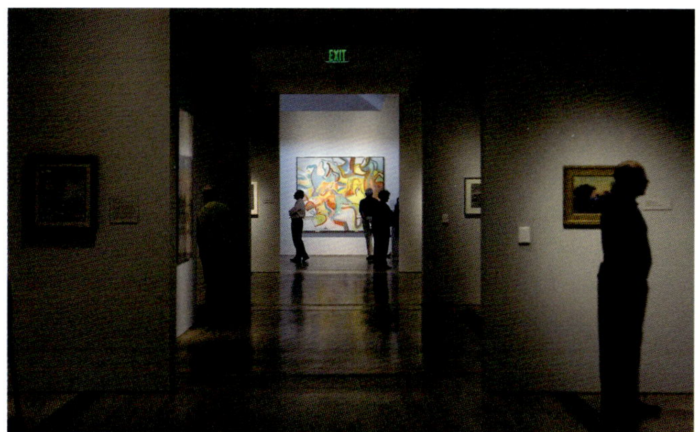 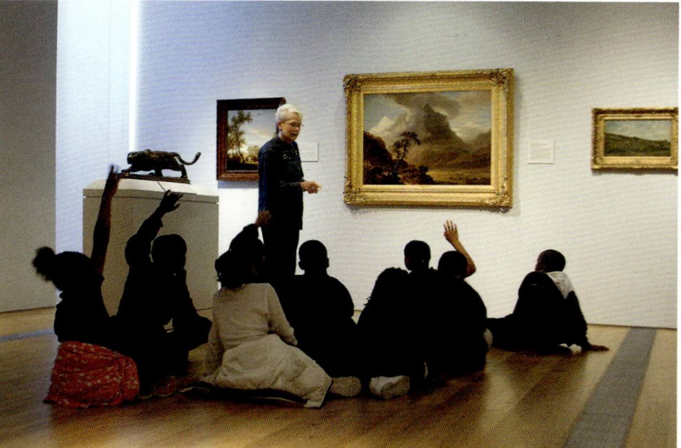 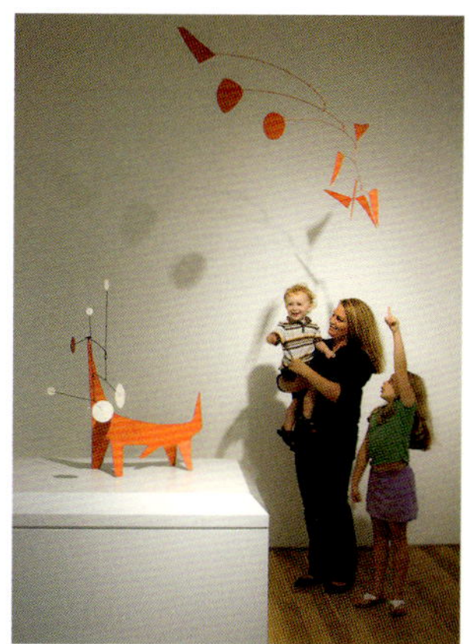

mind and spirit into the realization that art can be and should be an educational experience of huge proportions."

The educational experience is characterized by a sense of discovery, wonder, and exchange of ideas. Learning at the new Grand Rapids Art Museum is an active process, wherein a visitor's experiences are connected to and enhanced by the works of art that the institution holds in trust for the benefit of the community. This vision of a transformative encounter between individuals and the collection pervades the scope of the museum's education programming.

School tour participants enter the building with knowledge of the curriculum content that they have covered in their classrooms. New forms of literacy are developed, however, as they participate in docent-guided discussion about a work such as Frederic Remington's vibrant wash drawing entitled *Snow Indian of the Northern Type* (c. 1897). Thoughtful lines of questioning teach students how to read the artist's skillful manipulation of simple materials as a primary source document of a major moment in the history of the United States, namely the close of the Indian Wars. The artist's evocative use of ink wash to isolate his subject in a timeless setting creates a heroic, yet elegiac, mood. This drawing shows viewers how art can yield multiple yet complementary interpretations.

Family members of all ages share a stimulating afternoon exploring the galleries using an interactive guide designed to promote careful looking and dialogue about Alexander Calder's work. In the studio, grandparents, parents, and children are brought together in hands-on learning that allows them to understand the decision-making process that led to the creation of the artist's *Blunt-Tailed Dog* (1970).

Adult audiences enjoy a theater troupe's portrayal of the many sides of Andy Warhol's colorful life in Cook Auditorium. The performance creates a new connection to Warhol's art that enables participants to respond in a deeper manner to works such as his *Endangered Species* portfolio (1983). The viewer returns to the galleries with a broader sense of the artist's incisive response to the world around him.

In an important sense, however, a work of art also has a directness that engages the viewer before whatever else might be known about it in terms of the artist, the period in which it was created, or the various interpretations ascribed to it over time. T.S. Eliot's statement that "genuine poetry can communicate before it is understood" applies equally to visual works of art.

Richard H. Axsom, Senior Curator
Jon Carfagno, Education Director

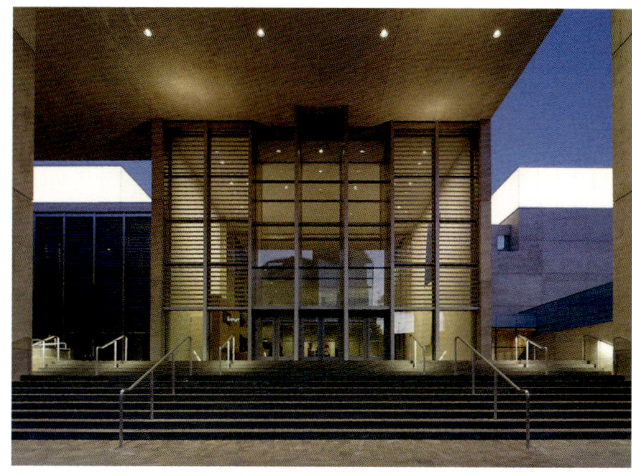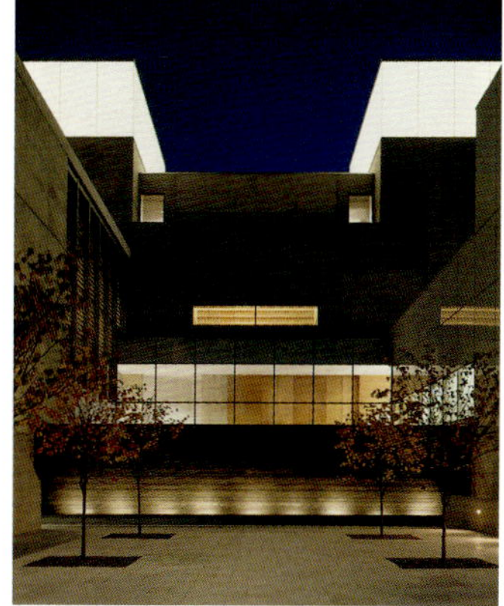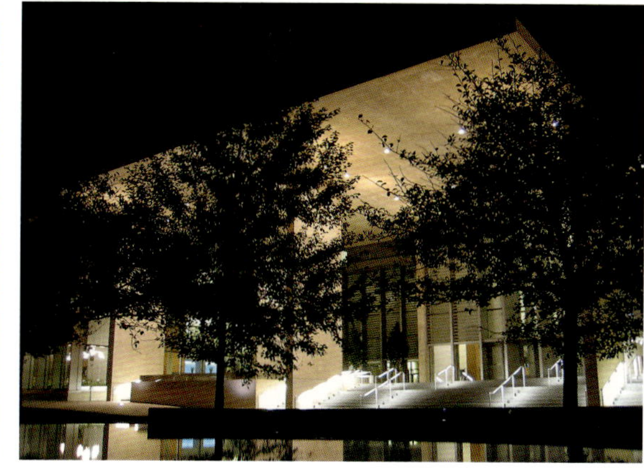

Mr. and Mrs. David G. Frey
Frey Foundation
William H. Gilbert Trust
Grand Rapids Community College
Grand Rapids Community Foundation
The Grand Rapids Press
Grand Valley State University
Ralph Hauenstein
Herman Miller Foundation
Herman Miller Inc.
Dorothy Tegner Hodgkins
Dirk and Victoria Hoffius
Howard Miller Company
J. C. Huizenga
Marilyn C. Hunting
Huntington Bank
Hylant Group
Beatrice Idema
Barbara and Thomas Jackoboice
Jade Pig Ventures

Michael and Susan Jandernoa
Cate and Sid Jansma, Jr.
kantorwassink
Miner S. and Mary Ann Keeler
John and Nancy Kennedy
KINSHIP Foundation
Scott and Linda LaFontsee
Herbert and Sharon Lantinga
Louis Padnos Iron and Metal Company
Mary Loupee
Thomas and Claudia Mabie
Meijer
The Meijer Foundation
Fred and Lena Meijer
Hank and Liesel Meijer
Michigan Council for Arts & Cultural Affairs
Jack H. Miller
Miller Johnson
Stephanie and Jack Neal
James and Mary Nelson

Norris, Perné & French LLP, Investment Counsel
Chris Stoffel and Greta D. Overvoorde
Martin and Enid Packard
Doug and Nancy Padnos
Richard and Mary Panek
Paul Goebel Group
PNC Financial Services Group
Porter Foundation
Richard L. and Ruth Postma
Rockford Construction Company Inc.
Rothbury Farms
Charles and Stella Royce
Sebastian Foundation
SeyferthPR
Nancy and Doug Slade
Smith Haughey Rice & Roegge
Spectrum Health
Steelcase Foundation
Steelcase Inc.
Frank Stella

Storytelling Pictures
Roger and Concy Thompson
Marilyn Titche
Triangle Associates, Inc.
Vander Waals Foundation
VanderWeide Family Foundation
Varnum LLP
Via Design
Warner Norcross & Judd LLP
Mitchell and Stacey Watt
Peter M. Wege
Wege Foundation
West Michigan Whitecaps
Scott and Rebecca Wierda
Greg and Meg Willit
Kate and Richard Wolters Foundation
Wolverine World Wide Inc.

. 100 Works of Art

. **Albrecht Dürer**
German, 1471–1528

In 1507, Albrecht Dürer began *The Engraved Passion*, a set of sixteen intaglio plates that he completed in 1513. This remarkable series constitutes Dürer's earliest work in the medium of engraving, and would later influence Rembrandt's prints. The engravings are somber and restrained in their presentation, while the fineness of the engraved lines enables Dürer to achieve incredible detail and to suggest in these scenes an almost spiritual light. The same delicacy also makes possible a greater exploration of facial expression, thereby expanding the psychological dimension of each scene. Despite their miniature size, the prominence of the figures gives the images a compelling forthrightness and grandeur, seen here in particularly brilliant impressions.

Albrecht Dürer was the first artist in Northern Europe to transform the arts from the product of the medieval workshop to a conscious expression of artistic genius. He understood the rules of perspective underlying Italian Renaissance art and applied them to depictions of individualized people and landscapes. Dürer became an international figure, his woodcuts and engravings supplying iconographic models to artists throughout Europe and setting new standards of technical mastery. CMB

The Engraved Passion 1507–1513
Set of sixteen engravings on off-white laid paper
4¾ × 3 inches (plate)
Jansma Collection, Grand Rapids Art Museum
2007.16a–p

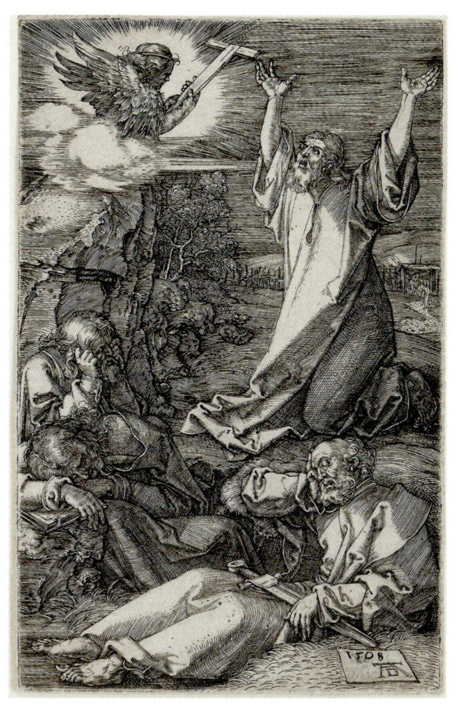
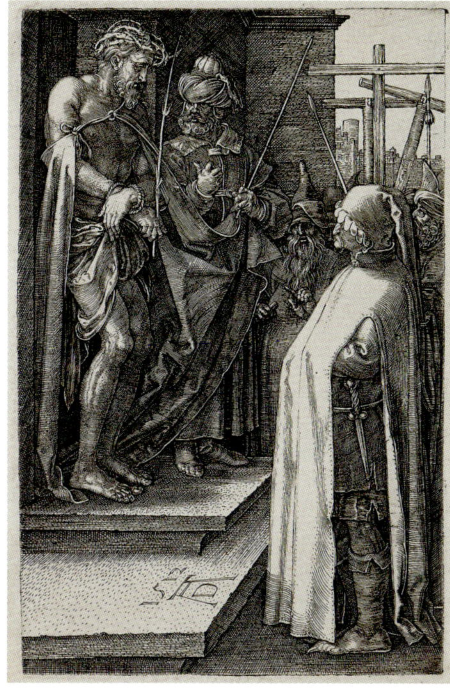
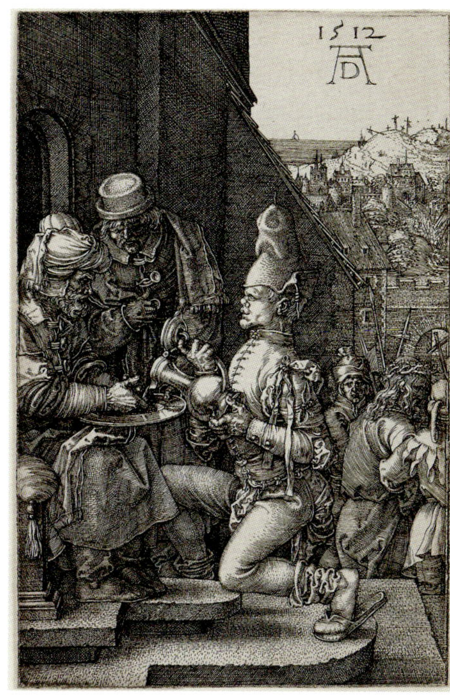
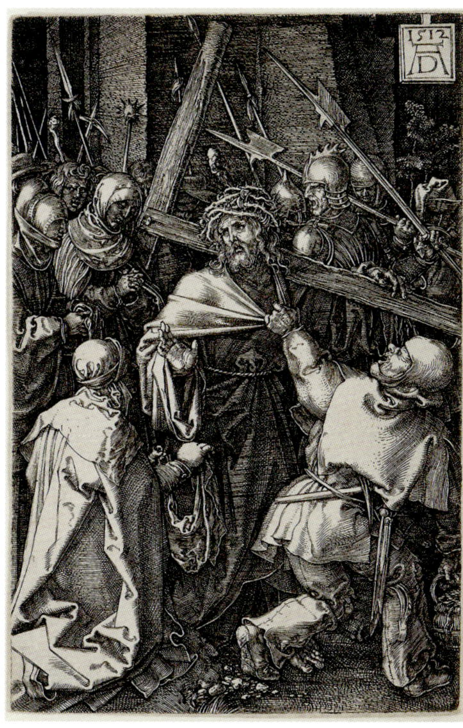
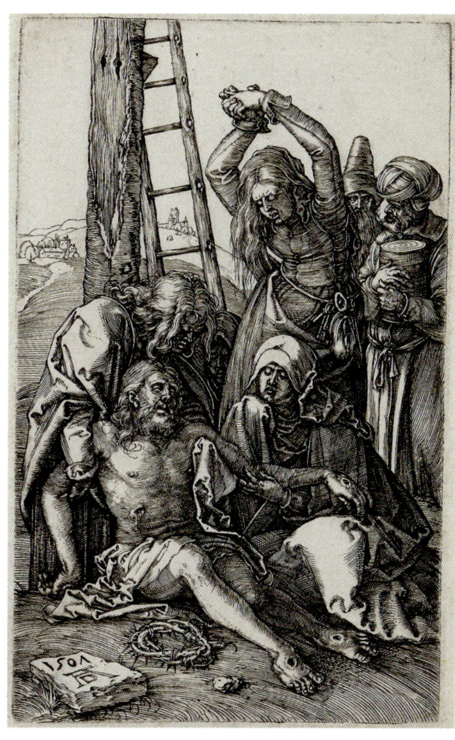
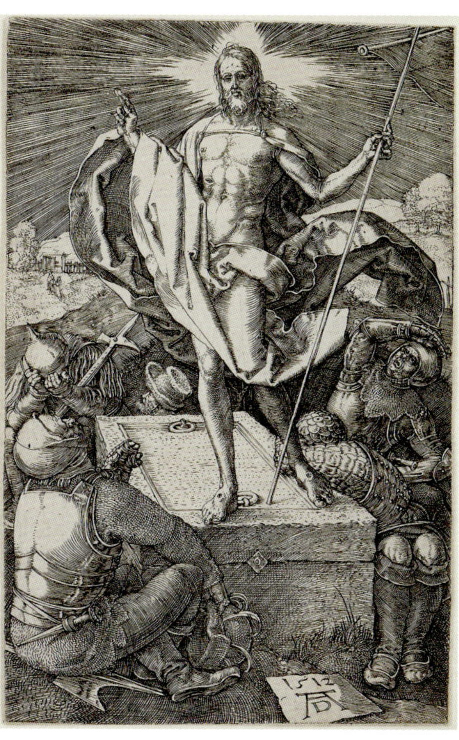

. **Rembrandt van Rijn**
Dutch, 1606–1669

As a painter and printmaker, the great Dutch artist Rembrandt van Rijn preferred subject matter drawn from Scripture. His interpretations of stories from the New and Old Testament were highly personal. With great compassion for his subjects, he sought universal humanity in the narratives of The Holy Bible.

Created ten years apart, these two etchings, later conceived by collectors as a pair, tell a profound tale of faith and redemption. To test his obedience, God commands Abraham to kill his son. *Abraham and Isaac* depicts the moment when Abraham, with unhesitating earnestness, tells his young son to prepare for a sacrifice. Isaac has gathered wood for the fire, innocently listening to his father's instructions. Abraham's sword is sheathed and the sacrificial stone is prominent in the left foreground. The psychological drama of the moment is in knowing what will follow. The tenderness with which Isaac is portrayed, a characterization that does not derive from the Biblical text, adds a deep poignancy to the moment.

Ten years later, Rembrandt etched *Abraham's Sacrifice*, portraying the moment when the angel stops the hand of Abraham from slaying his son. Abraham has aged, his eyes hollow with suffering—a figure in stark contrast to the smiling and richly attired Abraham of the earlier etching. These two prints, of superb quality, uniquely capture the power of Biblical stories through the eyes of one of the greatest artists in western art.   **RHA**

Abraham and Isaac 1645
Etching and drypoint on cream laid paper
6⅛ × 5¹/₁₆ inches (plate)
Jansma Collection, Grand Rapids Art Museum
2006.37

Abraham's Sacrifice 1655
Etching and drypoint on cream laid paper
6½ × 5¼ inches (plate)
Museum Purchase, Mabel H. Perkins Fund
1982.2.7

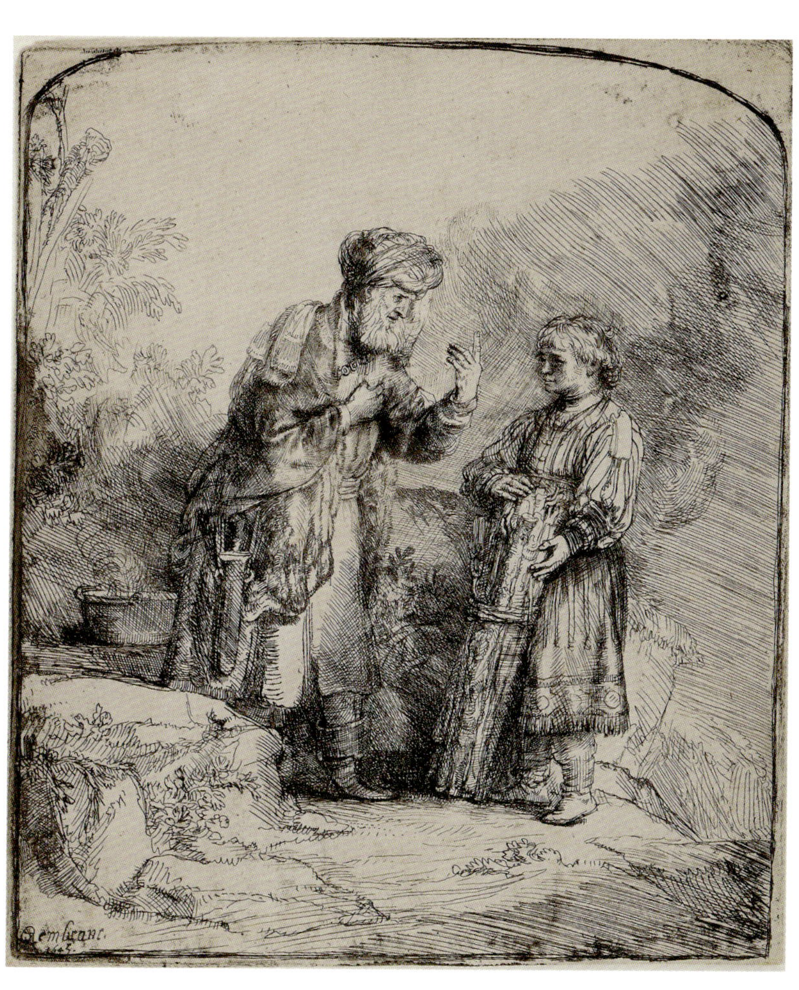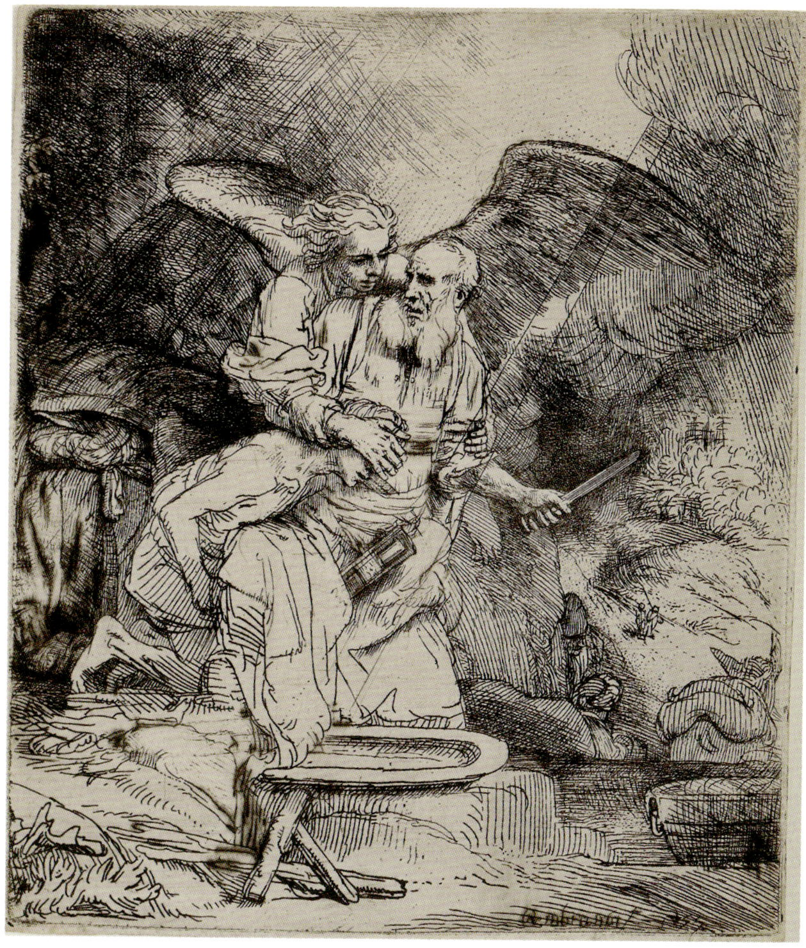

. **Rembrandt van Rijn**
Dutch, 1606–1669

In this moving scene of Christ's preaching, Rembrandt populates a city courtyard with a range of people, old and young, rich and poor, individually responding to a message of compassion. Only a small child playing in the foreground seems impervious to the spiritual drama taking place. Christ's placement in intimate proximity to the assembled crowd emphasizes the humanity of his teaching. Rembrandt conveys Christ's compassion through a gesture of blessing to those gathered around him in a scene that might be in Jerusalem or a street in seventeenth-century Amsterdam. Rembrandt here conveys the redemption of the New Testament as a potential experience of everyday life.

Rembrandt's use of etching and drypoint needles and the engraving burin masterfully creates striking effects of light and dark. The rich shadows and crisp articulation of detail mark this impression of *Christ Preaching* as a distinguished example of Rembrandt's printmaking. The parenthetical title, *La Petite Tombe*, is not an allusion to Christ's death. It is, according to recent scholarship, a reference to a family by the name of La Tombe in whose collection an impression of *Christ Preaching* was found.   **RHA**

Christ Preaching (La Petite Tombe) c. 1652
Etching, engraving, and drypoint on off-white laid paper
6$\frac{1}{16}$ × 8$\frac{1}{8}$ inches (plate)
Jansma Collection, Grand Rapids Art Museum
2006.30

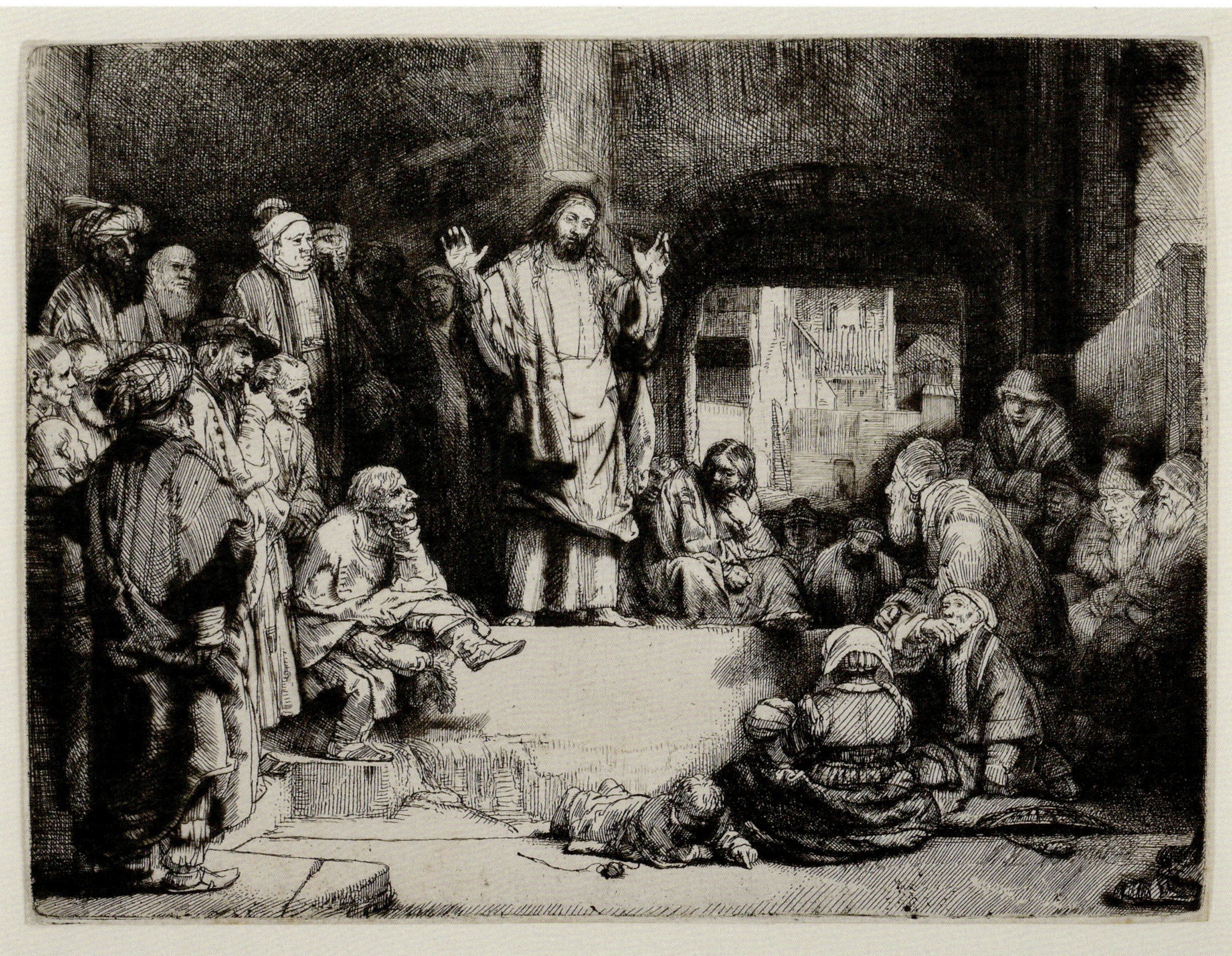

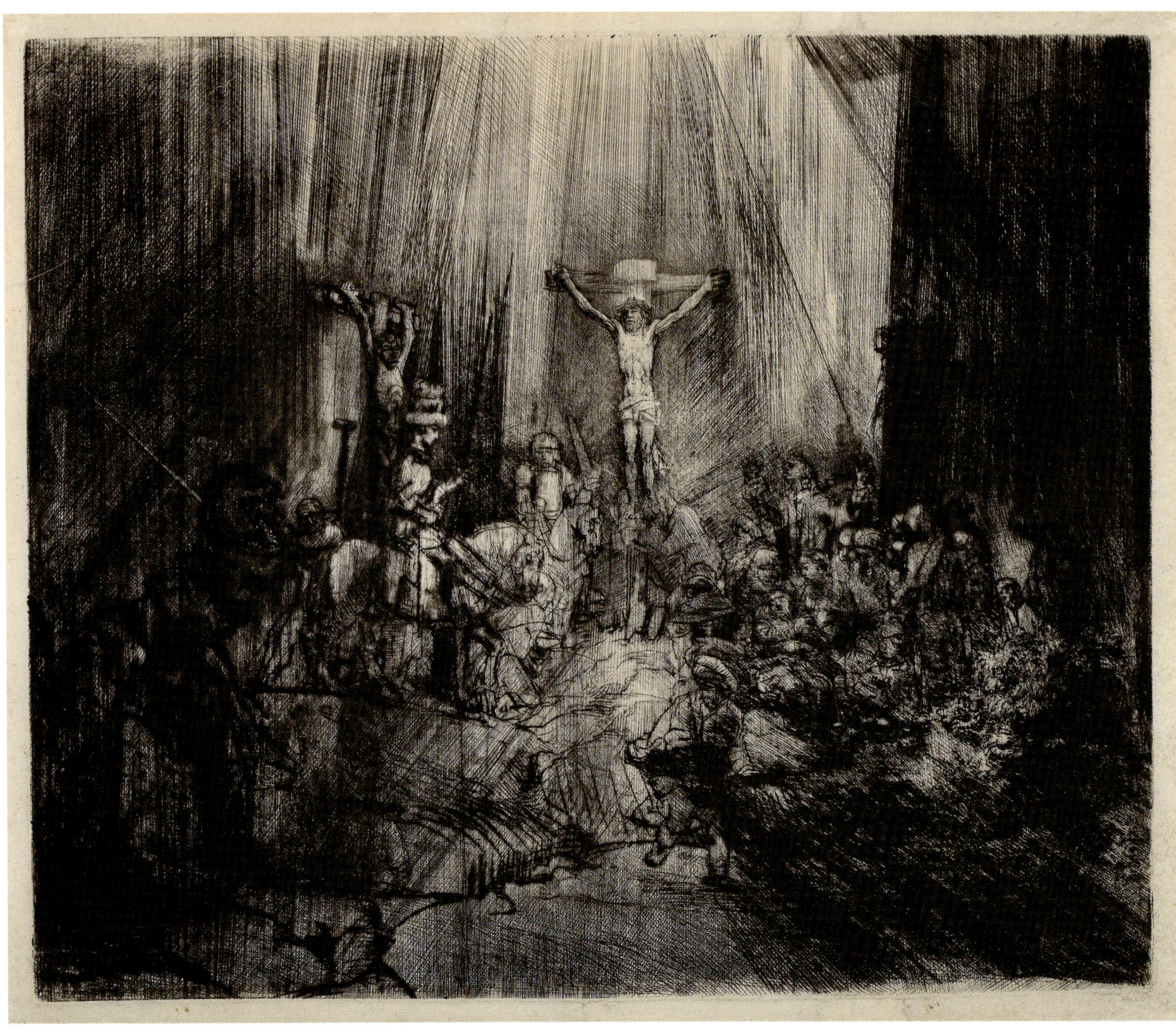

. **Rembrandt van Rijn**
Dutch, 1606–1669

*The Three Crosses
(Christ Crucified Between
Two Thieves),* fourth state
1653–1655
Drypoint with burin on off-white laid paper
16¼ × 19¾ inches (plate)
Jansma Collection, Grand Rapids Art Museum
2007.11

The fourth state of *The Three Crosses* represents one of the most profound depictions of death and redemption in the history of art. It is the culmination of four variations (or states) of the image that Rembrandt reworked on a single copperplate. In the first three states, executed in 1653, the narrative action is based upon St. Luke's account of the Crucifixion—when "darkness covered the earth."

Two years later, Rembrandt returned to the metal plate and dramatically altered the composition and meaning of the event depicted. He scraped, burnished, and polished extensive areas of the plate—removing figures, adding new ones, and scratching a dense network of lines that darkened the image. Beneath the crucified Christ to the left, Rembrandt placed a mysterious man on horseback. Without mention in the Scriptural passage, he is Rembrandt's invention. Attired in wealthy fashion, he may represent the temporal world and its vanities, contemplating the greater truths of Christ. The pictorial space explodes in a powerful contrast between the palpable darkness and the radiant shaft of light centered on Christ. These changes from the first three states transform the image into a meditation on inner spiritual meaning. This early impression is considered one of the finest in the world for its dark richness and tonal balance. It is the masterpiece of the museum's works on paper collection. RHA

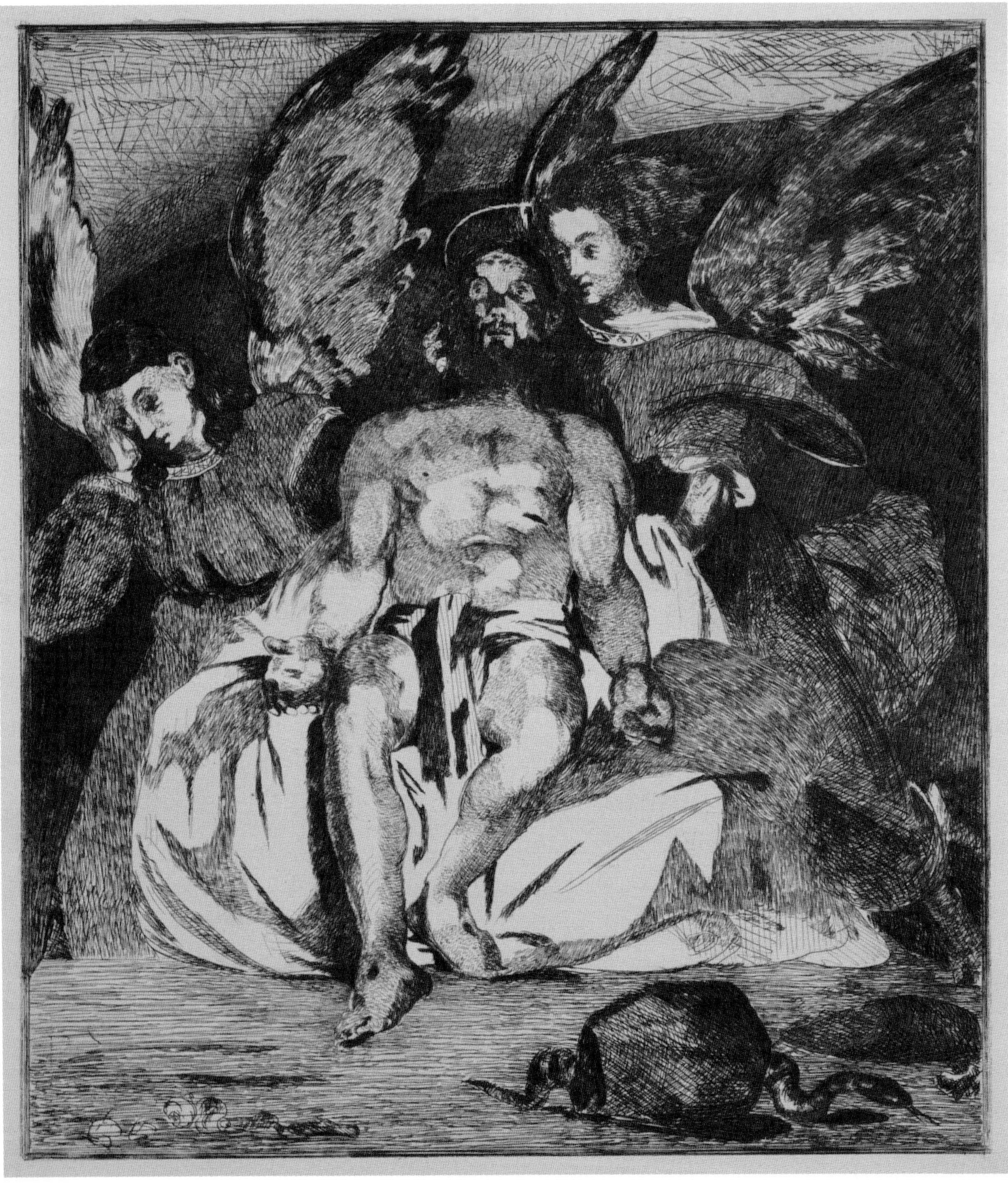

Édouard Manet

French, 1832–1883

The Dead Christ with Angels (Christ aux Anges), third state 1866–1867

Etching with aquatint printed in
brown ink on beige china paper
15⅞ × 13⅛ inches (plate)
Jansma Collection
Grand Rapids Art Museum
2010.12

Édouard Manet was the most important figure in the emergence of French Modernism in the 1860s. Always wishing to work through the annual state-sponsored exhibitions, he showed the painting *The Dead Christ with Angels* in the Salon of 1864. Three years later, Manet began work on an etching, conceived as a new interpretation of the painting. Unlike his contemporaries Mary Cassatt and Edgar Degas, who were prolific printmakers, Manet seldom executed prints, making the occasion of this print yet more significant.

The masterful print, *The Dead Christ with Angels*, was created from the largest copperplate Manet ever etched. Two elegantly rendered angels attend to Christ as he reveals the wounds of his Crucifixion. The intimate, atmospheric quality of the print, created by washes of aquatint, softens the lifeless physicality of Christ. The somber and elegiac tone of the scene anticipates the miracle of the Resurrection, a triumph over death and Satan, referenced by the slithering serpent in the foreground. Fewer than a dozen impressions of *The Dead Christ with Angels* exist. Exceedingly rare, this etching was privately published and never exhibited, only later claiming a distinguished place in the history of the western print. **RHA**

. Asher B. Durand
American, 1796–1886

This majestic landscape is one of four paintings that Asher B. Durand painted after a trip to Switzerland in 1840. Like other members of the Hudson River School of artists, Durand was inspired by the work of Claude Lorraine (c. 1600–1682), whose poetic rendering of light playing across idyllic scenes is echoed in this work. Durand's other three Alpine paintings have been unlocated since the nineteenth century, and it has previously been unclear which title matches this canvas. Two sketches by Durand in the collection of the New-York Historical Society relate to this painting: *On the Descent of the Susten Pass* and *Valley of Oberhasel*. Both are dated October 10, 1840. As discovered by scholar Corey Geske, the latter sketch matches the painting almost exactly, with the minor absence of the tree at the left.

Asher B. Durand was a prominent figure in the New York art community, and served as president of the National Academy of Design from 1845 to 1861. He was influenced by and worked alongside Thomas Cole, the founder of the Hudson River School. This group of artists sought to create a distinctly national style of painting incorporating highly detailed studies of nature into an idealized composition, emphasizing the smallness of human presence amidst the glory of divine creation. Durand wrote: "The true province of landscape art is the work of God in the visible creation, independent of man." CMB

*View in the Valley of
Oberhasle, Switzerland*
1842
Oil on canvas
32 × 45 inches
Museum Purchase
1986.1.3

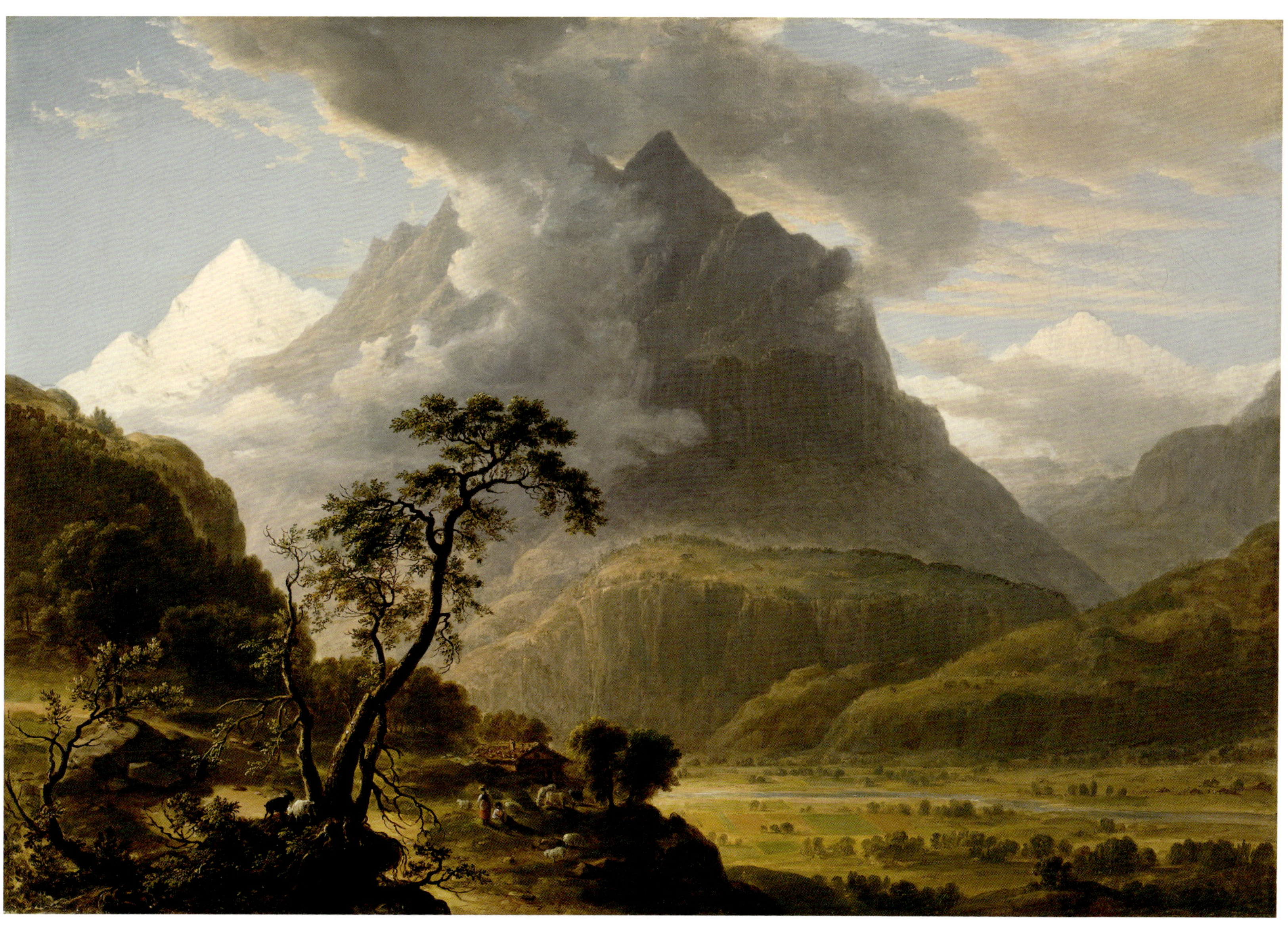

Herman Herzog was an established and successful landscape painter when he immigrated to the United States in the late 1860s. He soon began to paint scenes of America's natural landscape, influenced by the paintings of the Hudson River School. *Sketching on Beaver's Creek* calls to mind the forest interiors of Albert Bierstadt and Worthington Whittredge, who, like Herzog, had studied painting in Düsseldorf. The figure depicted working at his easel is most likely landscape painter George Cope (1855–1929). Herzog met Cope at the 1876 Centennial Exhibition in Philadelphia and the two formed a close alliance based on their love for nature, and took sketching trips together. In the 1880s, they painted extensively in the Delaware Water Gap area of Pennsylvania.

Born in Bremen, Germany, Herman Herzog enrolled in the Düsseldorf Academy at seventeen where he studied with Andreas Achenbach (1815–1910). Later he studied with painter Hans Frederick Gude (1825–1903), who was known for his wilderness landscapes. Herzog's work achieved recognition in Europe and his finely realistic landscapes attracted clients such as Queen Victoria of England and Czar Alexander II of Russia. Based in Philadelphia, Herzog traveled and painted extensively throughout the United States and Mexico. **CMB**

Sketching on Beaver's Creek c. 1880–1885
Oil on canvas
24 × 22 inches
Museum Purchase, Wege Foundation
2001.4

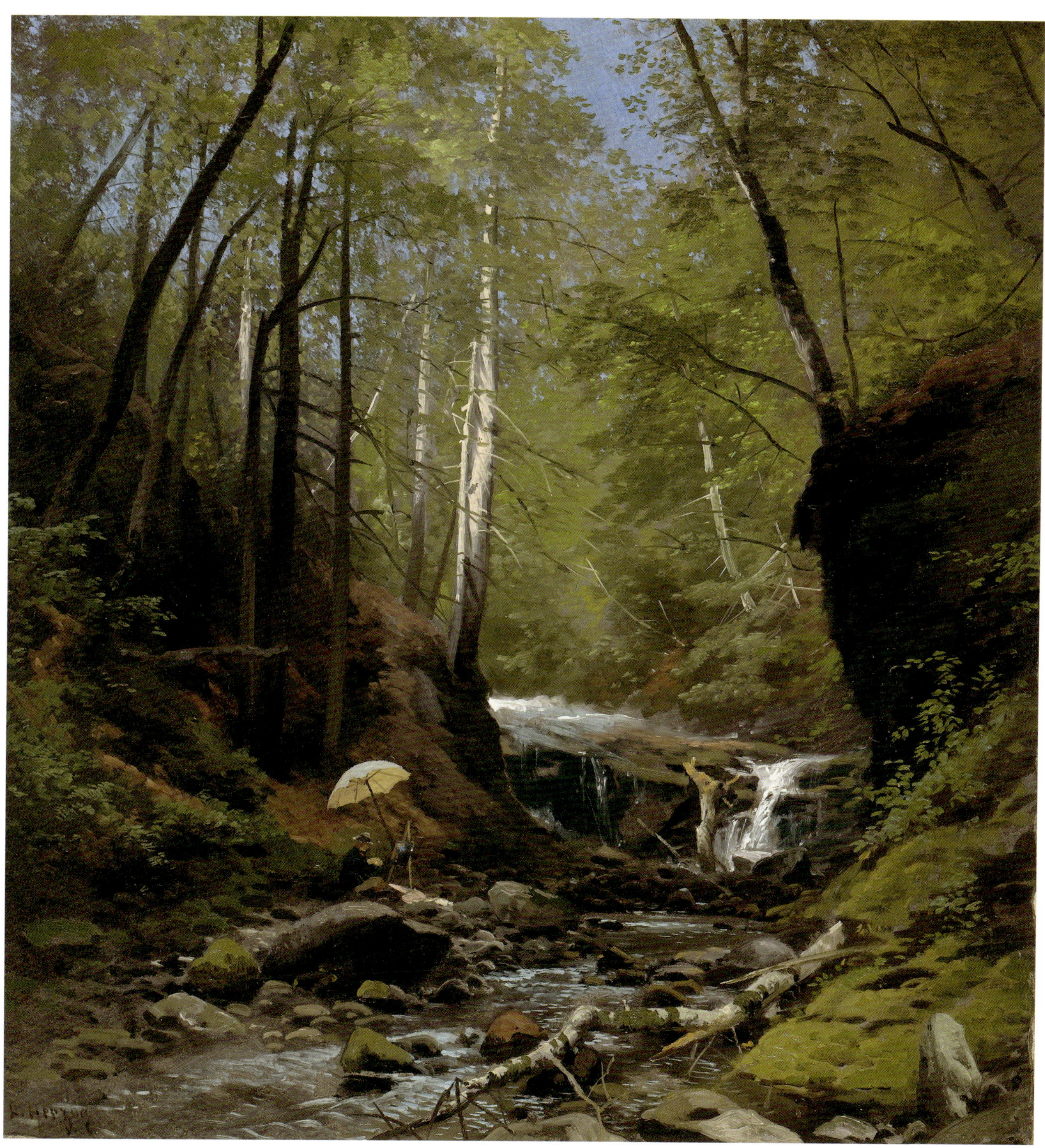

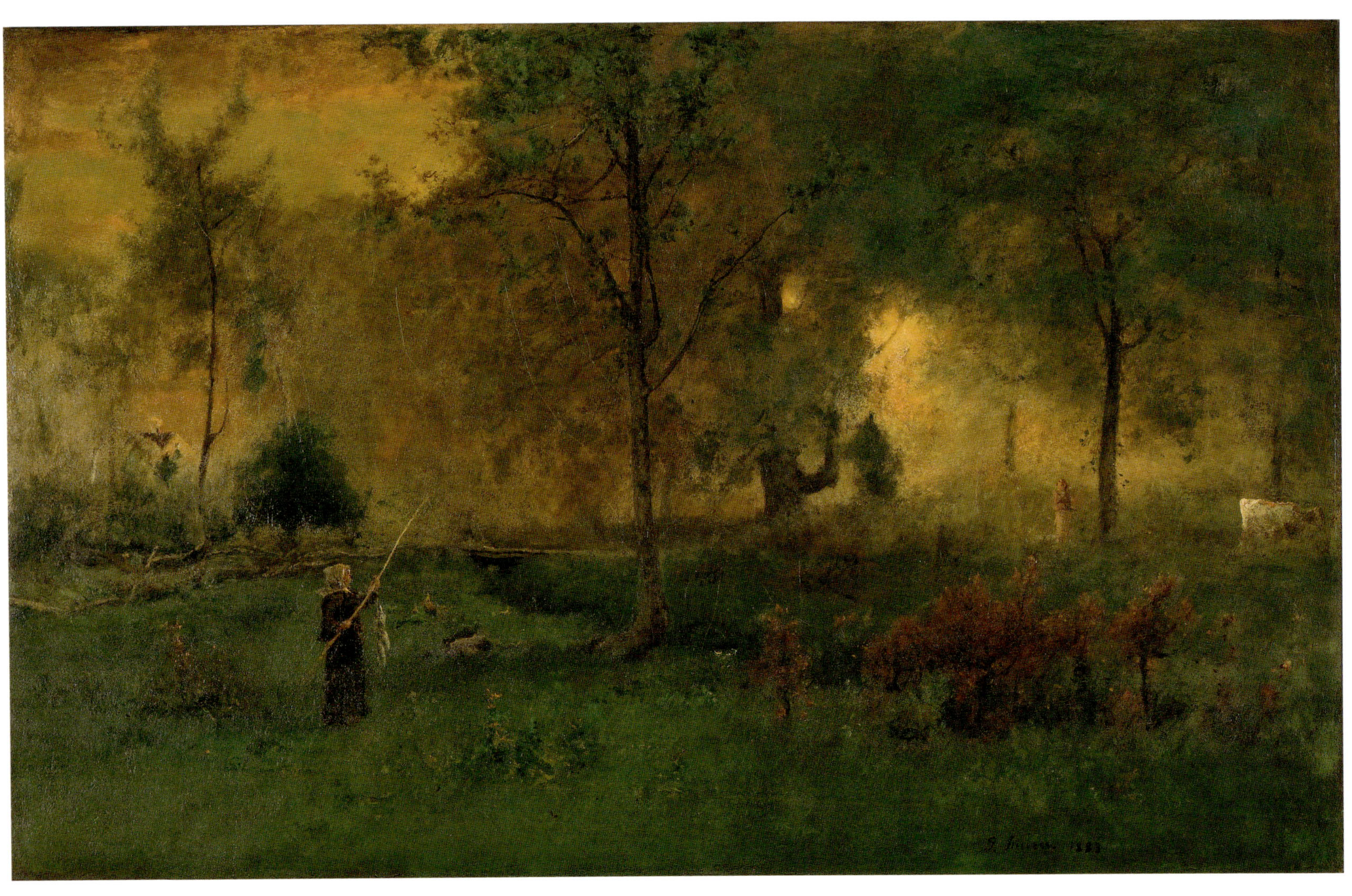

George Inness

American, 1825–1894

Sunset in the Woods 1883

Oil on canvas on board
22 × 34 inches
Museum Purchase, Frey Foundation,
Drake Quinn Family Foundation,
Mr. and Mrs. David G. Frey
2004.1.5

Sunset in the Woods marks the beginning of George Inness' late period, which focuses heavily on the mystical quality of landscape. Inness himself selected *Sunset in the Woods* for an important retrospective exhibition of his paintings at the American Art Galleries in New York in 1884. In relation to that exhibition, Inness described his current approach to painting. He sought to eliminate elaborate detail in order to convey "that subjective mystery of nature with which wherever I went I was filled."

As a disciple of the eighteenth-century theologian Emanuel Swedenborg, Inness believed that all objects in the natural world are imbued with a divine spirit but are nevertheless only reflections of the true reality of the spiritual world. Instead of carefully delineating individual forms such as facial features or leaves, the artist suggests them with color and indistinct form. The dim light of dusk seen in this painting contributes to this idea of being at a remove from reality.

George Inness was born in New York and spent most of his career in New York and Montclair, New Jersey. He considered himself primarily self-taught, though he studied briefly with French landscape painter Régis-François Gignoux and attended classes at the National Academy of Design. A pivotal figure in American art's transition from Tonalism to Impressionism, Inness' central stylistic influence came from the French Barbizon School artists, whose work he studied during his travels in France in the mid-1850s.   CMB

This early painting by Julian Alden Weir echoes the floral still lifes of Édouard Manet, whom Weir met in 1881. It is one of a number of still lifes that Weir painted in the 1880s, following his period of study in France, but before he fully embraced the Impressionist aesthetic. A popular subject for collectors, the still life also provided a convenient subject for addressing issues of color and composition.

Weir was the youngest of sixteen children, most of whom became artists. His father, Robert W. Weir, taught drawing at the U.S. Military Academy at West Point and his brother, John Ferguson Weir, served as head of the Art Department at Yale University. Julian Alden Weir studied in Paris from 1873 to 1877, where he became close friends with painters of the French Naturalist school, including Jules Bastien-Lepage. After 1890, he adopted an Impressionist style of painting and in 1898 became a founding member of The Ten American Painters, a group of artists that included Childe Hassam and William Merritt Chase. **CMB**

Still Life with Carnations 1880s
Oil on canvas
20 × 16 inches
Gift of William and Barbara Hyland in
memory of Edith Champion Goodspeed
1991.1.10

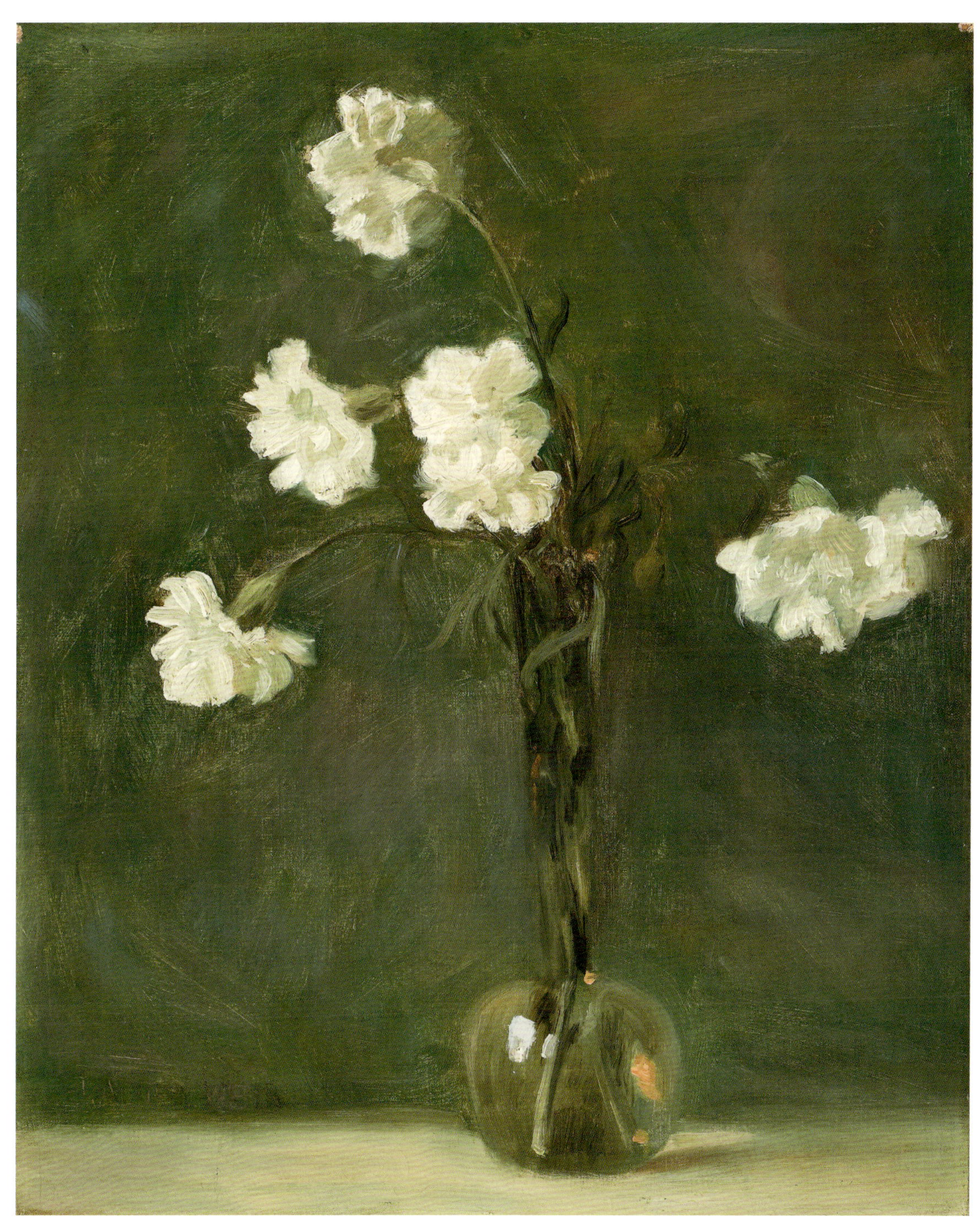

. **Winslow Homer**
American, 1836–1910

Winslow Homer was one of America's great artists of the nineteenth century and the sea was his greatest subject. The title of this etching, *Eight Bells*, refers to one of a series of on-deck watches conducted during a twenty-four-hour period. Two officers at the noon watch fix the position of their vessel, using sextants. Although this was an everyday scene of scientific measurement, Homer creates a gripping moment as two brave men seek their location in unruly high seas. This etching and the painting it is based upon declare the major theme of Homer's late seascapes set off the coast of Maine: humanity pitted against the dark forces of nature.

Early in his career, Homer made a name for himself as a graphic artist for *Harper's Weekly* and other publications, then turned seriously to painting after the Civil War. Homer's early work took everyday American life as a subject, but in his later art the sea became an increasingly favored motif. From the late 1880s to the end of his life, Homer lived and worked on the coast of Maine at Prout's Neck, producing the most dramatic seascapes in American art.   CMB

Eight Bells 1887
Etching on cream Japan paper
Proof before publication
19½ × 25 inches (plate)
Museum Purchase, Kate and
Richard Wolters Foundation
2005.15

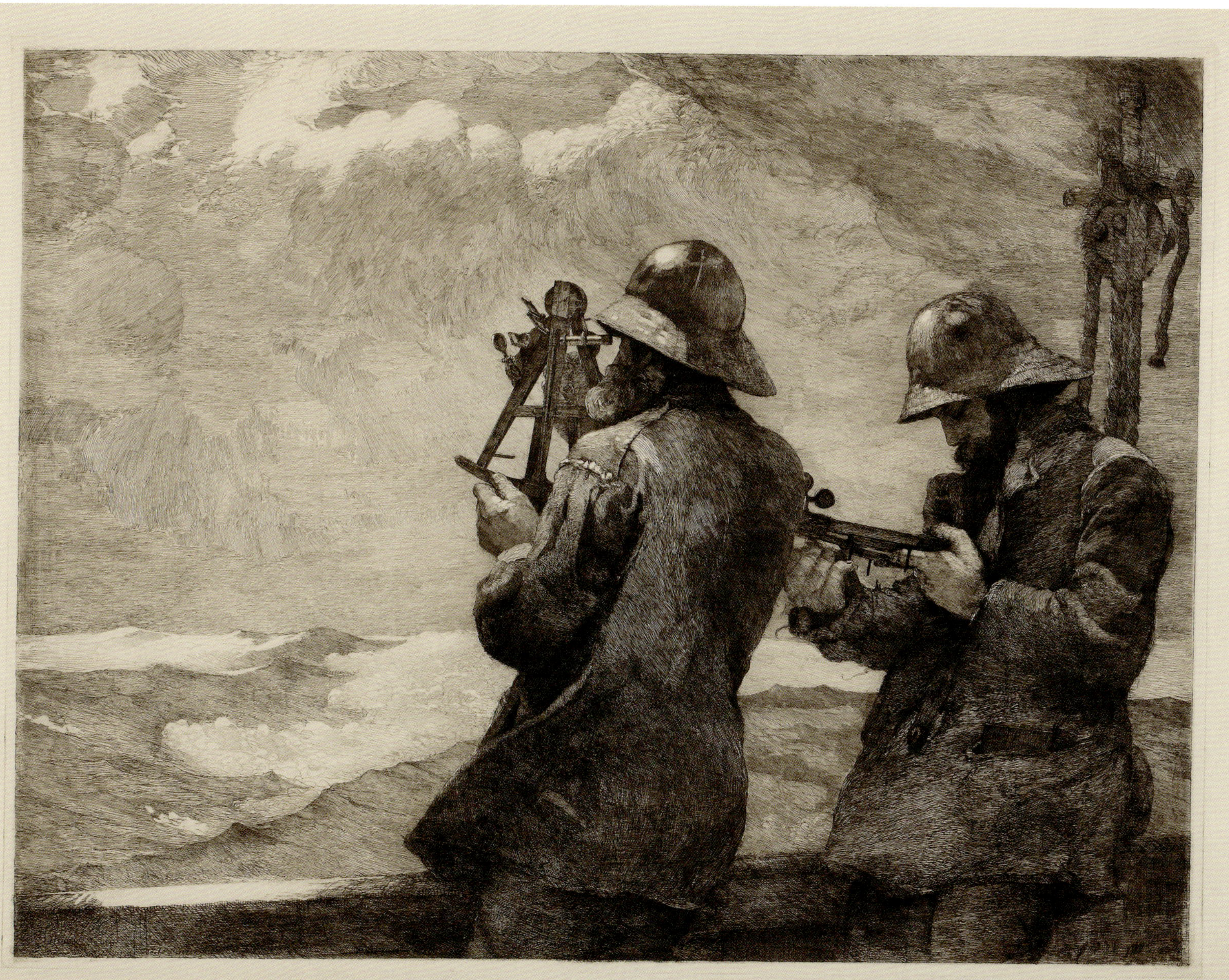

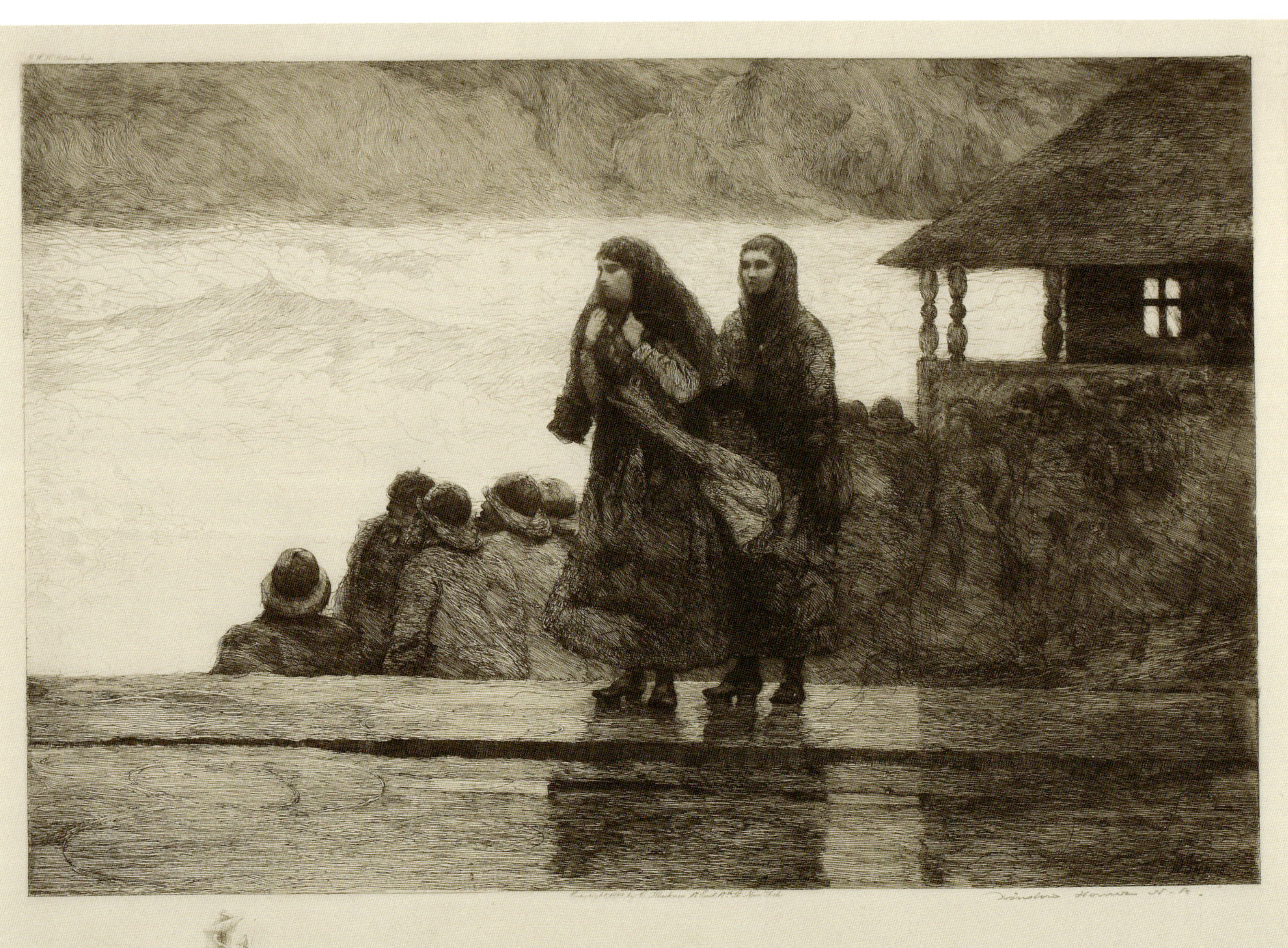

Winslow Homer

American, 1836–1910

Perils of the Sea 1888

Etching on cream Japan paper
16¾ × 21⅝ inches (plate)
Museum Purchase
James and Judy DeLapa
2007.1

Perils of the Sea is related to an ambitious watercolor Homer executed in the early 1880s while living on the northeast coast of England at Cullercoats near Tynemouth. This locale harbored a poor, hard-working community of fisherfolk who made their living and sometimes lost their lives on the sea.

In *Perils of the Sea*, a group of coastal men and women gather in foul weather at the Brigade's Watch House to witness a shipwreck they are powerless to reach. Homer derived the title from the refrain of "Eternal Father, Strong to Save," a contemporary hymn: "O hear us when we cry to Thee for those in peril on the sea." Focusing on the observers, Homer reserves special attention for two women whom he isolates in the immediate foreground for tragic effect, despair drawn across their faces. He uses a dense profusion of etched lines to create remarkable contrasts of light and dark.

The print is one of eight large etchings that he executed between 1886 and 1889, including *Eight Bells.* They are exceptional works that Homer regarded as equal to his paintings in quality and significance.   CMB

. **George Hitchcock**
American, 1850–1913

Purple Hyacinths brilliantly captures the vivid flower fields of Holland, in bands of purple and yellow receding into the distant horizon. Brightly colored Dutch landscapes became Hitchcock's primary painting subject following the success of his painting *La Culture des Tulipes* at the 1885 Paris Salon exhibition.

George Hitchcock was born in Providence, Rhode Island, the son of portrait painter Charles Hitchcock. After receiving his law degree from Harvard in 1874, Hitchcock decided to pursue a career as an artist. He left for Europe in 1877 and studied in London, Düsseldorf, and in Paris at the prestigious Académie Julian under Gustave Boulanger. He ultimately settled in the small town of Egmond aan Zee, just outside of Amsterdam. Egmond became an art colony, centered around Hitchcock and his fellow American artist Gari Melchers.   CMB

Purple Hyacinths c. 1890
Oil on canvas
17 × 22 inches
Museum Purchase, Frey Foundation, Mr. and Mrs. David G. Frey, Mr. and Mrs. Samuel M. Cummings, Daniel and Pamella DeVos Foundation and Richard and Helen DeVos Foundation in honor of Ethel DeVos
2001.1.3

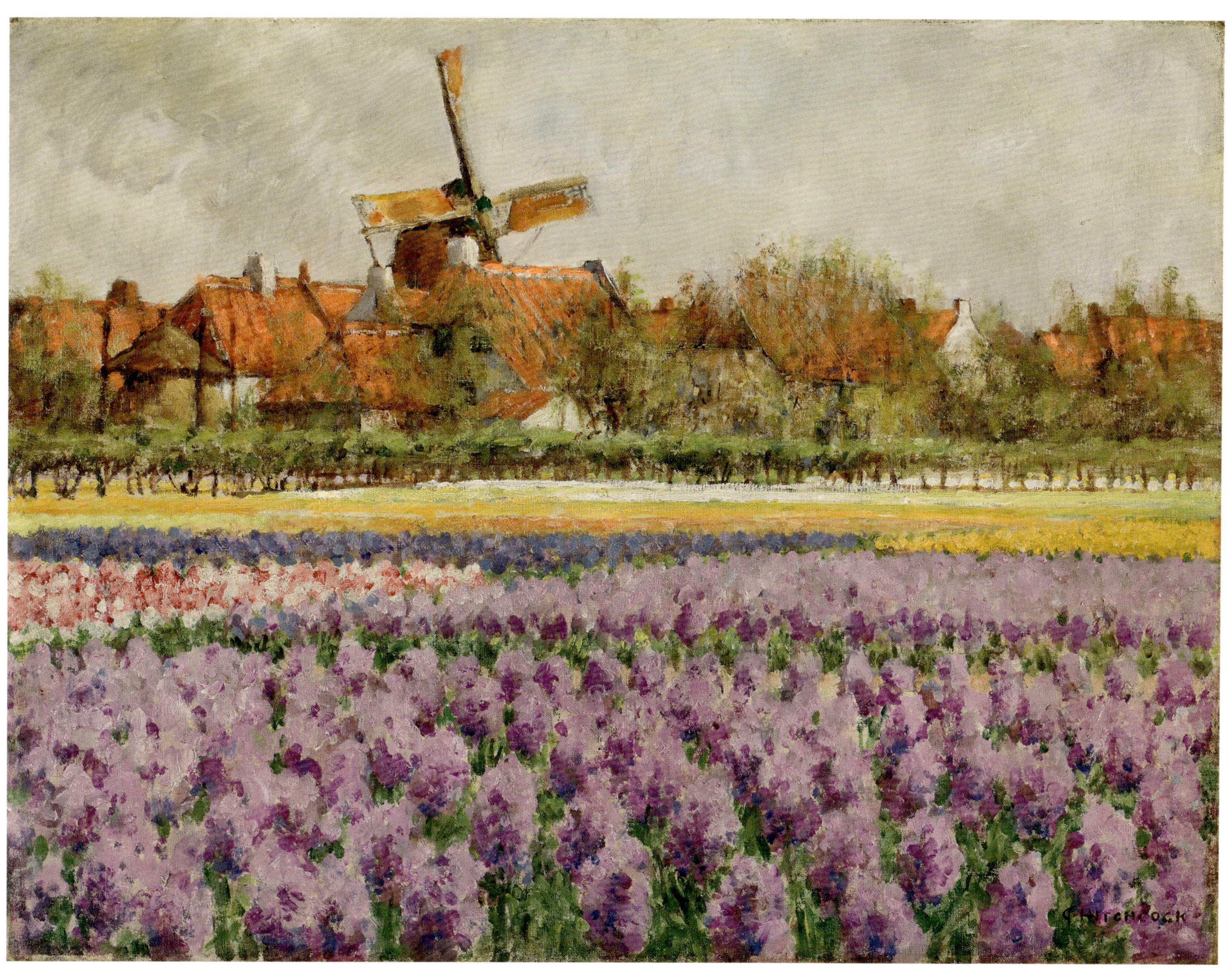

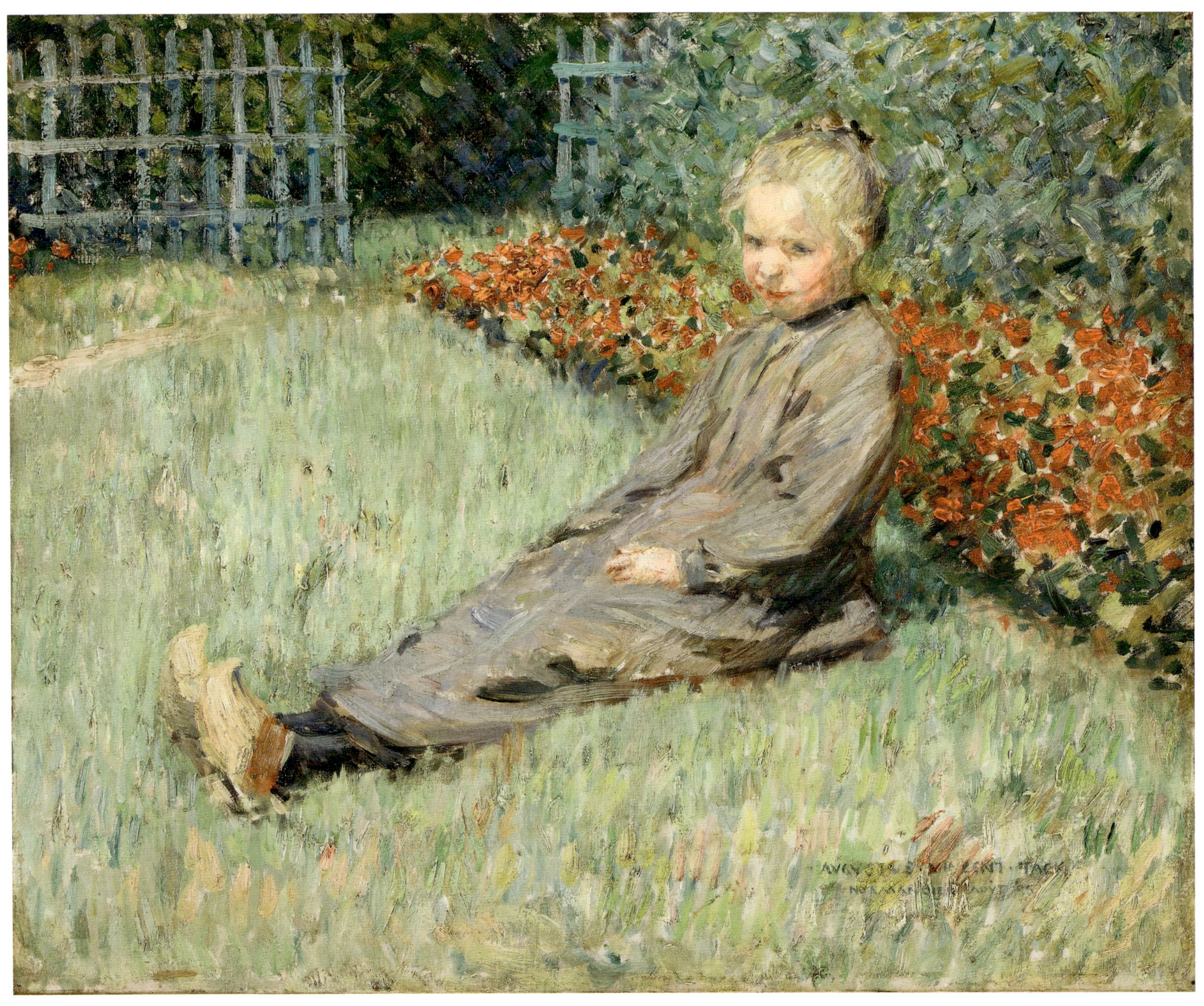

Augustus Vincent Tack

American, 1870–1949

Young Girl in Wooden Shoes 1895

Oil on canvas
18 × 22 inches
Museum Purchase in honor of
Babs Hoffius, Babs Hoffius Memorial
Fund and the Hoffius Family
1991.1.4

Painted in Normandy when Augustus Vincent Tack was just twenty-five years old, *Young Girl in Wooden Shoes* is strikingly close to the classic style of French Impressionism, utilizing precisely delineated quick brushstrokes and vivid color. The intersecting diagonals of the seated child and hedge of flowers set upon a tilting triangular field of grass form a sophisticated composition, reflecting the technical skill and talent of the young painter. The artist clearly recognized the success of this brilliant little painting as he carefully signed and dated the work in a formal manner. Tack had his first solo exhibition in New York the year following this painting, where he was applauded by critics for his feeling for color and spontaneous manner.

Tack began his study of art in 1890 at the Art Students League, of New York, under John Twachtman and H. Siddons Mowbray. He first exhibited in 1893 at the Society of American Artists in the same city. Tack made trips to Europe in 1890, 1893, and 1895, studying in Paris under Luc-Olivier Merson, at the École des Beaux-Arts, and visiting Claude Monet's studio at Giverny. Tack's style evolved drastically through the next two decades, and he is best known for his distinctive abstractions from the 1920s through 1940s, collected and commissioned by Duncan Phillips, with whom he is closely associated.   CMB

This dramatic portrait of a strikingly pale model in a luxurious fur-lined cloak is characteristic of William Merritt Chase's bravura painting style. In its pairing of white fabrics against an unadorned background it echoes the portraits of James McNeill Whistler. During the artist's lifetime the painting was exhibited under different titles: it debuted as *Portrait of Miss C.* at the 1893 Society of American Artists exhibition, then a few years later was shown as *Lady in Opera Cloak*. The artist himself described the model, Mrs. Clark (no relation to Emily J. Clark, the donor), as "the very subject I had long hoped to find—a perfect type of American womanhood. A clear-cut, classic face with splendid profile . . . and above all else, dignity and simplicity. . . ." She appears in four of Chase's paintings, all executed in or around 1893.

Born in Williamsburg, Indiana, Chase first studied under portrait painter Barton Hays (1826–1875). He continued his training from 1872 to 1877 in Munich at the Royal Academy. After five years of training, Chase returned to New York from Germany and taught at the Art Students League, the Brooklyn Art Association, and the Pennsylvania Academy of The Fine Arts. Chase was as exceptional a teacher as he was an artist, and in 1891 he founded the Shinnecock Summer School of Art near Southampton, Long Island. In 1896 he also founded the Chase School, which later became the New York School of Art. A very popular teacher, he taught his students to paint directly from nature, and outspokenly advocated that painting technique should take supremacy over subject matter. **CMB**

Portrait of Miss C. (Lady in Opera Cloak) c. 1893

Oil on canvas
48 × 48 inches
Gift of Emily J. Clark
1935.1.4

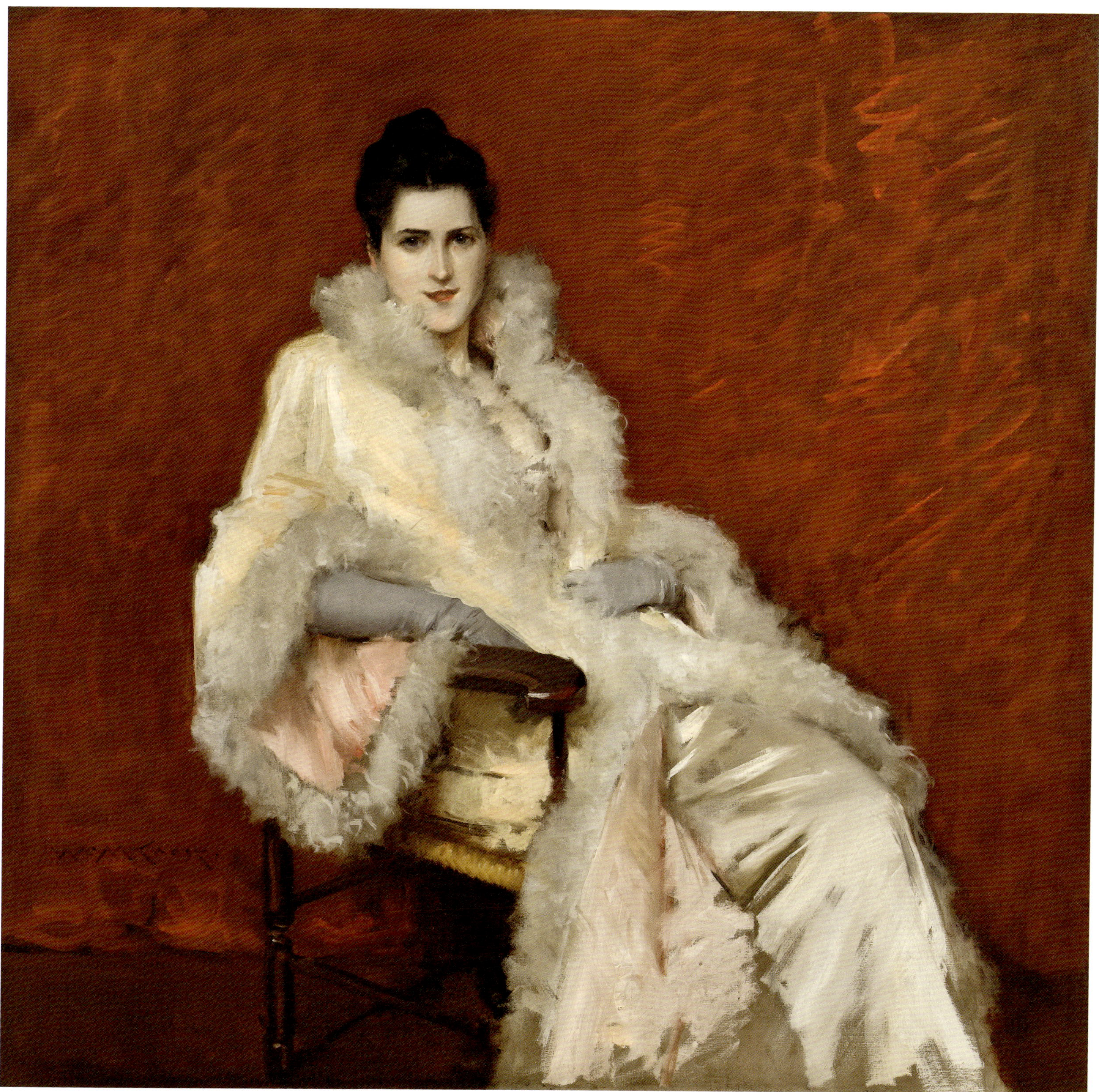

Mary Cassatt
American, 1844–1926

Like many of her fellow Impressionist artists in Paris, Mary Cassatt was drawn to and inspired by Japanese color woodblock prints. This influence, together with the knowledge she had gained in intaglio printmaking since 1879, resulted in a group of eighteen outstanding color prints she created in the 1890s.

One of twelve prints by Cassatt in the Museum's collection, *The Banjo Lesson* is directly related to the mural the artist was painting at this time for the Women's Pavilion at the 1893 World's Columbian Exposition in Chicago. Now lost, the mural's theme was "modern woman," and the right-hand panel included a personification of Music depicted by a young woman playing the banjo. The popularity of banjo playing among middle- and upper-class women of the 1890s made it an extremely modern scene, purposely chosen by Cassatt for that reason. She is quoted as saying that her image of Music would contain "nothing of St. Cecelia," referring to the patron saint of music traditionally depicted holding a lyre, harp, or other classical instrument. **CMB**

The Banjo Lesson c. 1893
Drypoint and aquatint printed in color
from two plates, on off-white laid paper
11¾ × 9⁷⁄₁₆ inches (plate)
Museum Purchase
1968.2.73

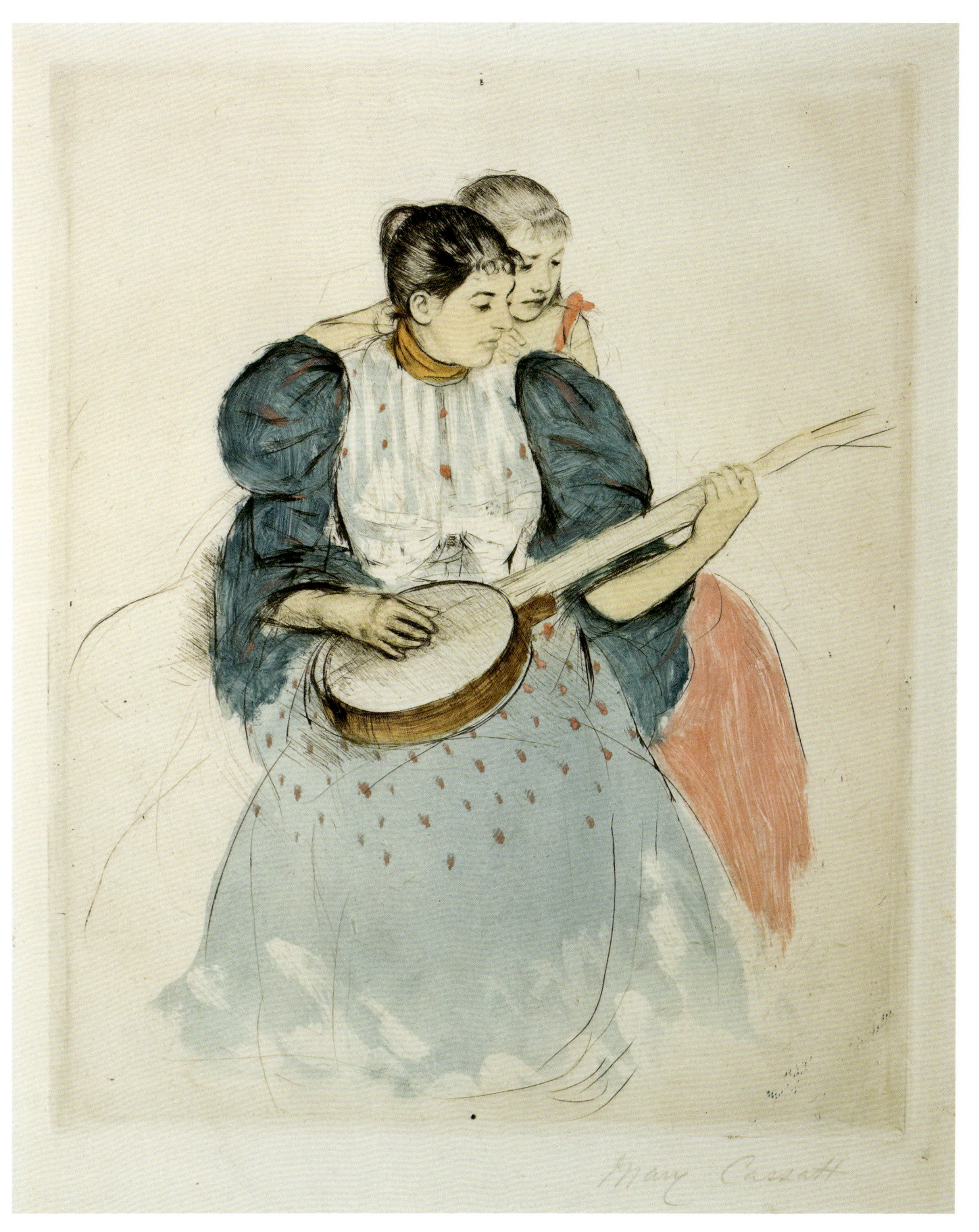

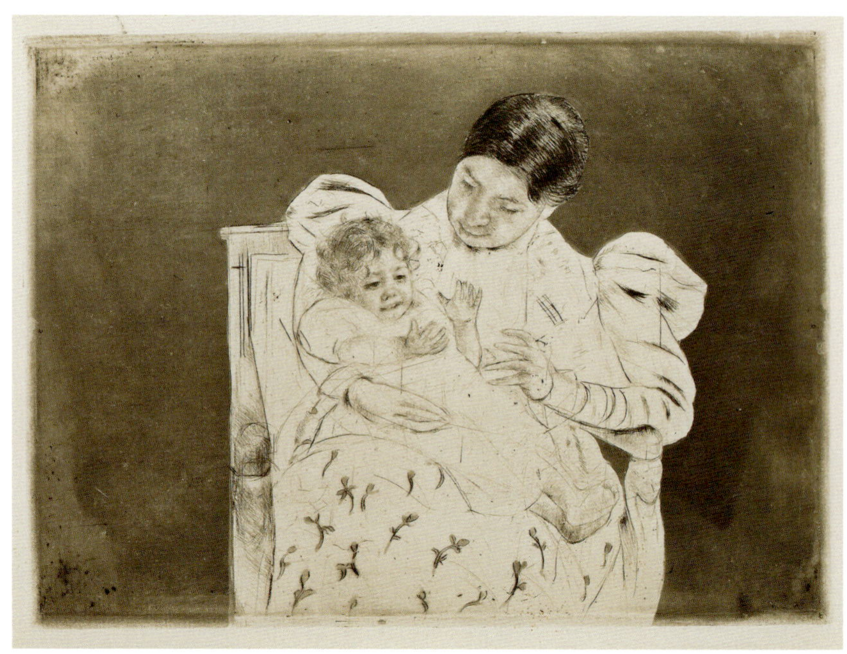

Mary Cassatt was an astute observer of the nurturing relationship between mother and child. Her many paintings, drawings, and prints of this theme are perceptive psychological studies of maternal instinct. In *The Barefooted Child*, the mother gazes intently at her slightly agitated child, while steadying the infant on her lap and calming it in the embrace of her arms. By isolating her figures from their setting and silhouetting them against a brushed ground of color, Cassatt's composition brings to mind traditional scenes of the enthroned Madonna and Christ Child. This allusion gives her modern, everyday subject of mother and child a spiritual dimension.

Of the three impressions in the Museum's collection, the color print with the green background is the final state of the image as it was published. The impression seen here printed only in black is different from the color impressions beyond just the color. It is printed from only one plate, whereas the other impressions are printed from three plates. Aquatinted tone is added in the areas of the flesh and chair on the second plate, and to the clothing on the third plate. The impression printed with an orange background is a unique color proof in which the artist experiments with color combinations, affecting the mood of the scene. CMB

The Barefooted Child c. 1896–1897

Fifth state, plate one only
Drypoint and aquatint on cream wove paper
9⅜ × 12½ inches (plate)
Museum Purchase
1968.2.71

Fifth state, unique trial proof
Color drypoint and aquatint on light blue laid paper
9⁹⁄₁₆ × 12⅝ inches
Museum Purchase, Dorothy Scott Gerber by exchange
2007.14

Fifth state, published edition
Color drypoint and aquatint on cream laid paper
9⁹⁄₁₆ × 12⁷⁄₁₆ inches
Museum Purchase
1968.2.72

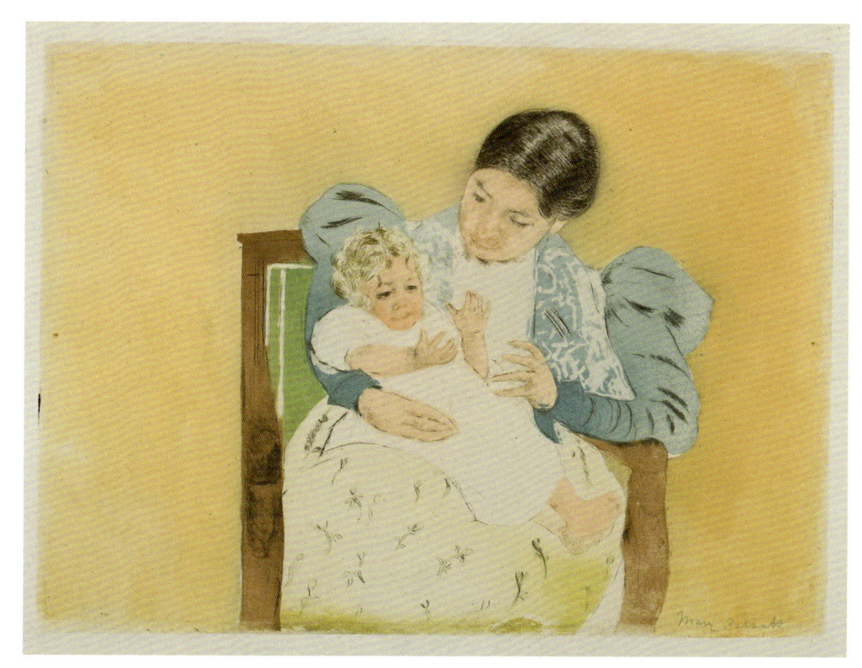 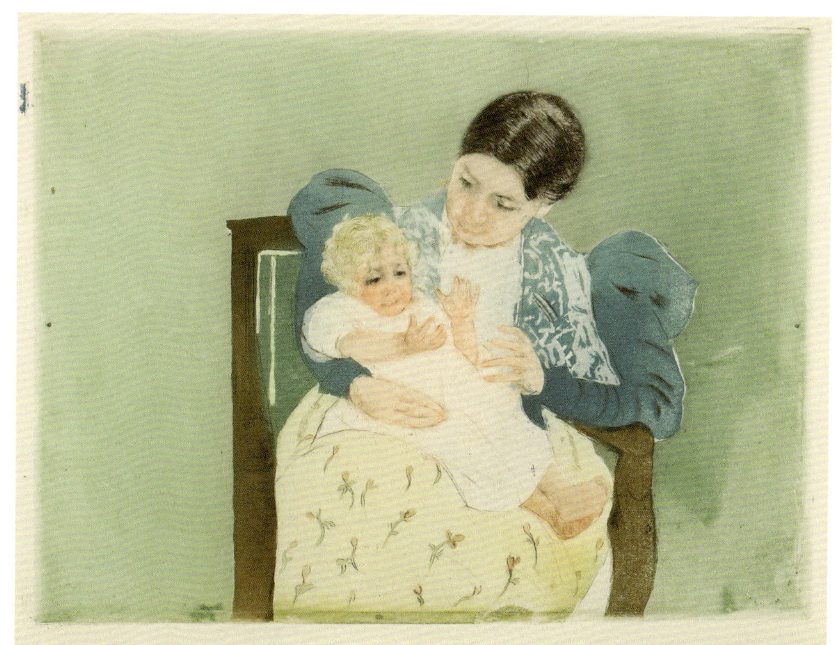

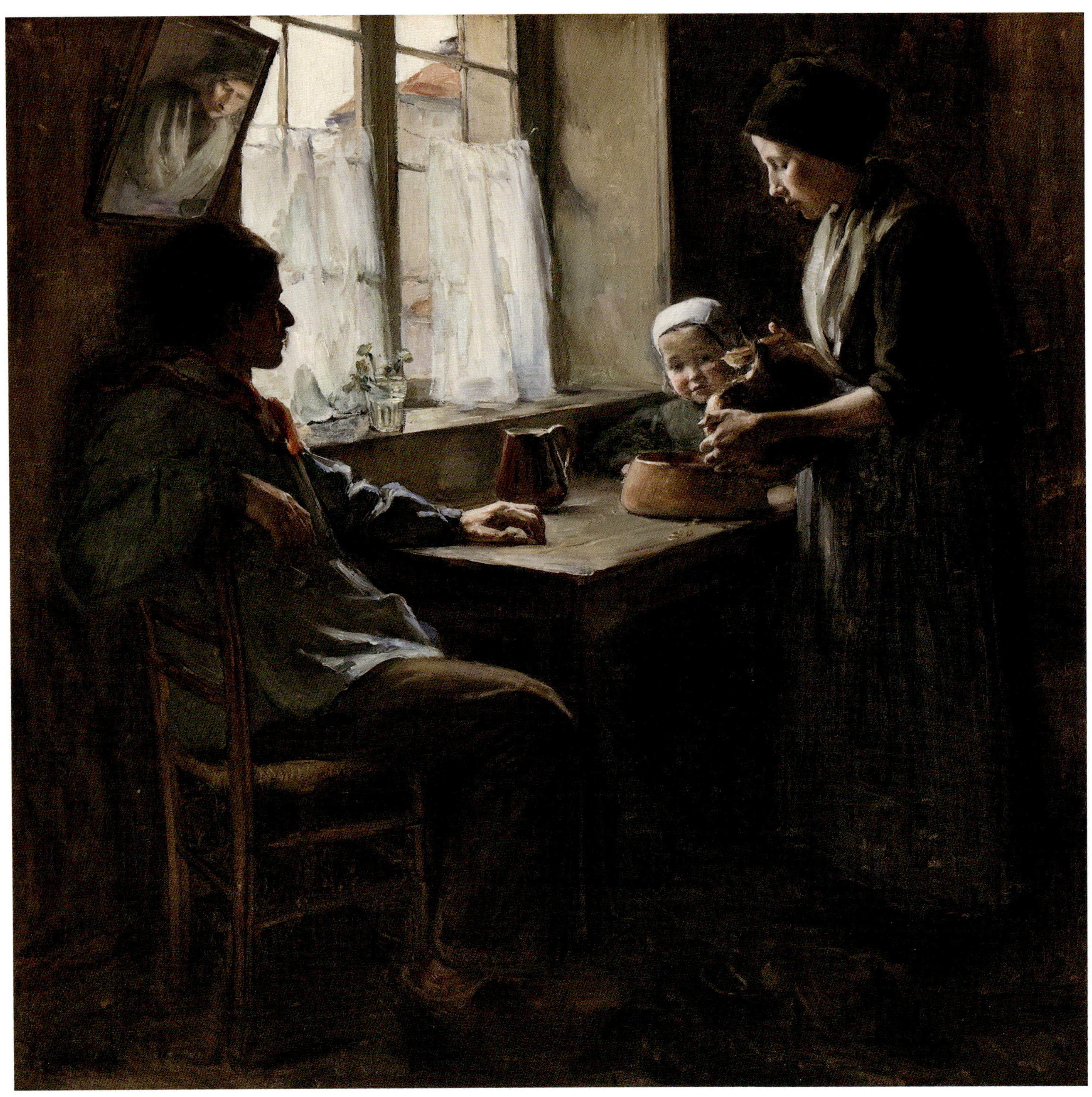

. **Elizabeth Nourse**

American, 1859–1938

Humble Ménage c. 1897

Oil on canvas
39½ × 39½ inches
Gift of Mrs. Cyrus E. Perkins
1911.1.4

Humble Ménage portrays Elizabeth Nourse's frequent subject of peasant women and their children. Depicted with a dignity she imbued in all her subjects, Nourse emphasizes the centrality of the mother's role within the family by reflecting her face in the mirror overhead. The rendering of figures highlighted by sunlight streaming in through the window reveals the strong influence of seventeenth-century Dutch and French painting. Nourse began this painting in Saint Léger-en-Yvelines, a village forty-five miles southwest of Paris. The village became a second home for Nourse and her sister Louise. The painting was shown at the 1897 Paris Salon exhibition and subsequently in Chicago and Philadelphia, where the artist titled it *A Humble Home*. One of the first paintings to enter the collection of the Grand Rapids Art Museum, it was a gift from one of the Museum's founders, and its first President, Mrs. Cyrus E. Perkins.

Elizabeth Nourse's impressive career includes the distinction of being the first woman elected an associate of the Société Nationale des Beaux-Arts. Nourse was born and trained in Cincinnati, but at age twenty-seven traveled to Paris with her sister Louise. Though she intended to stay only a few years, Nourse remained there a lifetime, returning only once to her native hometown in 1891 for an exhibition of her work at the Cincinnati Art Museum. Nourse chose to be buried in her beloved village of Saint Léger-en-Yvelines. **CMB**

Frederic Remington
American, 1861–1909

Frederic Remington was a painter, illustrator, sculptor, and writer who celebrated the American West in the later nineteenth century. Well known for his depiction of cowboys, American Indians, and the United States Cavalry, he constructed a mythological image of the wild frontier that defined American attitudes for nearly a century, most notably in western films.

Although he often depicted Indians endangering a cast of brave cowboys and cavalrymen, Remington also admired Native Americans for their valor and steadfastness in battle. He was particularly drawn to western Canada, where he visited Alberta and Saskatchewan several times. From these trips, he came to believe that the Blackfoot Indians were the most remarkable of all Northern Plains tribes. In 1895, Remington returned again to the region and made sketches to record a winter expedition. They were later the basis for an illustrated article that was serialized in *Harper's Monthly*.

One deftly executed ink and wash drawing from the expedition was *Snow Indian of the Northern Type*. With bridle confidently pulled back to control the gait of his horse, a Blackfoot man rides slowly and proudly forward. As evidence of contact with white civilization, he wears a Hudson Bay blanket capote—or hooded coat—and trousers. In another suggestion of an earlier age of French fur trapping, he wears a feathered beaver hat. Despite Remington's heroic portrayal, Indians at this point in the history of North America resided mostly on federal reservations, diminished by disease and massacre. **RHA**

Snow Indian of the Northern Type c. 1897
Pen and ink with wash on paper
21½ × 19 inches
Gift of Mr. Peter M. Wege
1967.5.1

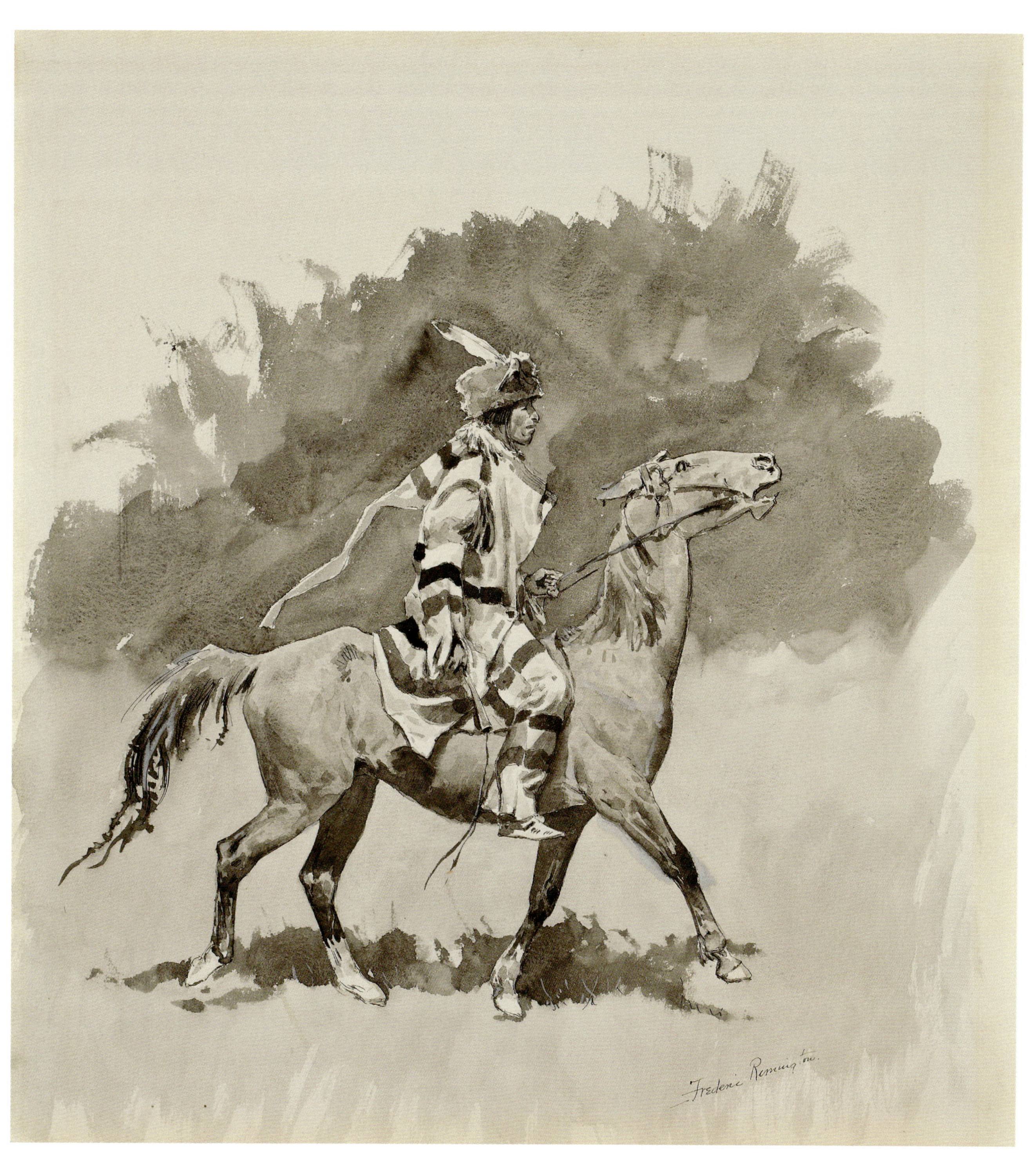

▪ **Paul Gauguin**
French, 1848–1903

In his increasing effort to reject the materialism of contemporary culture in favor of a more spiritual, unfettered life, Paul Gauguin moved to Tahiti in 1891. During his time there, he not only painted but also turned to wood sculpture, pottery, and woodblock prints. Ultimately his free and expressive cutting of the printing block helped to inspire a revival of the art of the woodcut.

Gauguin's undisputed woodcut masterpieces are the ten prints of the *Noa Noa Suite*. The images, drawing upon Tahitian myth and ritual, focus on elemental human experiences. They form a fluid cycle of divine creation, sexuality, birth, death, and rebirth. Far from seeking raw, flat forms, Gauguin strove for ambiguity, using over-printings and off-register printings, blending of inks on the blocks, hand rubbing the paper against the blocks, and inking the lower areas of the blocks so that the paper would pick up the soft, wavy marks made by the chisel. Gauguin himself printed no more than twelve impressions from any of the blocks, but editions were also pulled in collaboration with the printer Louis Roy. In 1921, Gauguin's son Pola reprinted eight blocks from the *Noa Noa Suite*, along with two additional woodcuts with Tahitian subjects, to form *Paul Gauguin 10 Traesnit*, posthumous editions of unsurpassed quality.

Gauguin's Post-Impressionist style evolved between 1886 and 1888 in his association with a group of artists known as the Pont-Aven School and during a short stay with Vincent van Gogh in the south of France. He rejected the tradition of western naturalism, using nature as a starting point from which to abstract figures and symbols. Gauguin stressed linear patterns, flat colors, and intense color harmonies, imbuing his art with a sense of mystery and expressive power that links him as a founding figure to the modern notion of "primitivism" in the arts.   CMB

Paul Gauguin 10 Traesnit
(Ten Woodcuts) 1893–1899
Te Po (Eternal Night)
Nave Nave Fenua (Fragrant Island)
L'Univers est créé (The Creation of the Universe)
Auti te Pape (Women at the River)
Maruru (Offerings of Gratitude)
Manau Tupapau (The Spirits of the Dead are Watching)
Noa Noa (Fragrant Scent)
Mahna no Varua Ino (The Devil Speaks)
Mahana Atua (The Day of God)
Le Sourire

Set of ten woodcuts on laid paper
Printed by Pola Gauguin, Paris, 1921
Various dimensions
Gift of Mabel H. Perkins
1949.2.24–33

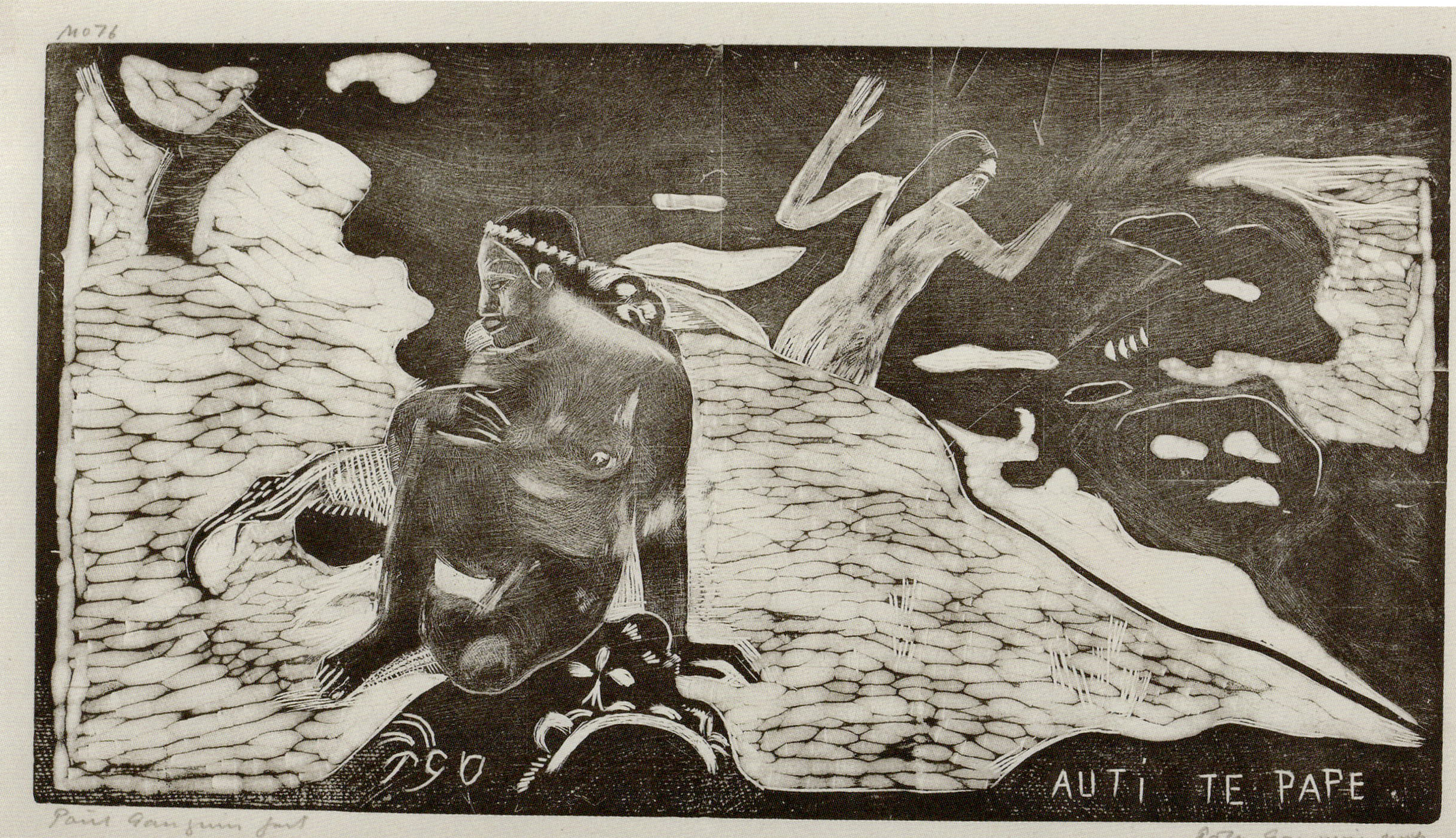
AUTI TE PAPE

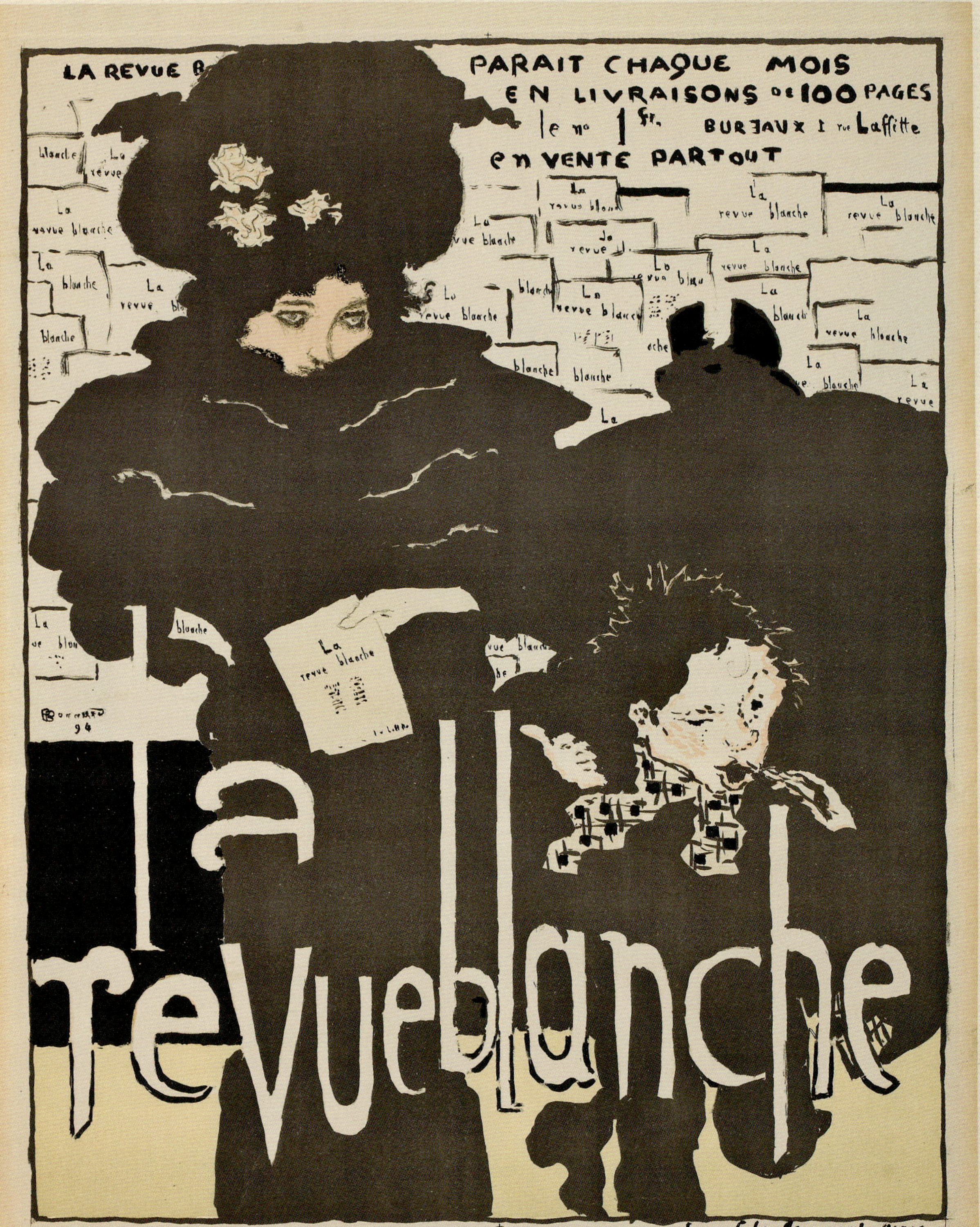

LA REVUE B...
blanche La revue
La revue blanche
La blanche La revue bl...
blanche
PARAIT CHAQUE MOIS
EN LIVRAISONS DE 100 PAGES
le no 1 fr. BUREAUX I rue Laffitte
en VENTE PARTOUT
La revue blanche
La revue blanche
La revue blanche
La revue blanche
La revue blanche
La revue blanche
La revue
La revue blanche
blanche
La revue blanche
La revue blanche
La
revue
La revue blanche
La
blanche
La revue blanche
blanche
La revue blanche
La
La revueblanche
Imp. Edw. Ancourt, PARIS

Pierre Bonnard
French, 1867–1947

Pierre Bonnard completed several lithographs for the literary review *La Revue blanche* between 1891 and 1903, as well as this color poster. *La Revue blanche (The White Review)*, published by the Brothers Natanson, was named for white light—which reflects all the colors of the spectrum. In the same fashion, the publishing house was open to a variety of ideas and schools, and invited Paris' leading writers and visual artists to contribute to its review.

In Bonnard's poster, a smartly dressed *parisienne* holds a new issue of *La Revue blanche*. The woman is Misia Sert, wife of Thadée Natanson and a notable figure in the circle of avant-garde artists in Paris. With boulevard wit, Bonnard pairs his fashionable woman with a rough-and-tumble newsboy. In a visual pun, the *l* of the word *la* hangs like a parasol from the woman's arm. In the background, the silhouette of a gentleman's top hat and evening cloak also plays in counterpoint to the figures. The bold flat shapes and stylized lettering, associated with Art Nouveau, are characteristic of the graphic designs of the Nabis artists.

The Nabis were a group of young Post-Impressionist avant-garde Parisian artists of the 1890s. This group, which included Bonnard, Édouard Vuillard, and Maurice Denis, was noted for the variety of media in which they worked. In addition to the fine arts, they worked in printmaking, poster design, book illustration, textiles, furniture, and theater design. The success of Bonnard's first color lithograph, an 1891 poster for *France-Champagne*, motivated him to continue working in lithography. In the same year, Bonnard introduced Henri de Toulouse-Lautrec to color lithography and its application to the commercial poster. **RHA**

. Henri de Toulouse-Lautrec
French, 1864–1901

Henri de Toulouse-Lautrec used the medium of the poster as a vehicle for personal expression that derived from his own private circle of acquaintances. With elements of caricature and sympathetic identification, he drew into his art the cabaret performers of Montmartre and close friends, whom he sketched and presented in their own social milieu.

May Milton was an English dancer with a pale, serious face and strong chin whose signature costume was a white débutante's dress with puff sleeves. Promoted as the "English Miss," Milton performed for only one season in Paris, on a small, undistinguished stage. She then departed for New York never to be heard from again. This five-color poster was printed in Paris by Ancourt to publicize the dancer's tour of the United States.

During the 1890s, the last decade of his life, Toulouse-Lautrec became a master of lithography, amassing a body of original lithographs that number among the most important in the history of the modern print. Between 1891 and 1899 he produced thirty-one posters that are the foundation for his reputation as the greatest of all poster artists. His posters epitomize the avant-garde styles of the fin-de-siècle in their flat forms enlivened by bold color and curvilinear contours. **RHA**

Poster for *May Milton* 1895

Color lithograph on beige wove paper
31⁵⁄₁₆ × 24³⁄₁₆ inches
Museum Purchase, Drake Quinn Family Foundation
2005.6

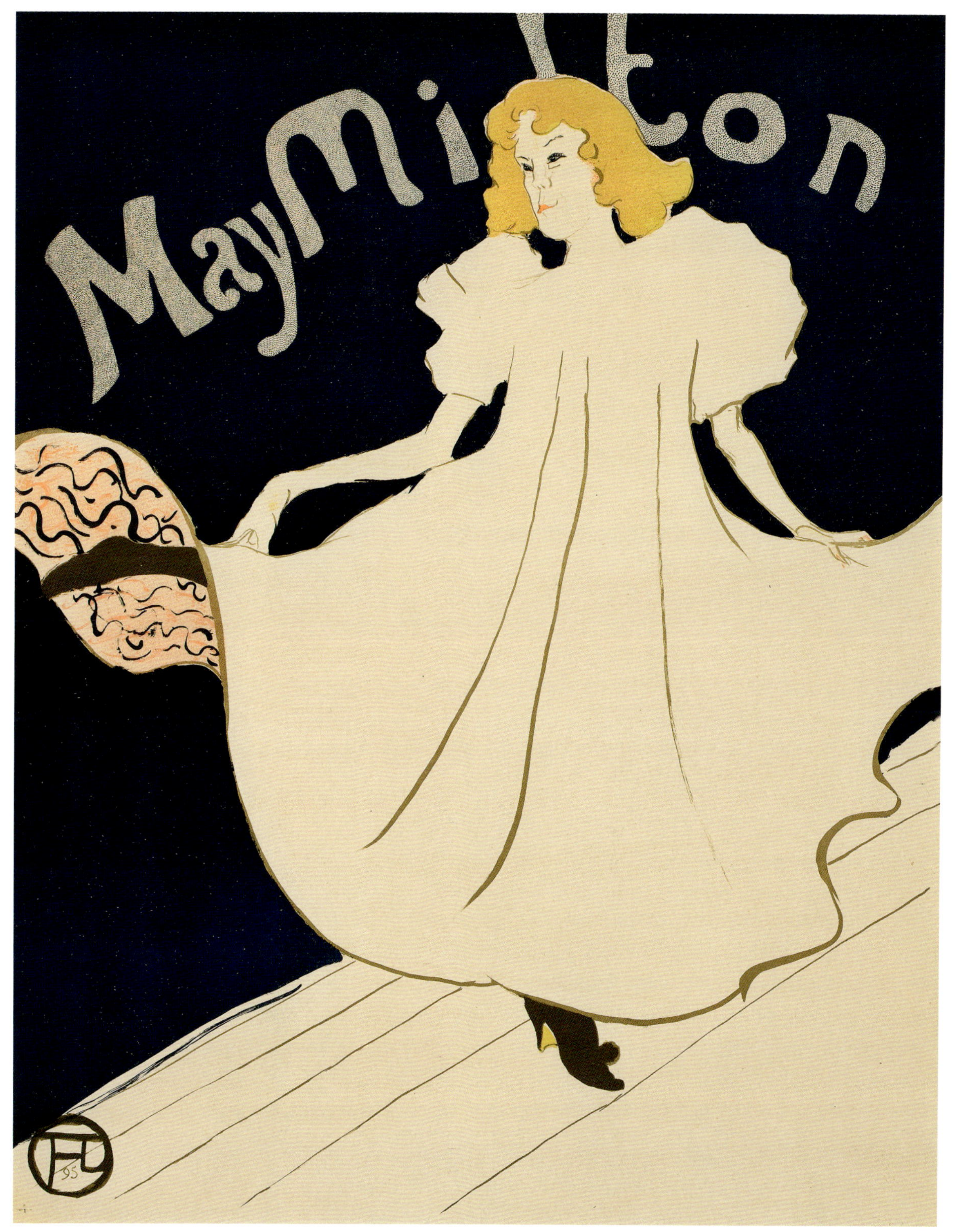
May Milton

. **Henri de Toulouse-Lautrec**
French, 1864–1901

Jane Avril, a star performer in the cabarets of Montmartre, commissioned this poster for the Églantine dancers' first and only London appearance. It shows the members of the high-kicking Parisian troupe—Jane Avril, Cléopatre, Églantine, and Gazelle. They are engaged in the lively can-can—a leg-baring, risqué dance that was the rage in the cabarets of Montmartre. Although Toulouse-Lautrec made a preparatory oil sketch for the poster, he based the composition on a photograph. From both photograph and sketch he extracted the simplified lines for the poster and created a sharp caricature of each dancer. Jealousies divided the dancers into two camps: Avril and Églantine against Cléopatre and Gazelle. Toulouse-Lautrec seems to have enjoyed choreographing their rivalry in an iconic image of Parisian nightlife.

Henri de Toulouse-Lautrec was born into an aristocratic French family. Against his family wishes, he pursued art as a profession, studying with established academic painters and then joining more progressive artists' circles in Paris. Although a sensitive portraitist of his bohemian friends and cabaret performers in Montmartre, Toulouse-Lautrec is best known for his color lithography.   **RHA**

Poster for *La Troupe de Mademoiselle Églantine (The Troupe of Mademoiselle Églantine)* 1896
Color lithograph on beige wove paper
24 1/16 × 31 3/16 inches
Museum Purchase, Peter M. Wege
2005.4

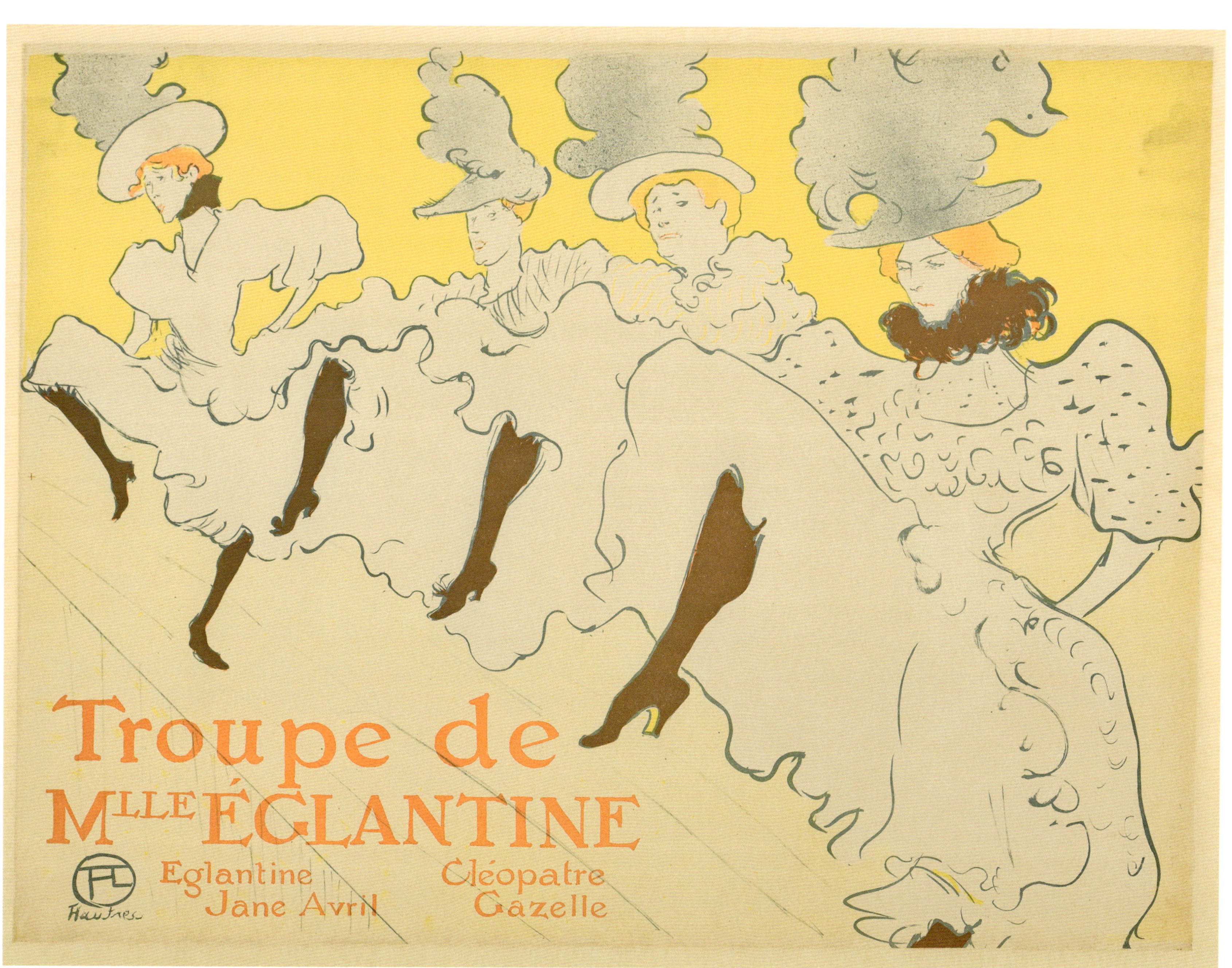

Troupe de
Mlle EGLANTINE
Eglantine   Cléopatre
Jane Avril   Gazelle

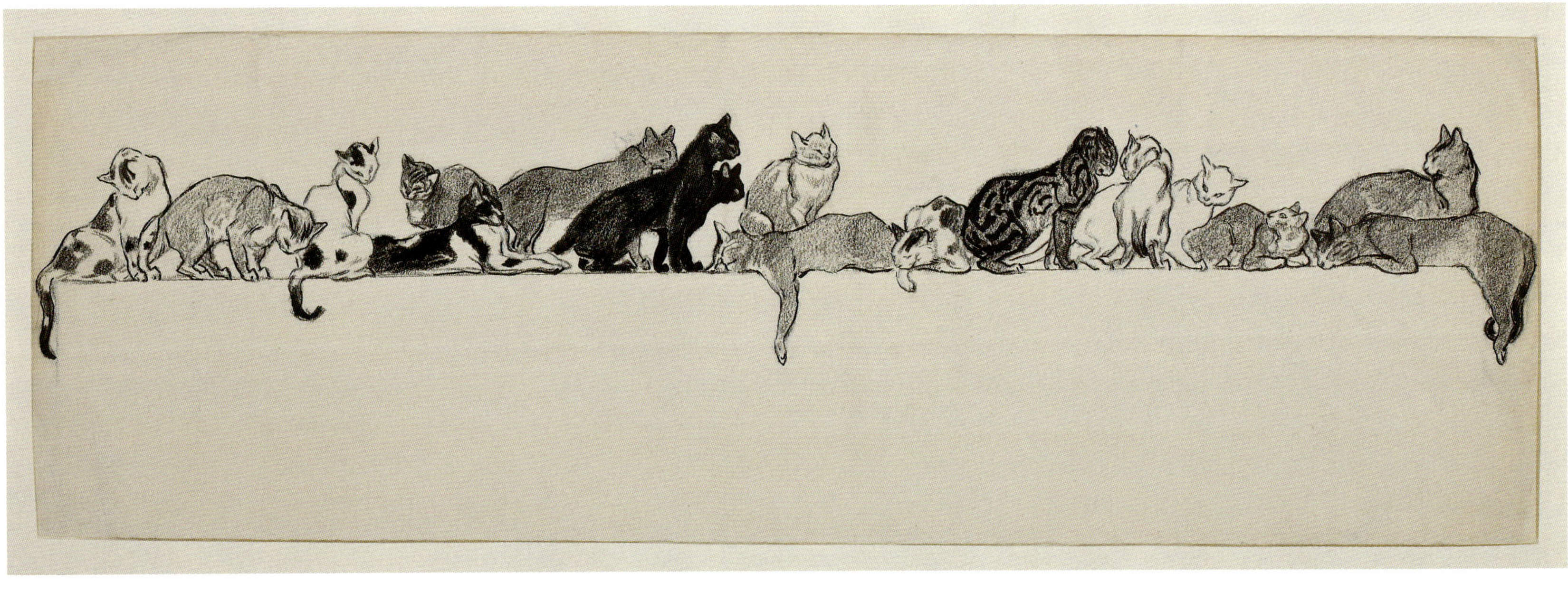

Théophile Alexandre Steinlen

Swiss, 1859–1923

Seventeen Cats on a Ledge was created to illustrate the margins of a special four-page supplement of the weekly journal *L'Illustration*. The March 1901 issue, for which this was drawn, featured an article on cats by Jacques Dalbray. Théophile Steinlen's drawing presents seventeen cats in varied poses that represent the many characteristic postures of cats. Like Degas' dancers at the bar, the cats stretch and bend, relax and extend their agile limbs in an engaging and syncopated line of feline display. Steinlen painted this subject often and became increasingly known for his depictions of cats. They were his most notable subjects and he rendered them in prints, drawings, paintings, and sculpture with an exceptional level of accuracy and understanding.

Seventeen Cats on a Ledge

1901

Graphite, black chalk, and black ink
over traces of blue chalk on paper
7½ × 21⅞ inches
Museum Purchase, Stuart and
Babs Hoffius and Jon and Carol Muth
2006.38

When Steinlen moved to the Montmartre quarter of Paris in the early 1890s, he was introduced to the artists' community at *Le Chat Noir* (The Black Cat), the first great literary cabaret of the era. Steinlen was commissioned to create poster art for the cabaret's owner, Aristide Bruant, and produced the signature poster image of a black cat for the cabaret. He became well known in the art circles of Montmartre that included Pierre Bonnard, Félix Vallotton, Edgar Degas, and Henri de Toulouse-Lautrec.   CMB

Robert Henri
American, 1865–1929

Portrait of Gertrude Kaska, also known under its previous title *Young Girl with a Bonnet*, is characteristic of Robert Henri's broad brushwork and use of strong illumination against deep shadow. It is not known whether this striking painting was a commissioned portrait, but its presence in the artist's studio at the time of his death suggests this was not the case. Henri was known for expressive portraits such as this. He wrote the following advice regarding portraying children in his 1923 publication *The Art Spirit*: "If you paint children you must have no patronizing attitude toward them. Whoever approaches a child without humility, without wonderment and without infinite respect, misses in his judgment of what is before him, and loses an opportunity for a marvelous response. Children are greater than the grown man."

Robert Henri was born in Cincinnati, Ohio, as Robert Henry Cozad. He changed his surname to Henri after his father was charged with murder (although later exonerated). He chose to pronounce this variant of his middle name as "hen-rye" to rhyme with buckeye, in honor of his Ohio roots. Henri studied with Thomas Anshutz at the Pennsylvania Academy of The Fine Arts during the mid-1880s and traveled to France, studying first at the Académie Julian and later at the École des Beaux-Arts. Henri's most significant influence on American art was as a teacher, writer, and organizer. He taught at the New York School of Art, then founded his own art school in New York in 1909. He was a driving force behind the important 1908 exhibition of a group of artists known as The Eight at the Macbeth Gallery. This event marked an important move away from the hegemony of the National Academy of Design, and featured the work of artists later known as the Ashcan School, so named for their gritty depictions of contemporary urban life. **CMB**

Portrait of Gertrude Kaska 1904
Oil on canvas
23 × 19¼ inches
Gift of Mr. and Mrs. Hyman J. Bylan
1962.1.8

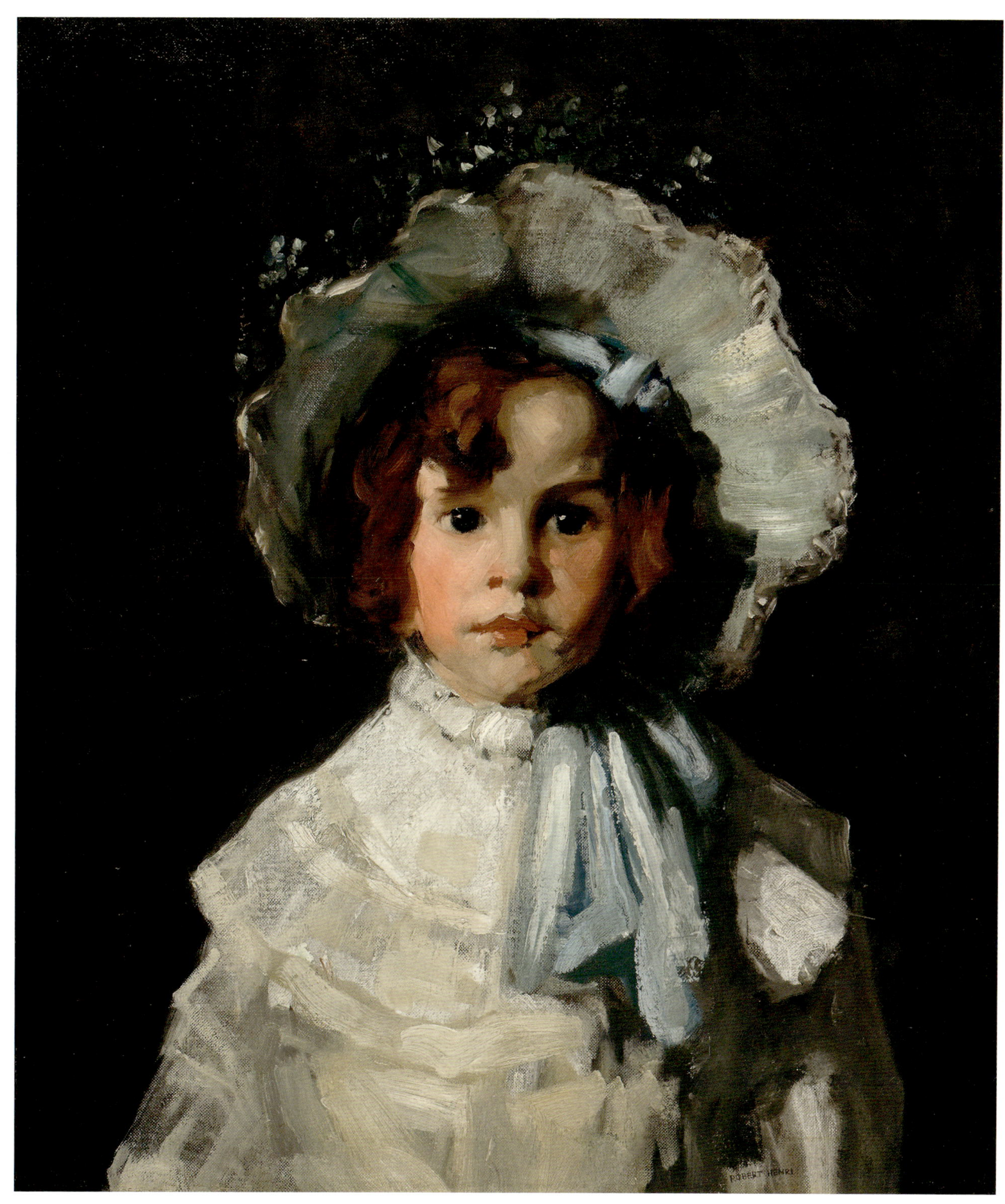

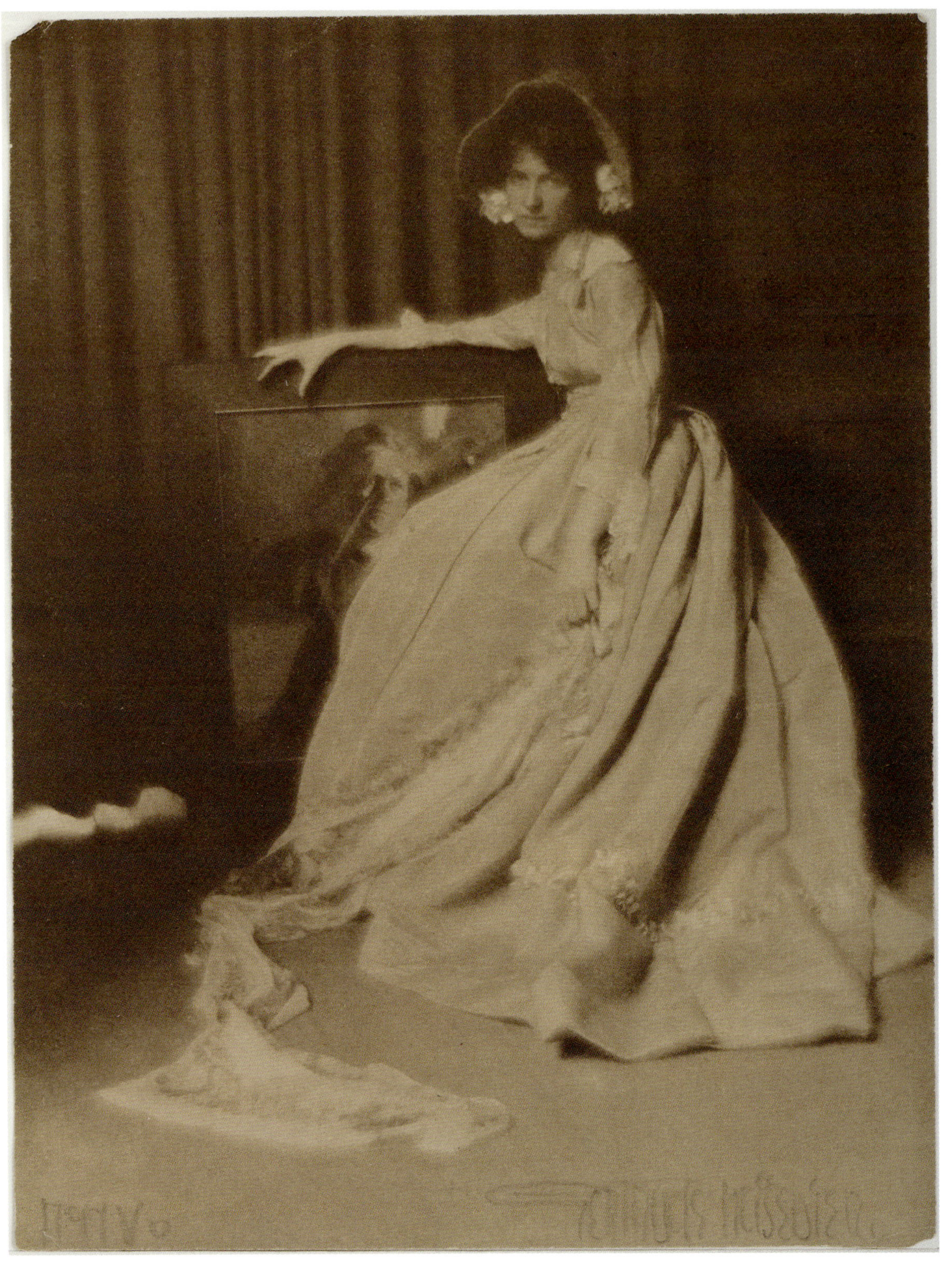

Gertrude Käsebier

American, 1852–1934

Portrait of Eulabee Dix 1910

Vintage toned platinum print
7¹⁵⁄₁₆ × 5¹⁵⁄₁₆ inches
Gift of Frederick P. Currier
1986.14.24

In 1895, Eulabee Dix rejoined her family in Grand Rapids, Michigan, following her art studies at the St. Louis School of Fine Art. She began to teach art classes and to paint portrait miniatures, the genre for which she became nationally known. Moving to New York at the turn of the century to become a professional artist, Dix achieved a reputation as an accomplished society portrait painter, dividing her time between New York and London. Dix's sitters included Ethel Barrymore, Mark Twain, and Gertrude Käsebier. Dix, herself, was the subject of two portraits by the American artist Robert Henri. Käsebier, a close friend, photographed her on at least four occasions.

As a portrait photographer, Käsebier sought the character and beauty of her sitters. This is reflected in her photograph of Dix in which she wears a voluminous dress and flowered bonnet suggestive of early Victorian fashion. Dix is reported to have had a love for self-dramatization in hand gesture and clothing; it was her idea to dress up when she posed for Käsebier. Subtle lighting stresses the long folds of the dress and the downward spill of a shawl that Dix has nonchalantly dropped to the floor. As a contrived image of timeless elegance, the photograph accentuates Dix's slender beauty with the extended and elegant line of her right arm resting on a framed portrait painting of Käsebier. **RHA**

Léon-Augustin Lhermitte is known for his poetic scenes of rustic life that incorporated Impressionist techniques into Realist compositions. In a similar vein to that of Jules Bastien-Lepage, Lhermitte specialized in depicting individualized peasants working in bountiful fields and spacious landscapes. Lhermitte played an active role in the resurgence of pastel painting. As an active member of the Société des Pastellistes Français, he exhibited with them often and mentored younger artists in the technique.

Lhermitte was a native of Mont-Saint-Père, in the Picardy region of northern France. He spent every summer in his native village, while maintaining a studio during the rest of the year in Paris. His 1881 monumental series of paintings on the life of the agricultural worker contributed to his reputation as the next Jean-François Millet, and illustrations of his work reproduced in *Le Monde Illustré* were greatly admired by Vincent van Gogh.

His paintings, charcoals, and pastels were appreciated by an international audience during his lifetime, and over the past twenty years have received renewed attention. CMB

Landscape (Shepherd and Flock at the Farm of Ru-Chailly) c. 1905–1910
Pastel on paper mounted to canvas
16½ × 20½ inches
Gift of Emily J. Clark
1935.1.17

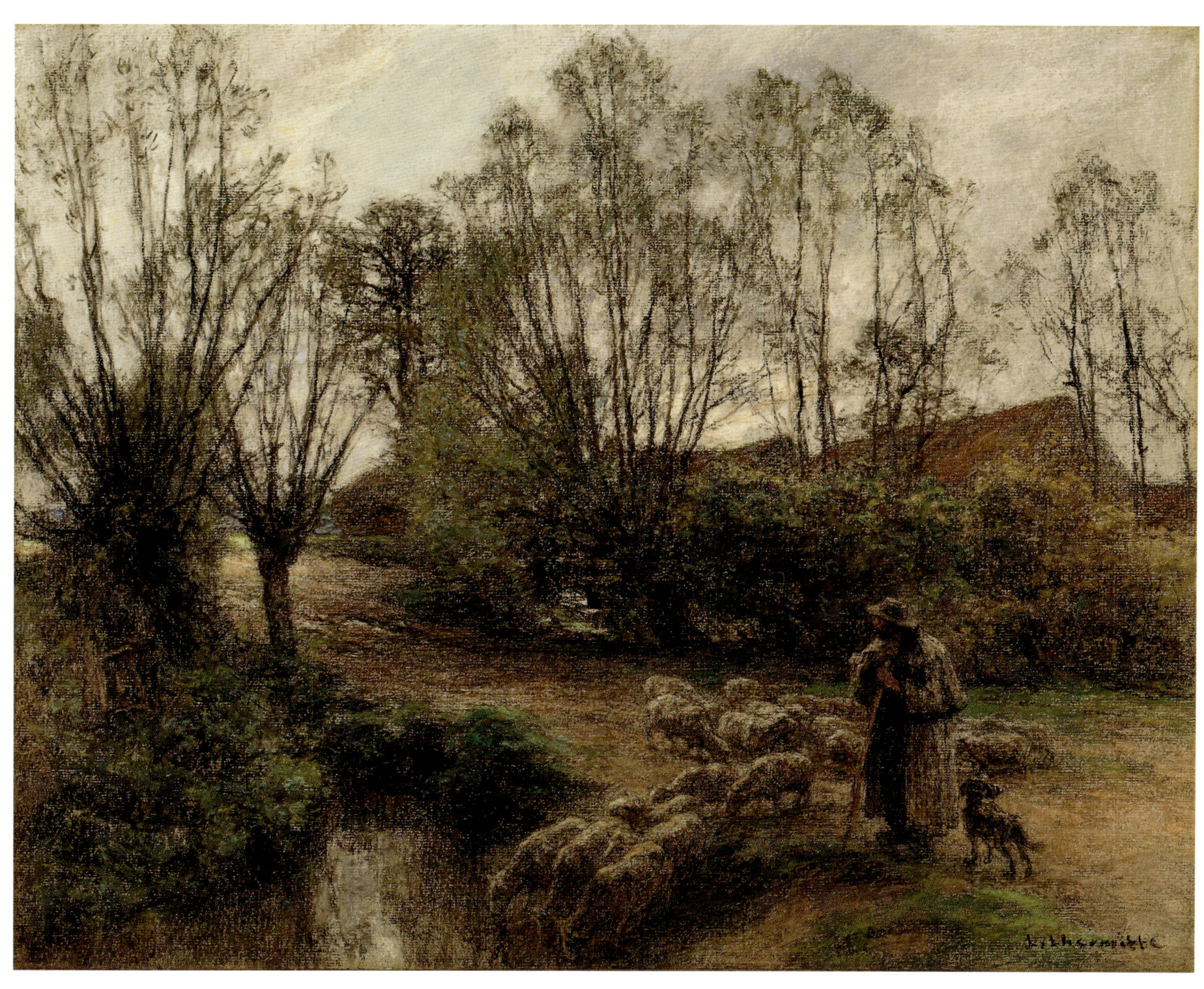
L. Lhermitte

. **Armand Guillaumin**
French, 1841–1927

In *View at Rouen,* Armand Guillaumin portrays a view across the river from Rouen Cathedral, the spires of the cathedral barely visible behind a large tree. A pair of cranes on the quay in the foreground anchor the composition and visually unite the near and far banks of the river. Guillaumin is best known for his paintings of the urban landscape, frequently depicting workers and yards. These were scenes with which he became very familiar while working for the French railroad.

Guillaumin began his formal artistic training at the Académie Suisse in Paris, and later exhibited with Paul Cézanne and Camille Pissarro at the Salon des Refusés in 1863. The continued friendship he shared with these artists introduced him to the style of Impressionism and he contributed to all but two of the Impressionist exhibitions. As his style developed in the 1880s, he became more interested in expressing the mood and feelings induced by nature through use of complementary colors and dramatically lit scenes. In 1891, Guillaumin won 100,000 francs in the state lottery, allowing him to retire from municipal service and devote all of his time to painting. CMB

View at Rouen 1904
Oil on canvas
21⅞ × 25⅞ inches
Gift of the Estate of Martin A. and Carrie Ryerson
1939.1.4

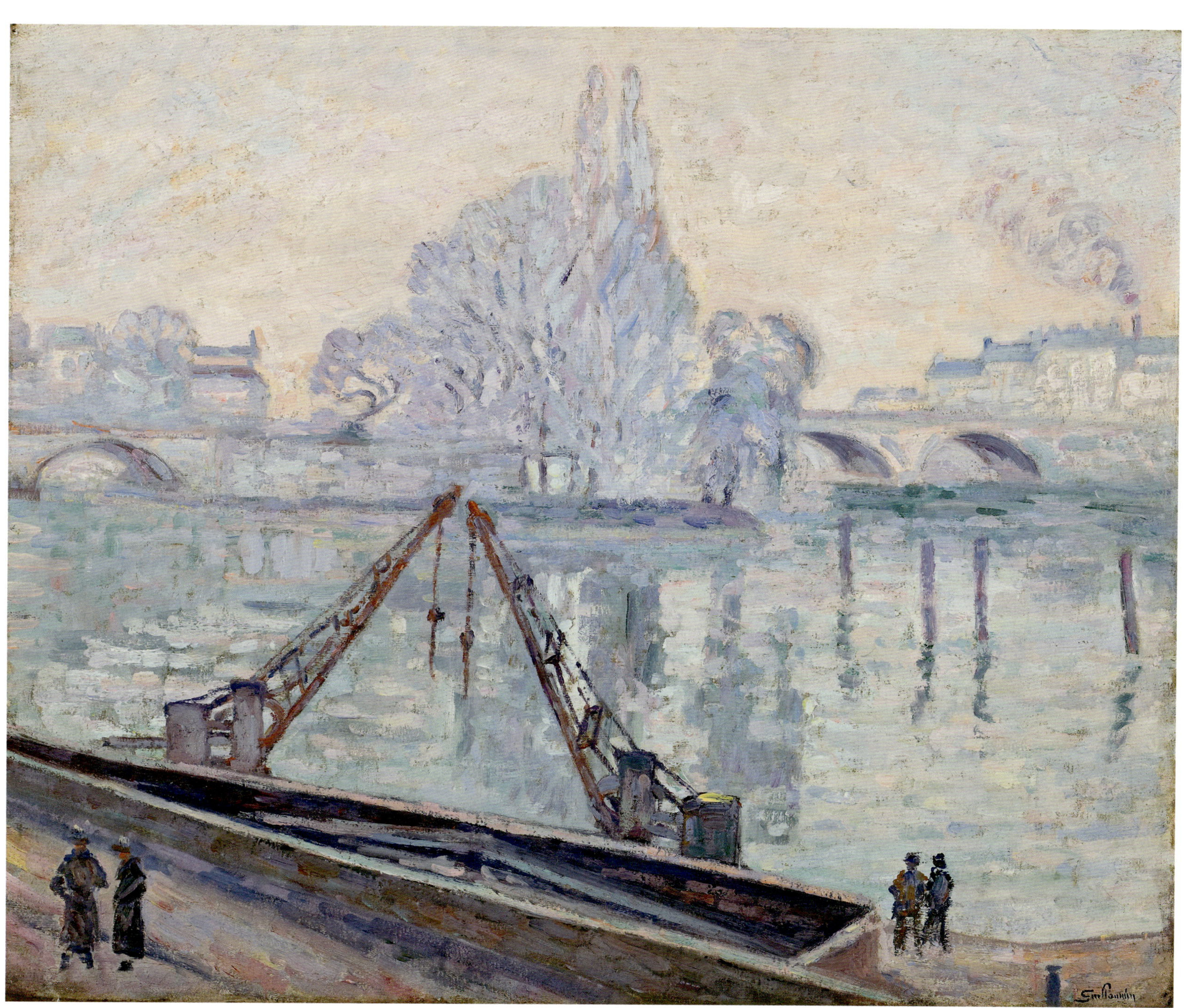

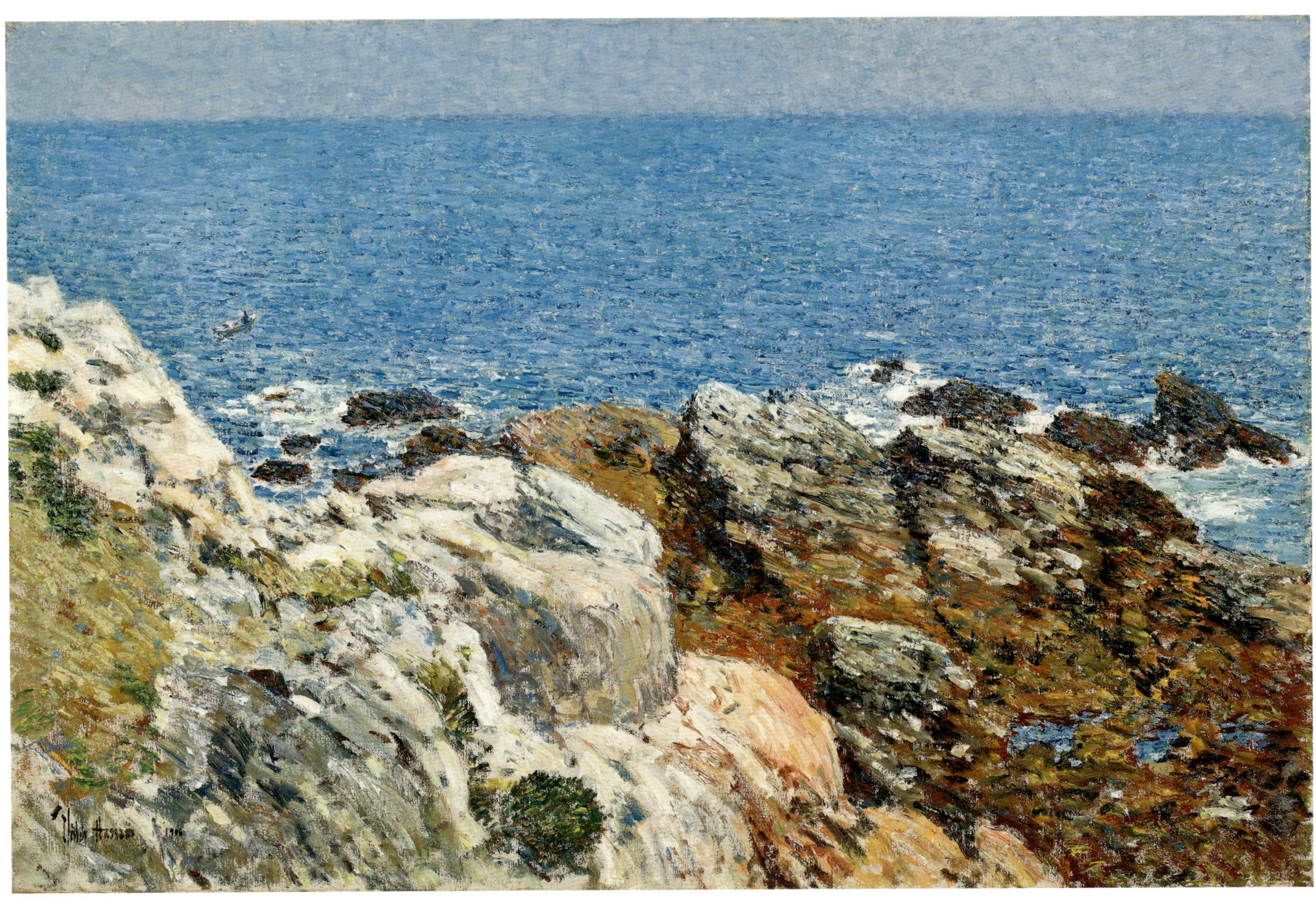

Childe Hassam

American, 1859–1935

Summer Sea 1906

Oil on canvas
19½ × 29½ inches
Gift of Mr. and Mrs. Hyman J. Bylan
1964.1.6

Summer Sea is a painting of the Isles of Shoals in which Childe Hassam captures the sparkle of vivid blues and whites across the ocean surface. Beginning in 1890 Hassam traveled each summer to this group of nine islands located ten miles off the New Hampshire and Maine coasts. Celia Thaxter, a poet and longtime friend of Hassam, ran House, a summer resort on Appledore, the largest island of the area. She encouraged Hassam's first visit to the Isles, and he continued to return to the wild and rugged area until 1916, completing over four hundred paintings, watercolors, pastels, drawings, and prints of the region. In contrast to the approach of Monet and other French Impressionists who painted multiple canvases of one subject in varying conditions of light, Hassam delighted in painting the sea and rocks in the midday sun.

Hassam was a leader among the first generation of American Impressionist painters. After studying in Boston and Paris, he settled in New York and in 1898 became a member of a group of American Impressionists known as The Ten. Hassam strongly identified with his American roots and his sense of patriotism continually led him back to his local landscapes.   CMB

. **John Singer Sargent**
American (b. Italy), 1856–1925

The Brook, set in the Val d'Aosta in the mountains of northern Italy, depicts the brilliant play of light on water, becoming nearly abstract as it is interpreted by dazzling brushwork and brilliant color. John Singer Sargent's early watercolor sketches served as studies for many of his oil paintings, but after 1900, watercolor became his preferred medium. The quick, spontaneous quality of watercolor fulfilled his desire to capture the light, air, and reflections that he observed in the landscape around him. Sargent often worked outdoors, and the portability of watercolor allowed him to produce a large and spontaneous body of work. Sargent's watercolors were often bold and experimental in manner. His friendships with the French Impressionists, particularly Claude Monet, also influenced his rapid and fluid brush technique.

Sargent was born in Italy to expatriate parents. His family moved their household across Europe during Sargent's youth and instilled wanderlust in his spirit. He began his formal artistic education at the age of thirteen in the studio of Carl Welsh, another American expatriate based in Rome. Sargent also attended classes at the Accademia delle Belle Arti in Florence and learned portraiture in the school of Carolus-Duran in Paris. During the 1880s, Sargent became a significant presence at the Paris salons, gaining notoriety for his portraits, *El Jaleo* (1882) and *Madame X* (1884). Though he spent much of his career in Europe, Sargent obtained official American citizenship during his first trip to America in 1876.   CMB

The Brook c. 1906–1908

Watercolor and gouache over graphite
on white wove paper
16½ × 13¹⁵⁄₁₆ inches
Gift of Mr. and Mrs. Hyman J. Bylan
1962.1.6

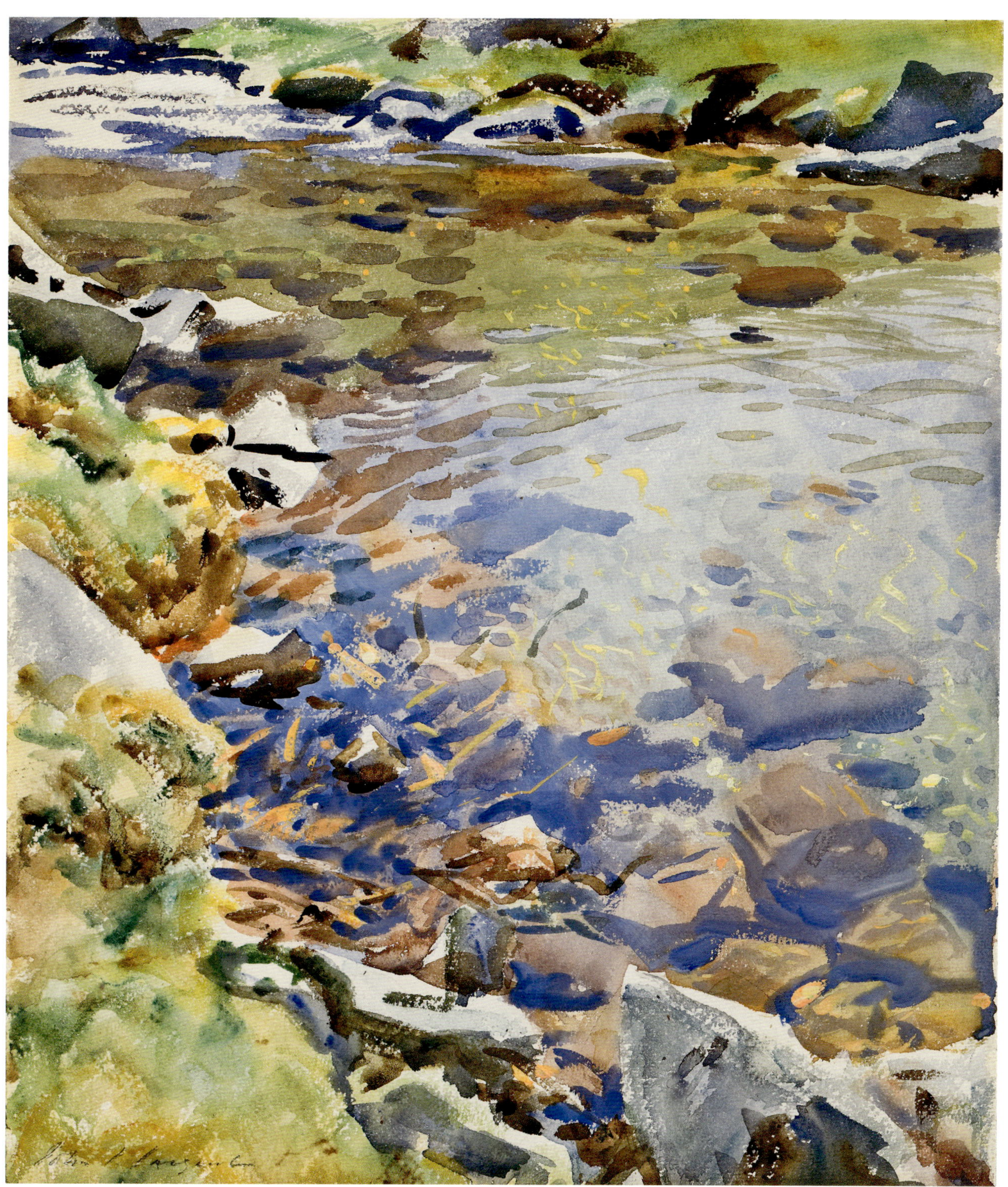

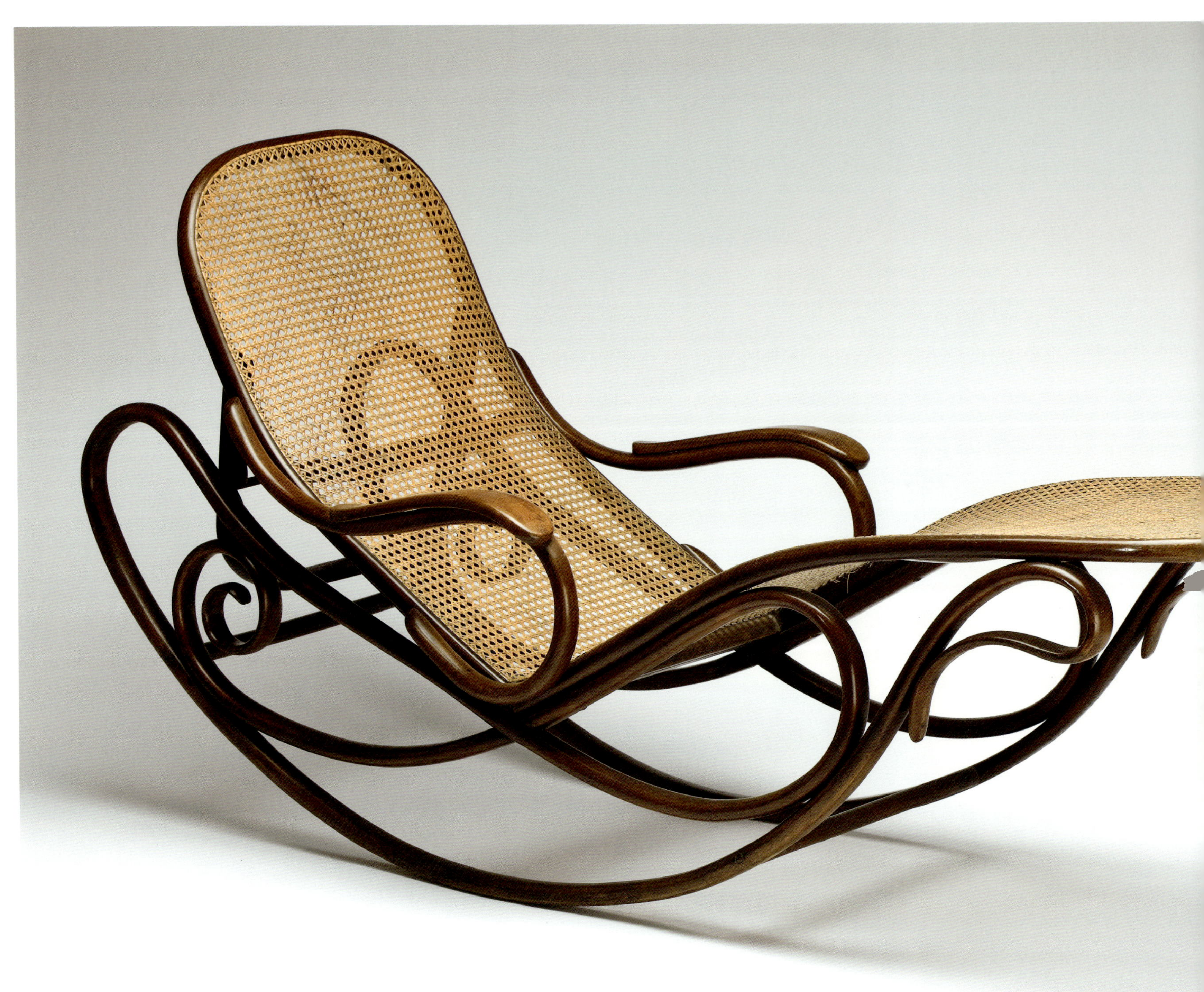

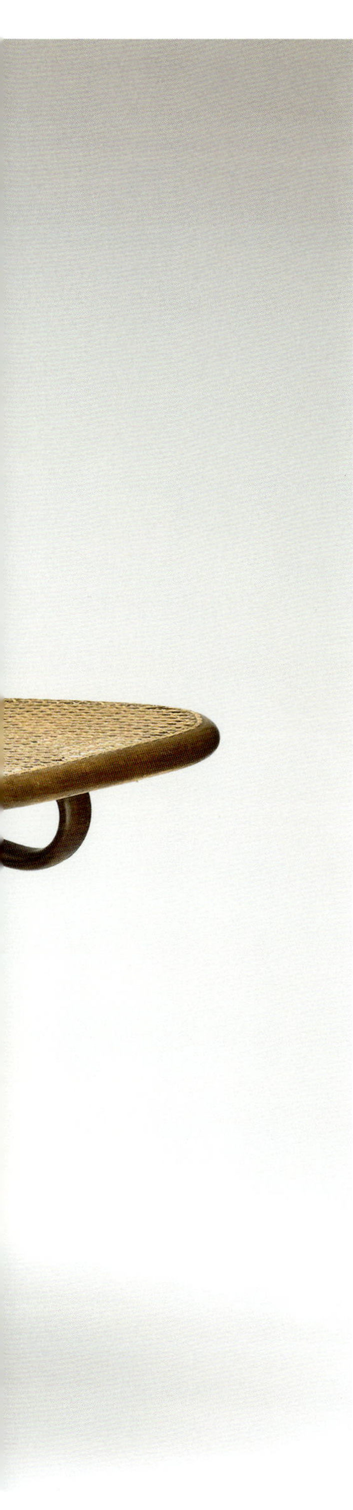

Gebrüder Thonet, Manufacturer
Austrian, founded 1849

Rocking Chaise (model #7500) c. 1890
Bent beechwood and chair caning
30½ × 68½ × 27⅜ inches
Museum Purchase, Hollis Baker Fund
2006.25

Founded in 1849 by Michael Thonet, the Gebrüder Thonet firm was directed by his five sons after 1871. The company is best known for the invention and manufacture of bentwood furniture. Prior to the establishment of the firm, Thonet experimented with bentwood furniture in the mid-1830s. By the 1850s, he had refined the process and found a way to bend solid beechwood with steam. The highly stylized, curvilinear forms of the rocking chaise based on plant and organic forms signal the growing influence of Jugendstil, a German art movement that began in the 1880s as part of the international Art Nouveau style. The graceful, long lines of the armrests along the sides of the rocking chaise are among the longest lengths of bentwood in any of Thonet's chairs.   **RHA**

Hector Guimard
French, 1867–1942

The influential work of architect and designer Hector Guimard defined the Art Nouveau style in Paris at the turn of the twentieth century. Art Nouveau, also known as Jugendstil and Stile Liberty, was an international style in art, architecture, and the decorative arts that dominated the arts from the 1890s to the advent of World War I in 1914. With this contemporary style applied to exterior and interior architecture, the decorative and graphic arts, artists aspired to unite all aspects of daily life in an aesthetic and harmonic whole.

Art Nouveau is characterized by flowing curvilinear motifs derived especially from floral and plant forms, which are epitomized in this cast-iron balcony railing, whose centered motif is an abstracted vase and exuberant spray of flowers and tendrils. In 1907, balcony railings such as this began to appear in buildings around Paris. Guimard's graceful and brilliant designs are associated with the era of the Belle Époch, embodied by his landmark stations of the Paris Métro (1900–1904) that became a symbol of the city itself. In 1938 Guimard and his American wife, Adeline, moved to New York City, where he became acquainted with Alfred H. Barr, Jr., the first director of the Museum of Modern Art. RHA

Balcony Railing 1909–1911
Patinated cast iron
35½ × 64 × 7 inches
Saint-Dizier Foundry
Museum Purchase
John H. Booth by exchange
2007.9

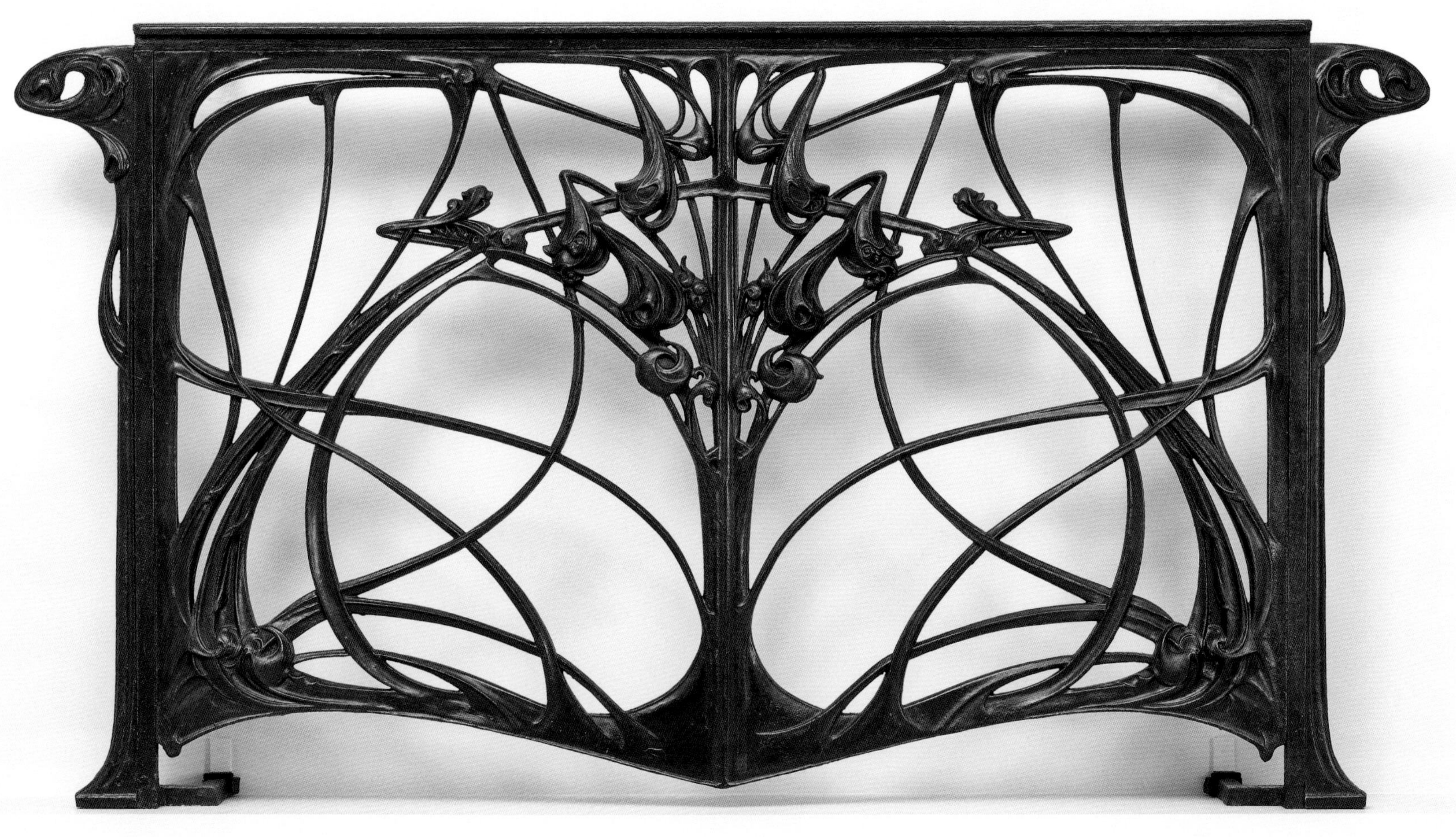

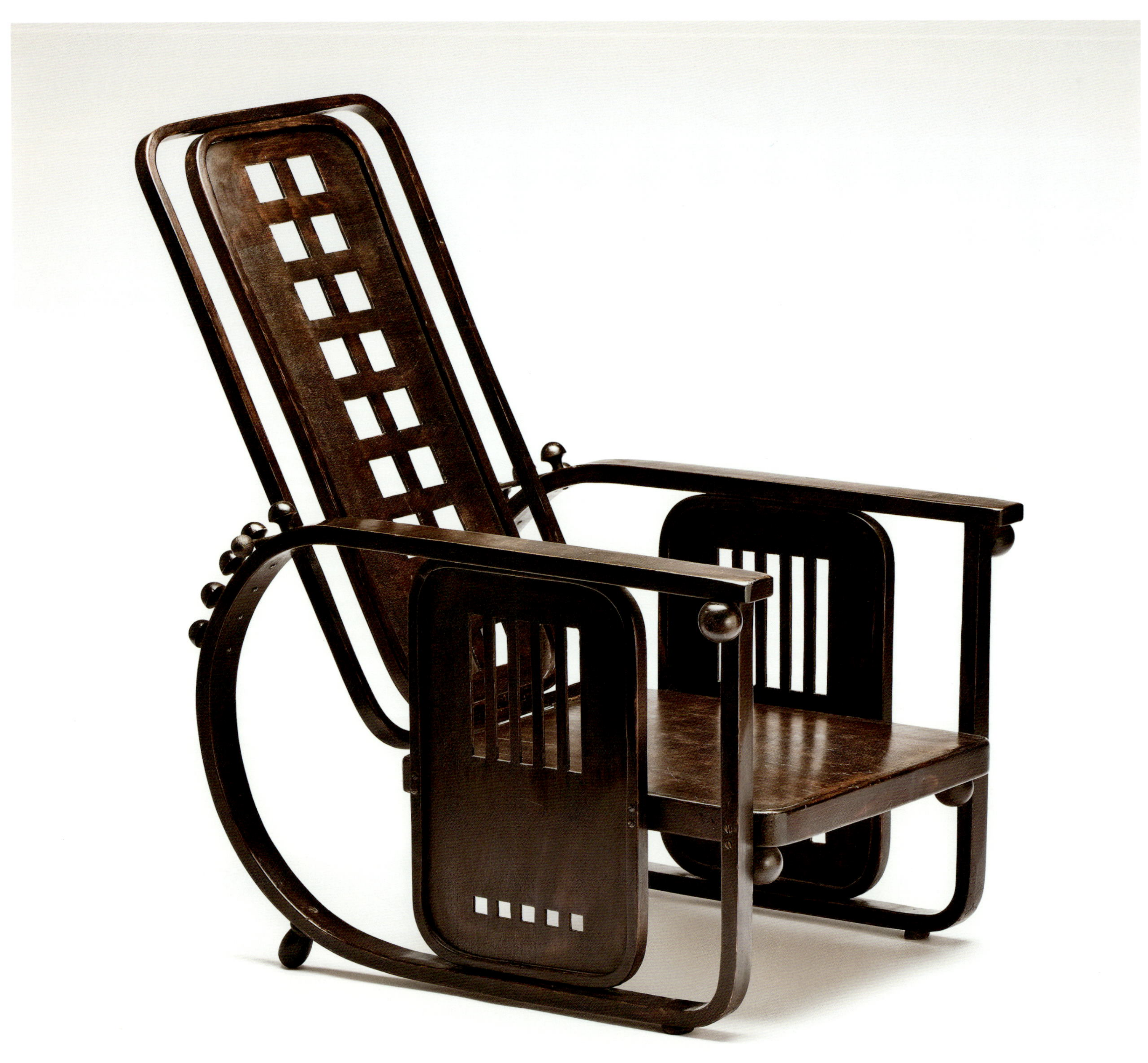

Josef Hoffmann

Austrian, 1870–1956

Sitzmachine (Machine for sitting) c. 1910

Bent and stained beechwood, plywood, and metal
41¾ × 26½ × 36½ inches
Museum Purchase
Baker Fund by exchange
2006.27

Josef Hoffmann, a renowned Viennese architect and designer, and Koloman Moser founded the *Wiener Werkstätte* in 1903. As a community of architects, artists, and designers that addressed the applied arts, the "Vienna Workshop" aspired to produce objects of a superior quality and craftsmanship and to unite all aspects of life.

One of the earliest commissions received by the *Wiener Werkstätte* was for the Purkersdorf Sanatorium in Vienna. Hoffmann was the architect for the building, his first major work, and was also responsible for designing the interiors. The *Sitzmachine* is one of many pieces of furniture and other decorative objects that Hoffmann created for the project. The *Sitzmachine* was manufactured in Vienna by the highly respected J. & J. Kohn firm, which also produced many of Hoffmann's other furniture designs. Hoffmann devised the chair using the basic forms of the rectangle, square, and sphere. With its adjustable back and visible nuts and bolts, the *Sitzmachine* reveals Hoffmann's interest in simplified forms, machine technologies, and concern for function. The *Sitzmachine* is among the first manually adjustable reclining chairs in the history of design. It remained in production until 1916 in a number of versions that included back and seat cushions.   **RHA**

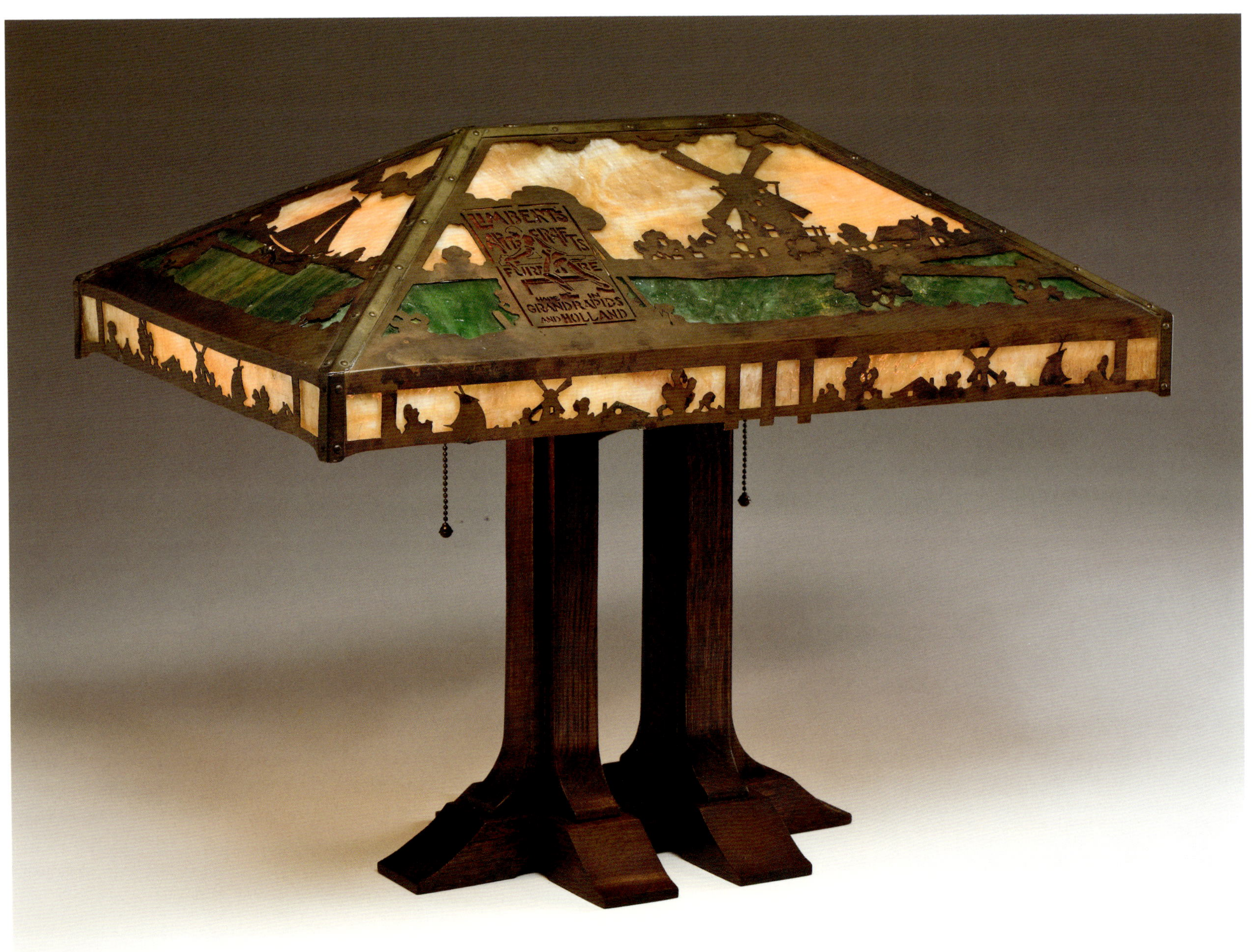
LIMBERTS
ARTS & CRAFTS
FURNITURE
MADE IN
GRAND RAPIDS
AND HOLLAND

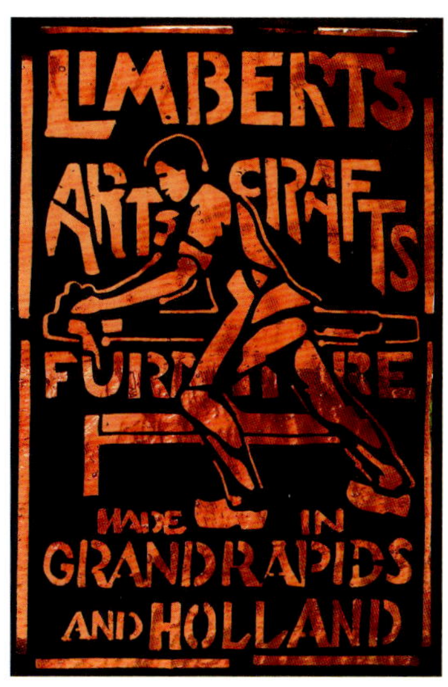

Charles P. Limbert

American, 1854–1923

Advertising Lamp c. 1910

Slag glass on oak base
19 × 24 × 16 inches
Museum Purchase, Samuel M.
Cummings, Frank and Ann Battistella
Fund, Porter Fund
2004.18

Charles Limbert founded a furniture company in Grand Rapids in 1894 and began producing Dutch Arts and Crafts–style furniture and lighting at his factory in 1902. Under the name Limbert's Arts and Crafts Furniture, the company's production line was influenced by Northern European Arts and Crafts design, American Prairie School, and Gustav Stickley. In 1906 Limbert opened a factory in Holland, Michigan, where he produced furniture until 1922.

Limbert's *Advertising Lamp* reflects the core philosophy of the American Arts and Crafts movement: to create a harmonious home environment. This one-of-a-kind lamp is also closely linked with Limbert's contemporary furniture design, especially in the construction of the pegged oak base. The lampshade of opalescent, colored art glass with stylized designs is set behind copper panels and depicts a Dutch windmill scene and sailing boat, which are repeated on the lower series of panels. The Limbert mark "Limbert's Arts and Crafts Furniture: Made in Grand Rapids and Holland" also appears on the lampshade and directly ties the lamp to its West Michigan origins. The presence of the Limbert lamp in the museum's collection of Design and Modern Craft highlights the contributions of the West Michigan region to other masters of the Arts and Crafts movement, including Frank Lloyd Wright.   RHA

. **Mathias J. Alten**
American, 1871–1938

Grand Rapids artist Mathias J. Alten journeyed to the Netherlands in August 1910, taking his family and his student Norman Chamberlain with him. Alten spent about a year in Katwijk and other coastal towns, producing seascapes and beach scenes almost every day. Among these was *The Broken Mast*, which describes a team of three horses straining to pull a boat ashore on the rugged coast. In the Netherlands, three-horse teams were used to pull in boats either for the season or for repair, as is the case in this painting. The composition, which celebrates the dignity and power of men and animals working together, was influenced by contemporary Hague School artists Hendrik Willem Mesdag and Willem Maris. Alten utilizes a pervasive blue-gray tonality to convey the damp, heavy air as the mighty horses labor over the wet beach.

Mathias Alten immigrated to this country with his family in 1889 at the age of seventeen. Apprenticed as a painter in Saint Wendel, Germany, he continued to study painting with local instructors in Grand Rapids. In 1898, Alten, like many of his contemporaries, traveled to Paris to study at the Académie Julian and the Académie Colorossi. When he returned nine months later, Alten's profession as a painter of standing was established, and he would continue painting for the next forty years in Grand Rapids. CMB

The Broken Mast 1910–1911
Oil on canvas
32 × 42 inches
Gift of Peter C. and Pat Cook
1998.1.2

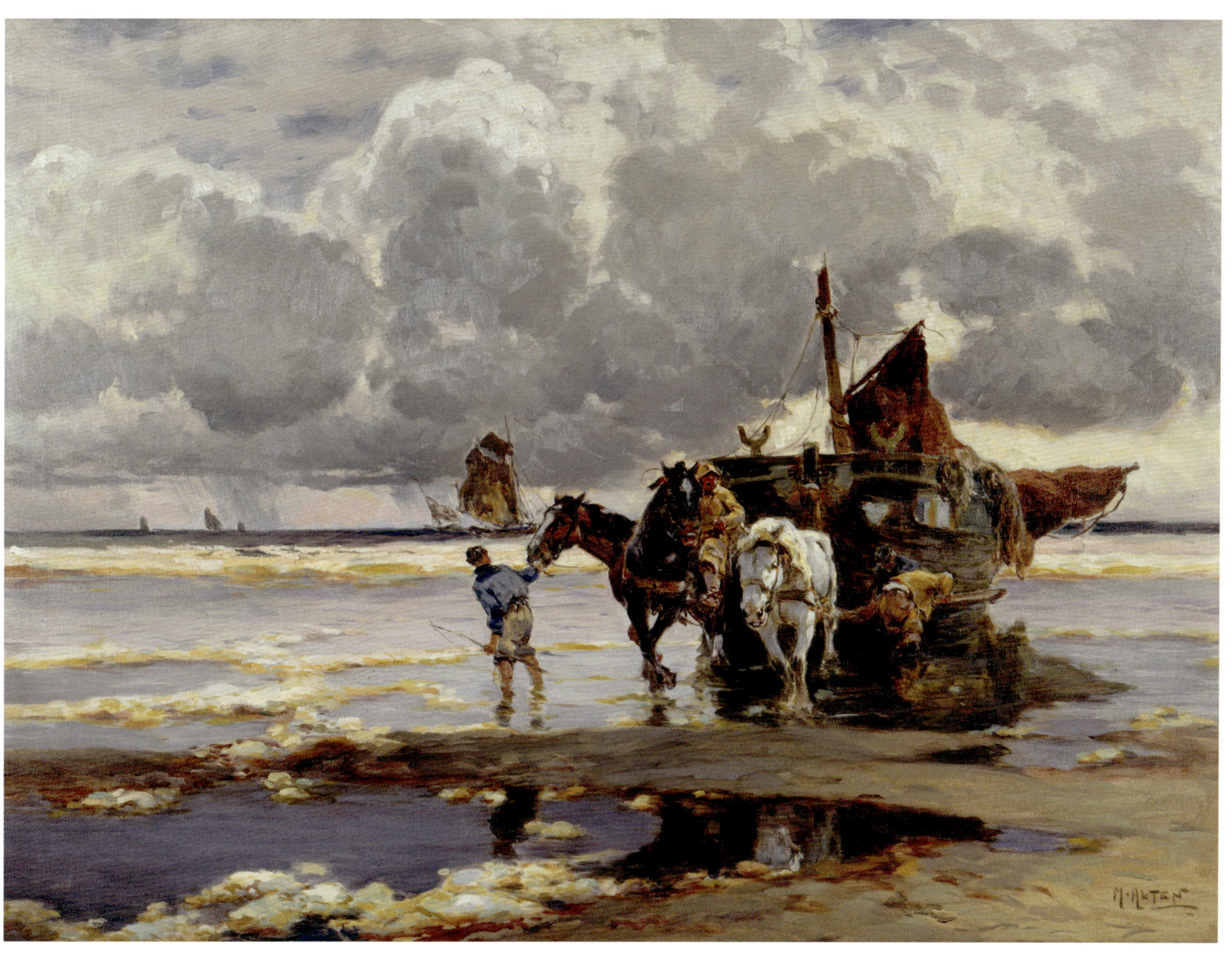

Will Howe Foote
American, 1874–1965

In *Sunlit Interior*, Will Howe Foote depicts a domestic scene within his home in Old Lyme, Connecticut. Located on the east bank of the mouth of the Connecticut River, the town became the site of an artist's colony for American Impressionists. Foote first visited Old Lyme in 1901. The following year he was hired as an assistant to Frank Vincent DuMond, the director of the Lyme Summer School of Art. Foote continued to teach privately in Old Lyme and settled there permanently in 1907, working alongside Henry Ward Ranger, Childe Hassam, and Willard Metcalf.

Born in Grand Rapids, Foote was the son of furniture industry executive E. H. Foote, and the nephew of the well-known painter William Henry Howe. In addition, his aunt was Grand Rapids Art Museum founder Mrs. Cyrus E. Perkins. In 1894 Foote studied at the Art Institute of Chicago, becoming friends with fellow Michigan native Frederick Frieseke. The following year both Foote and Frieseke moved to New York City, where they enrolled in the famous Art Students League of New York, Foote studying with Kenyon Cox and H. Siddons Mowbray. In 1897 Foote was again accompanied by Frieseke to Paris, where both enrolled in the Académie Julian and studied briefly with James McNeill Whistler. **CMB**

Sunlit Interior c. 1914
Oil on canvas
30 × 30 inches
Gift of Mabel H. Perkins
1965.1.12

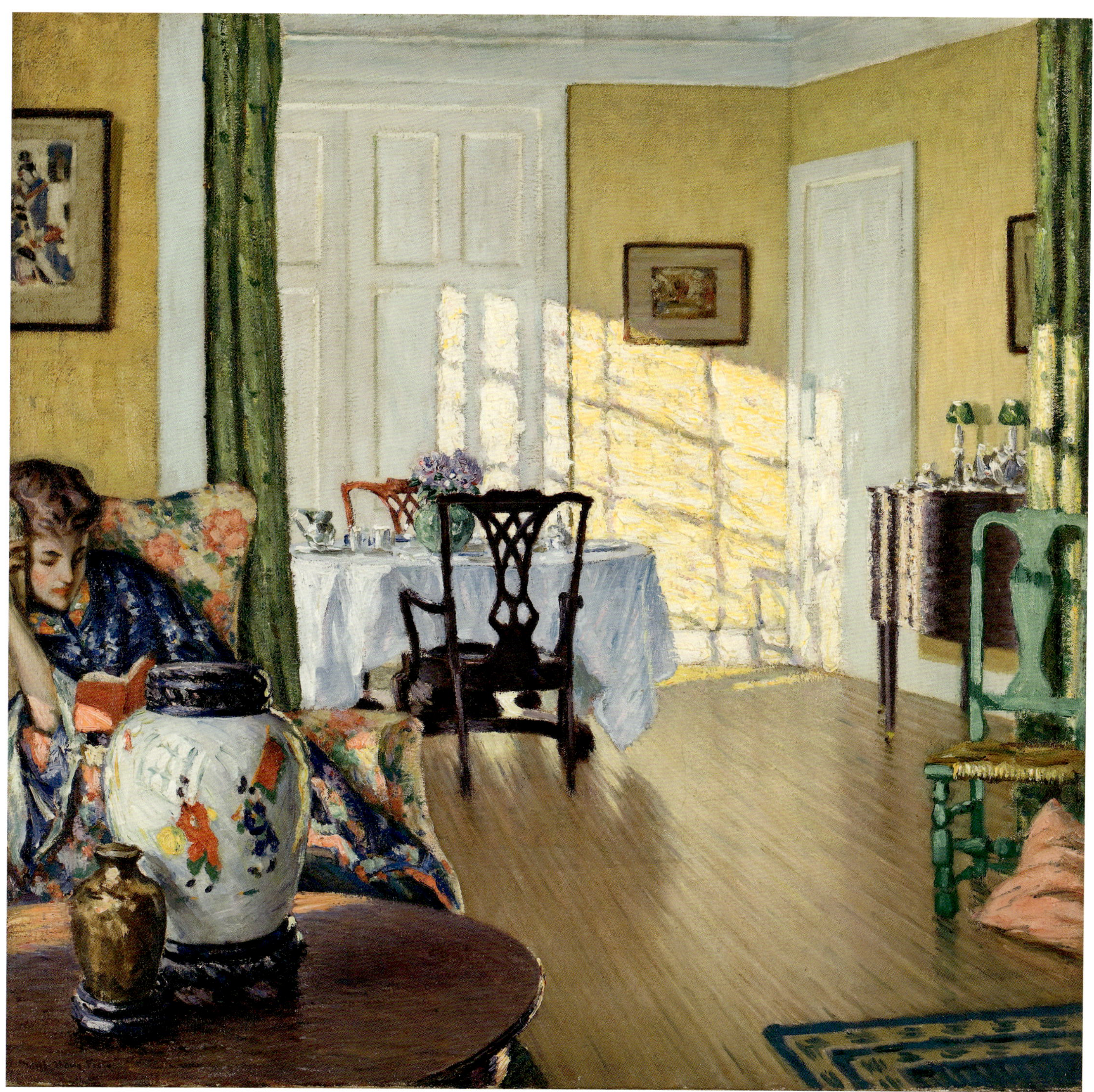

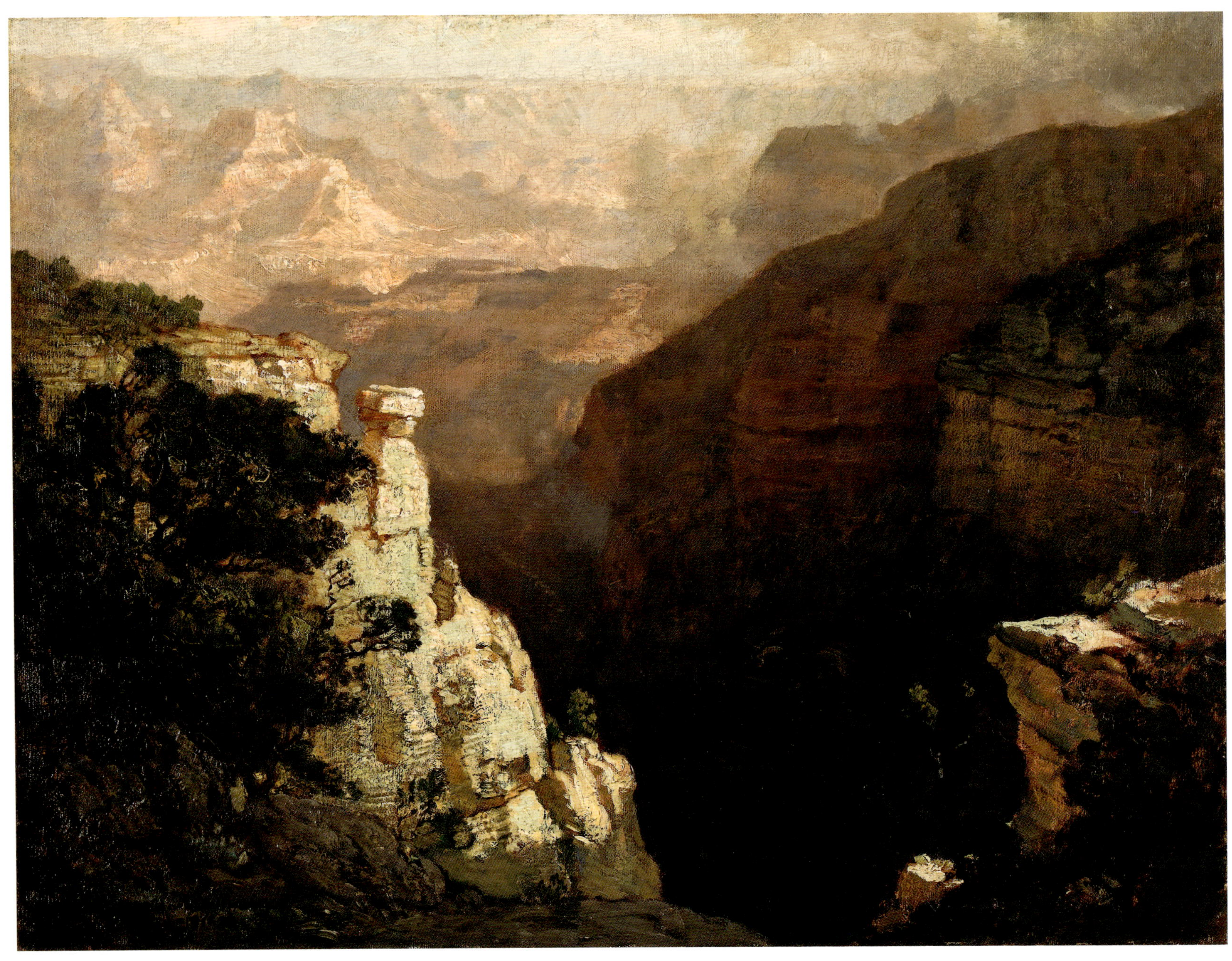

Frederick Ballard Williams

American, 1871–1956

The Grand Canyon 1910

Oil on canvas
28 × 36 inches
Gift of Emily J Clark
1923.1.2

In 1910 the Sante Fe Railway and the American Lithographic Company commissioned five artists to paint scenes of the Grand Canyon. Frederick Ballard Williams accompanied Thomas Moran, Elliott Daingerfield, DeWitt Parshall, and Edward Potthast to Arizona, where they spent ten days painting in and around the Grand Canyon.

The Grand Canyon is among the many works that Williams produced during this journey. Williams descended into the canyon to capture this particular scene. The hazy, flat rim of the canyon rises along the distant high horizon. The deep shadows that loom to the right suggest the immense depth of the canyon, while the thickly painted foliage in the left foreground is illuminated with the golden light of autumn. Williams captures the mystery and awe of the Grand Canyon's infinite span and its rich, remarkable colors.

Williams was born in Brooklyn, New York, where he lived until moving to New Jersey in 1895. He studied painting at the Cooper Union, the New York Institute of Artists and Artisans, and at the National Academy of Design. He was elected to the Academy as an Associate in 1907 and a full Academician in 1909, and showed his work regularly at Macbeth Gallery in New York. Williams was a conservative painter, employing a Realist approach to his landscapes that was strongly influenced by the French Barbizon school.   CMB

Dating to 1911, *The Hunt* describes a winter night in a forest where three Indians gather around the fire after a day of hunting. A deer they have killed lies on the snow before their lean-to. While the fire's glow dramatically lights the forms of the central figures, the moon reflecting off the blue-white snow illuminates the larger surrounding landscape. The scene suggests a Nativity in its quiet humanity and sacred stillness. Farny was known for finely executed small paintings such as this that elevated the daily life of the Plains Indians to a timeless stature. After 1900, as the golden era of the West was fading, general fascination with Native American subjects by both American and European audiences grew.

Henry François Farny was born in Alsace, France. In 1853 his family immigrated to the United States, settling in Cincinnati, Ohio, in 1859. Cincinnati remained Farny's home city for the remainder of his life. Fascinated by Native American culture while still a boy, Farny made his first trip west in 1881 and returned many times until his death in 1916. He worked as an illustrator and lithographer for *Harper's Weekly* for thirty years and exhibited his work in Europe and the United States. Farny was adopted by a Sioux tribe and often signed his pictures with his name and a Native American symbol. That symbol, composed of a dot surrounded by a circle, may reflect the name the Southwest Zuni gave him: "White Medicine Bead." CMB

The Hunt (*Moonlit Indian Encampment*)

1911
Gouache and watercolor on academy board
9½ × 5⅞ inches
Gift of Peter M. Wege
2007.5

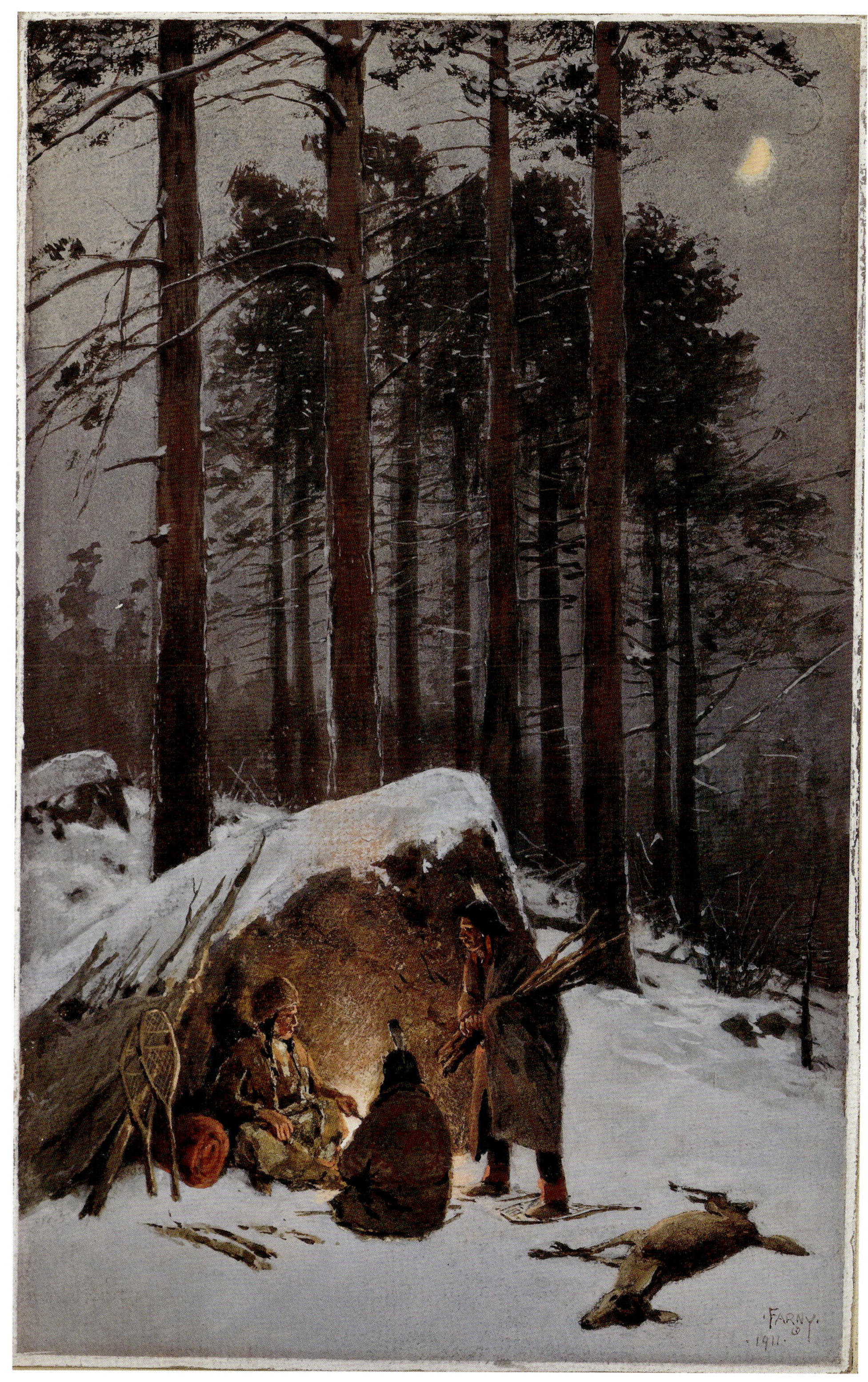

Walter Elmer Schofield
American, 1867–1944

This painting of a cottage in the English countryside exemplifies Walter Elmer Schofield's accomplished painterly approach to depicting the landscape. The purple shadows cast by the three tall trees unite the man-made structures with the fields beyond. The texture of broken brushwork is applied to every surface, while the overall palette of yellows, greens, and browns is punctuated by touches of brilliant blues and purples. The subject is a typical Cornish farmhouse, with a thatched roof and walls made of a stone, mud, and straw mix known as "cob." Schofield took pride in completing his canvases entirely out-of-doors in front of his subject, even in the most severe weather.

Born in Philadelphia, Schofield attended Swarthmore College and the Pennsylvania Academy of The Fine Arts and later the Académie des Beaux-Arts and Académie Julien in Paris. Initially associated with American Realist artists Edward Redfield, George Luks, and Everett Shinn, Schofield painted extensively in the New Hope area of Pennsylvania along the Delaware River. He married an Englishwoman, Murielle Redmayne, in 1897 and seven years later the couple settled in the artists' colony of St. Ives in Cornwall, England. Schofield traveled frequently, both in England and in the United States, painting landscapes in California and Maine.   CMB

English Cottage c. 1925
Oil on canvas
30 × 36 inches
Gift of Emily J. Clark
1935.1.23

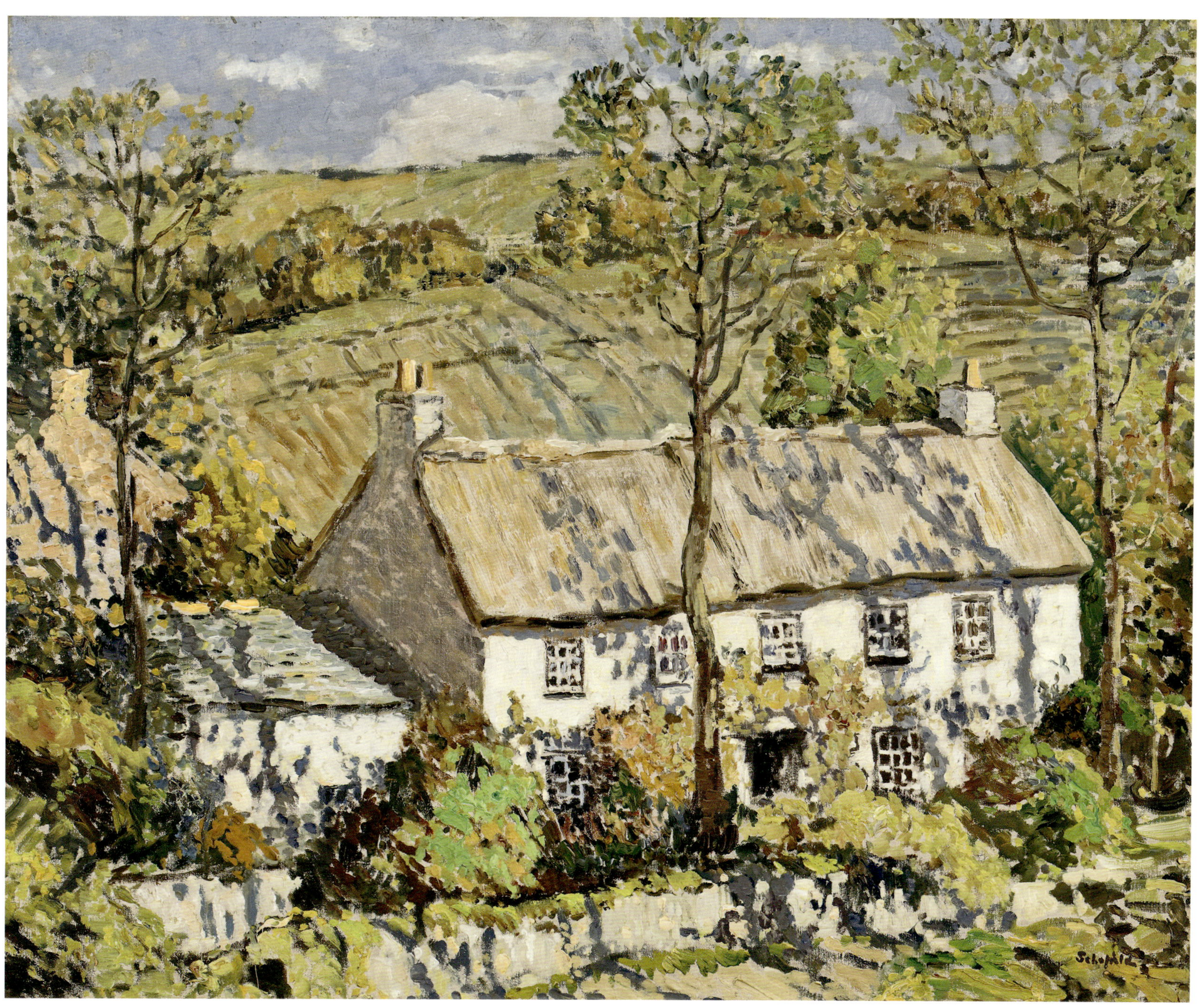

Frederick Frieseke
American, 1874–1939

Reflections was painted in the garden of Frederick Frieseke's own house, which was next-door to Claude Monet's home at Giverny. Contemporary photographs of the garden document the same trellised walls, garden alley, and round pool, which, in the painting, the artist has taken the license of relocating to the front of the house. The female figure, wearing a white kimono with bright red flowers, is shown looking at her own reflection in the pool in front of her. Frieseke's flickering brushwork is thinly applied to the canvas, resulting in a delicate pastel tonality of green and lilac. The lush flower garden sparkles with color, reflecting the sunlight of a summer day. Frieseke moved to Giverny in 1906 to join a large artists' colony where many American painters and writers settled, calling themselves the "Giverny Group." Unlike many of the other artists who moved to Giverny, Frieseke formed a friendship with the increasingly reclusive Impressionist Monet. In contrast to the work Frieseke had produced in his Paris studio, his work at Giverny is painted *en plein air*, out of doors in the surrounding gardens.

Frieseke, an important American Impressionist painter, was born in Owosso, Michigan, and studied at the Art Institute of Chicago and the Art Students League of New York. He left for Paris in 1898, and settled in France for the remainder of his life, though he frequently traveled to the United States. While in Paris, Frieseke joined his Michigan friend Will Howe Foote in studying at the Académie Julian and the Académie Carmen under James McNeill Whistler. **CMB**

Reflections (The Garden Mirror) c. 1912

Oil on canvas
25 × 32 inches
Gift of Emily J. Clark
1935.1.9

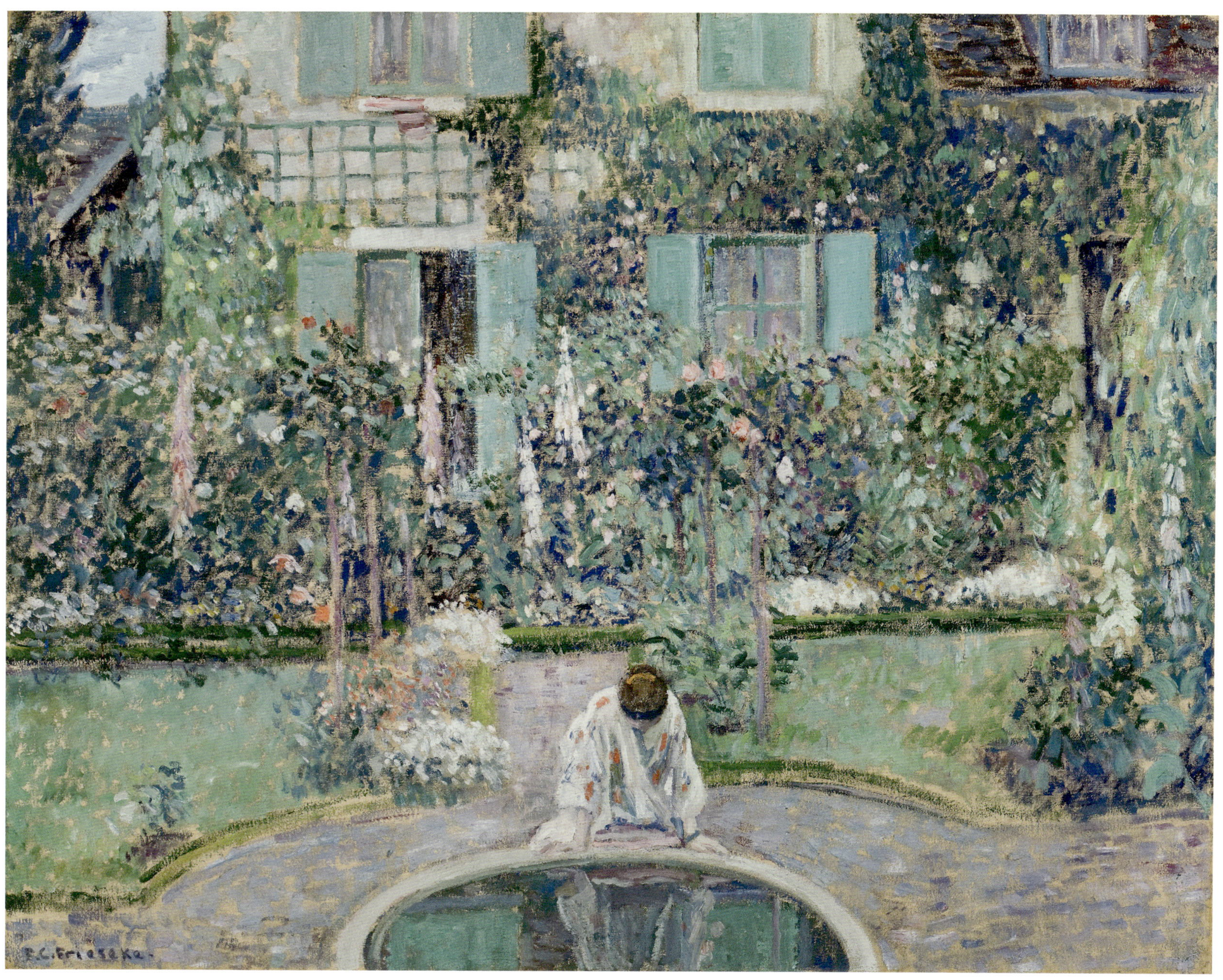

. Ernest Lawson
American, 1873–1939

Traveling to Cape Cod, Massachusetts in the summer of 1913, Ernest Lawson passed through Middletown, Rhode Island. The small country church situated off the main road must have caught his eye, and he depicts it in his only known Rhode Island landscape. Built in the early 1880s by renowned Philadelphia architect Wilson Eyre, St. Columba's was a local architectural landmark. The Episcopal church was designed in an English Gothic style, with stained glass windows designed by David Maitland Armstrong, a John LaFarge associate, and manufactured by Tiffany Studios in New York. This painting features juxtaposed diagonal elements in the foreground, a compositional device Lawson often used. However, the light palette and soft brushwork are less typical for the artist, most likely reflecting the influence of his mentor, fellow Impressionist John Twachtman.

Lawson was born in Nova Scotia and raised in Ontario. After studying in Paris for two years where he met Alfred Sisley, he returned to the United States and settled in New York City.   CMB

Middletown, Rhode Island 1913
Oil on canvas
24½ × 29½ inches
Museum Purchase, John and Marilyn Drake,
Frey Foundation, and Mr. and Mrs. David G. Frey
2009.129

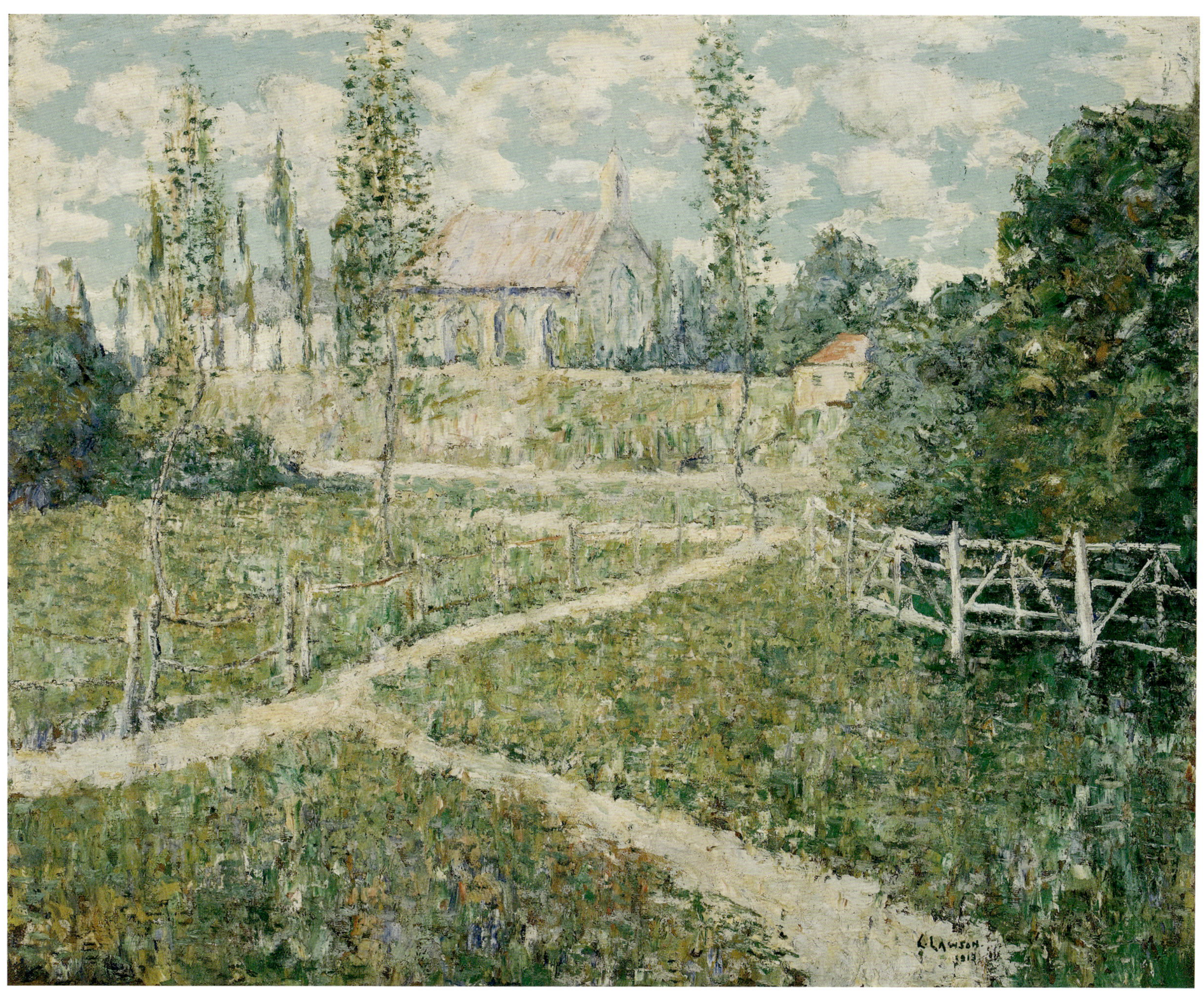

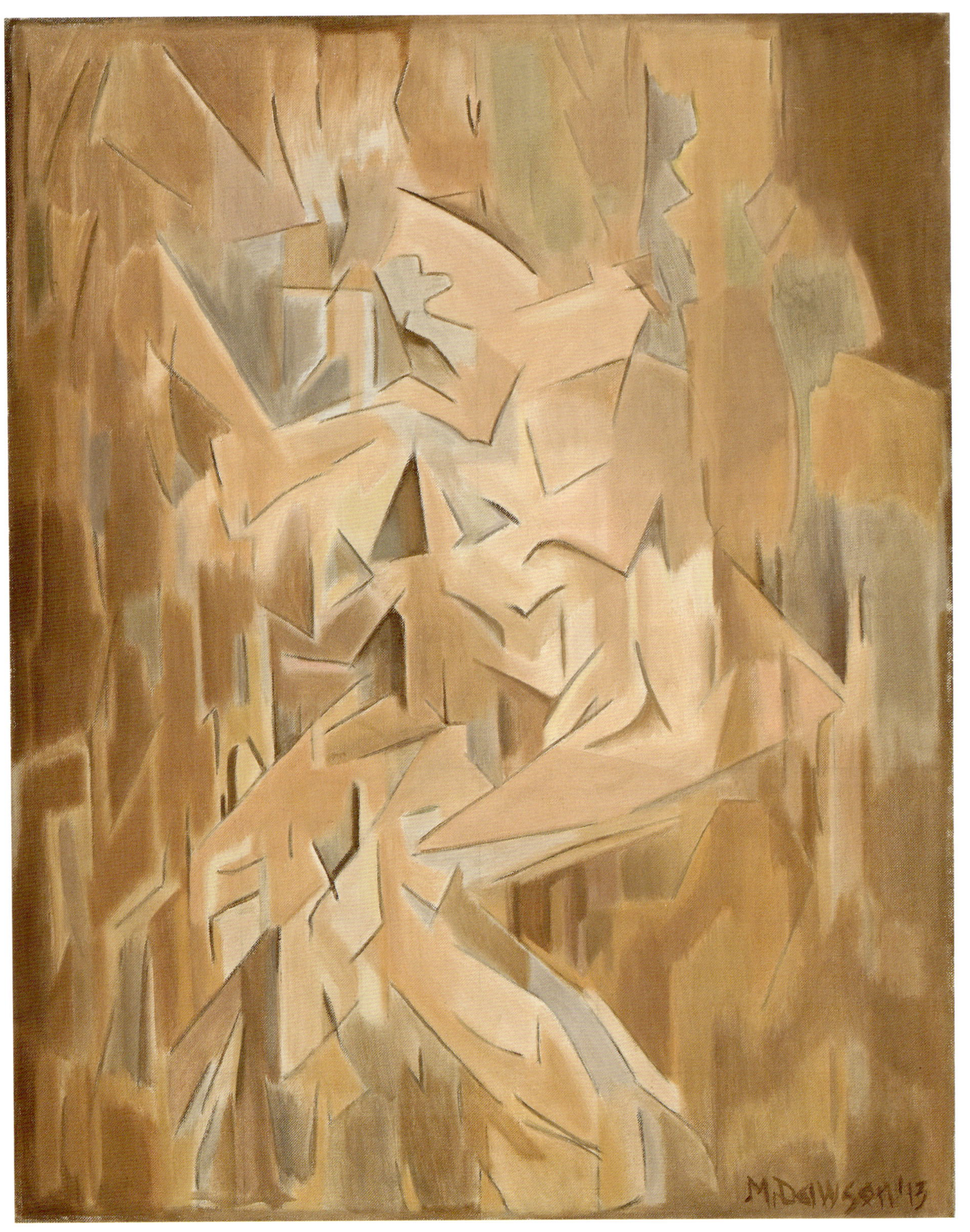

M.Dawson'13

 # **Manierre Dawson**

American, 1887–1969

Hercules II 1913

Oil on canvas
36 × 28 inches
Museum Purchase, Mr. and Mrs. David G.
Frey American Art Endowment Fund,
Dorothy Scott Gerber Fund, and Sam
and Janene Cummings
2006.31

Born in Chicago, Manierre Dawson pursued a career in architectural engineering before turning to art. After trips to Italy and France in 1910, where he met John Singer Sargent and saw Gertrude Stein and Alice B. Toklas' collection of modern art in Paris, he began to paint in earnest. From 1910 to 1914, Dawson produced over two hundred paintings that were highly accomplished and strikingly modern in style. In 1913, he was invited to submit a painting to the landmark Armory Show. First presented in New York and then in Chicago, the Armory Show introduced European Modernism to the United States.

Hercules II is a heroic American Cubist painting that is remarkably early in date. The painting echoes the monochromatic palette of Pablo Picasso's Analytic Cubism (1910–1911). It focuses on the motion of a figure through space—the mythical Greek hero Hercules. The painting completely integrates the figure into the space that surrounds it, forming one dynamic field of movement. Dawson noted in his journal of 1913 that he was painting three pictures of Hercules, all of which were inspired by Marcel Duchamp's controversial *Nude Descending a Staircase No. 2* exhibited the same year.

Dawson numbers among very few American painters who absorbed and embraced the philosophy and technique of Modernism before 1920. Though his painting career was brief, his early achievement was so impressive that it invites speculation about the role he might have played in American art had he seriously pursued a lifelong artistic career. In 1914 Dawson purchased a fruit farm in Ludington, Michigan, near his family's summer retreat where he lived for the rest of his life. He continued painting until 1920.   **RHA**

Edvard Munch
Norwegian, 1863–1944

Edvard Munch was a Symbolist painter and printmaker whose work, along with that of Vincent van Gogh, marked the origins of the expressionist tradition in modern art. *Death Chamber* is Munch's postscript in print media to *Death in the Sick Chamber*, a painting he executed the year before. The composition depicts a dying woman who is seated to the rear and attended to by an older man and woman, while other members of the family stand or sit. The painting and print are remembrances of the deaths of Munch's mother and later his older sister, when the artist was a young boy of five and fourteen, respectively. The gathering of family members mixes past and present time. Munch and his siblings are shown as adults with their father, who had already died.

Munch's lithograph is a highly personal and alienated response to death. The artist isolates each of his figures from one another, preventing any sense of consolation. In black attire, their shapes blend into one another and visually lock the family together in fear and melancholy. The exaggerated staring eyes of the woman facing out anchor the psychological climate of the room in unrelieved anxiety. Without any source of redemption in sight, each surviving figure must individually come to terms with death. **RHA**

Death Chamber 1896
Lithograph on cream wove paper
15⁵/₁₆ × 21¹³/₁₆ inches
Gift of Mabel H. Perkins
1955.2.11

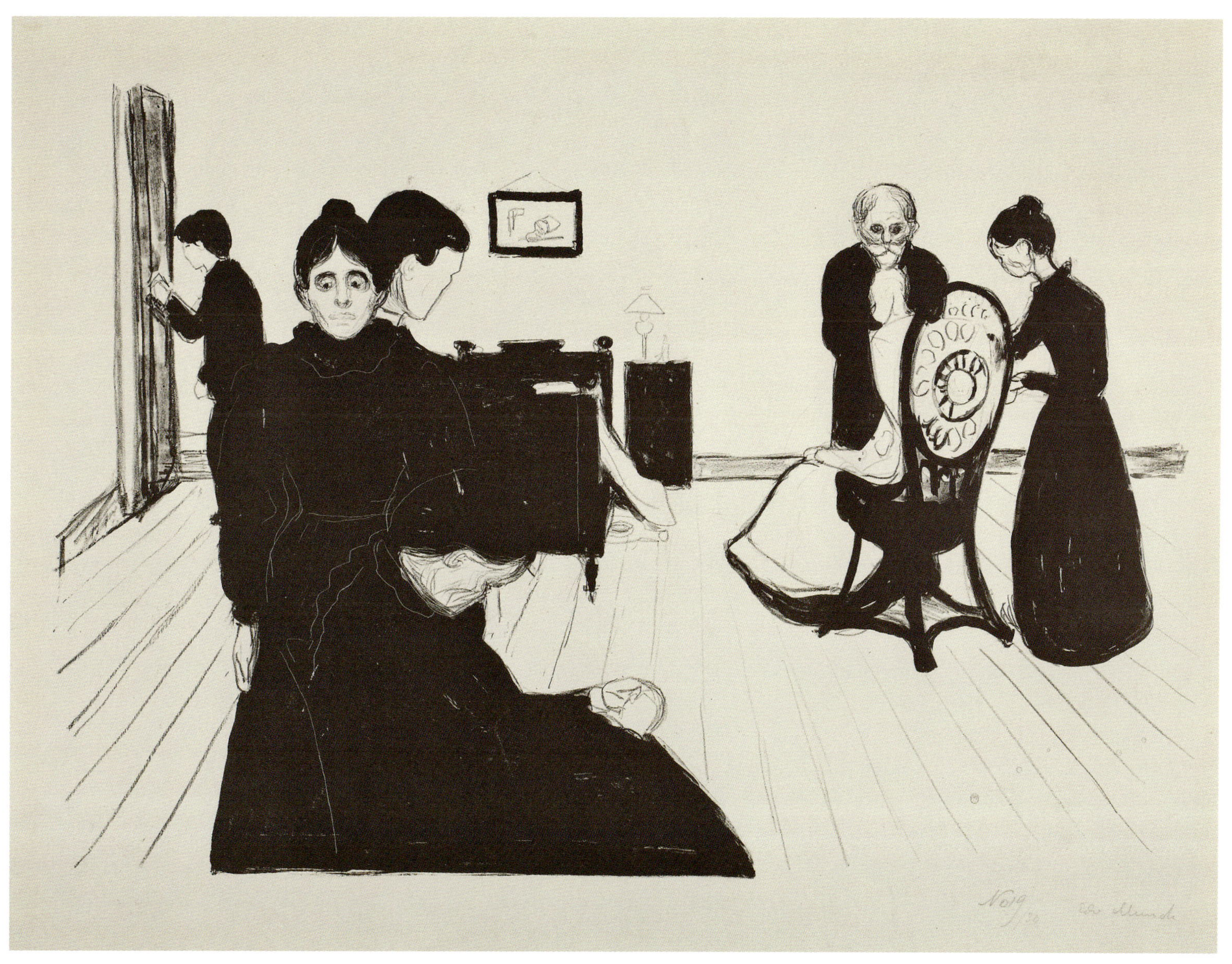

 Egon Schiele
Austrian, 1890–1918

The Vienna Secession was founded in 1897 by Josef Hoffmann, Gustav Klimt, Koloman Moser, and other artists seeking to establish a modern movement in the arts, including design and architecture. In 1903 Hoffmann and Moser founded the Wiener Werkstätte as a fine arts society for crafts, an offshoot of the Vienna Secession.

This poster, considered Egon Schiele's greatest print, announces the forty-ninth and final Vienna Secession exhibition that featured the artist's last solo exhibition. It depicts members of the Secession group working around a table, evoking The Last Supper with Schiele himself in the place of Christ. This religious reference suggests the tight-knit nature of the artists' community and their prophet-like role in bettering the world. An empty chair may reference the recently deceased Klimt, Schiele's friend and mentor. Schiele himself died of the Spanish influenza at the age of twenty-eight in the fall of 1918.   RHA

Secession 49 Ausstellung (Secession 49th Exhibition) 1918
Color lithograph and offset lithograph
on thin wove paper
25¼ × 19 inches
Museum Purchase, Hollis Baker Fund
2009.25

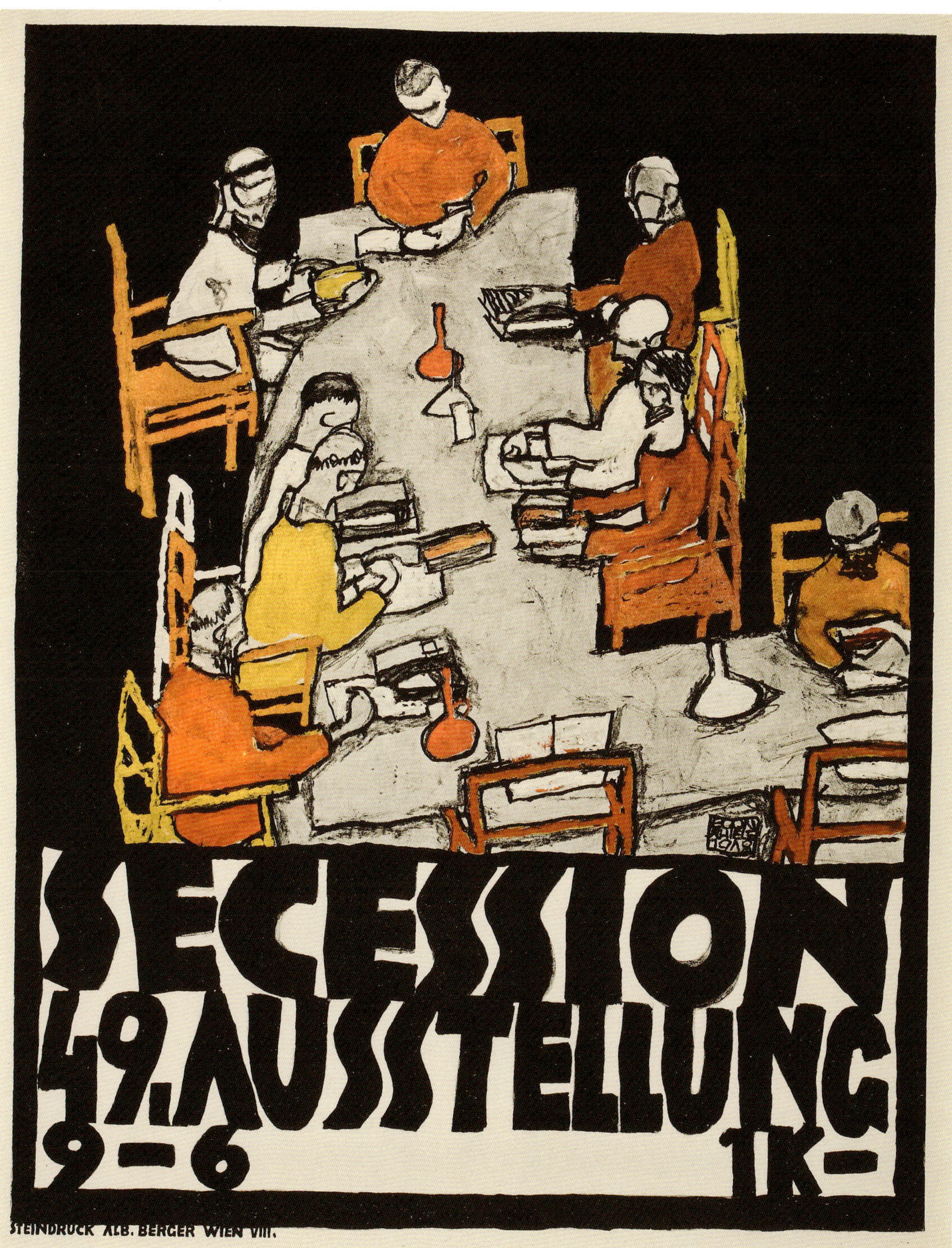

SECESSION
49. AUSSTELLUNG
9-6
1 K -
STEINDRUCK ALB. BERGER WIEN VIII.

In *Harvest*, Karl Schmidt-Rottluff depicts field hands at work in a rural setting. The artist saw nature as pure, consoling, and an antidote to the alienating aspects of urban life. Schmidt-Rottluff's harvesters use pre-modern tools to cut and bundle wheat, suggesting traditional practices. Bold oranges, yellows, and blues with green accents evoke the colorations of folk art. Used for emotional effect rather than realistic appearances, strong color and simplified, painterly forms celebrate a seasonal and primal ritual of the countryside. The effect of Schmidt-Rottluff's unusual handling of color and form is a poetic tribute to the unity of nature, man, and work.

Schmidt-Rottluff, Fritz Bleyl, Erick Heckel, and Ernst Ludwig Kirchner founded the Brücke group in Dresden, Germany, in 1905. Marking the beginnings of German Expressionism in the visual arts, Brücke was the first modern art movement of the twentieth century. The original members of the group and other artists who later joined the group, such as Emile Nolde and Max Pechstein, took the modern city and the natural landscape as their primary subjects. Their revolutionary style incorporated jagged forms, dissonant colors, and broad gestures to record each artist's personal responses to his subject. In highly expressive paintings, drawings, prints, and sculptures, this young generation of German artists wished to provide a *brücke,* or bridge, to a fresh and creative future.   **RHA**

Harvest c. 1910
Oil on canvas
38½ × 44 inches
Gift of John L. Booth
1956.1.1

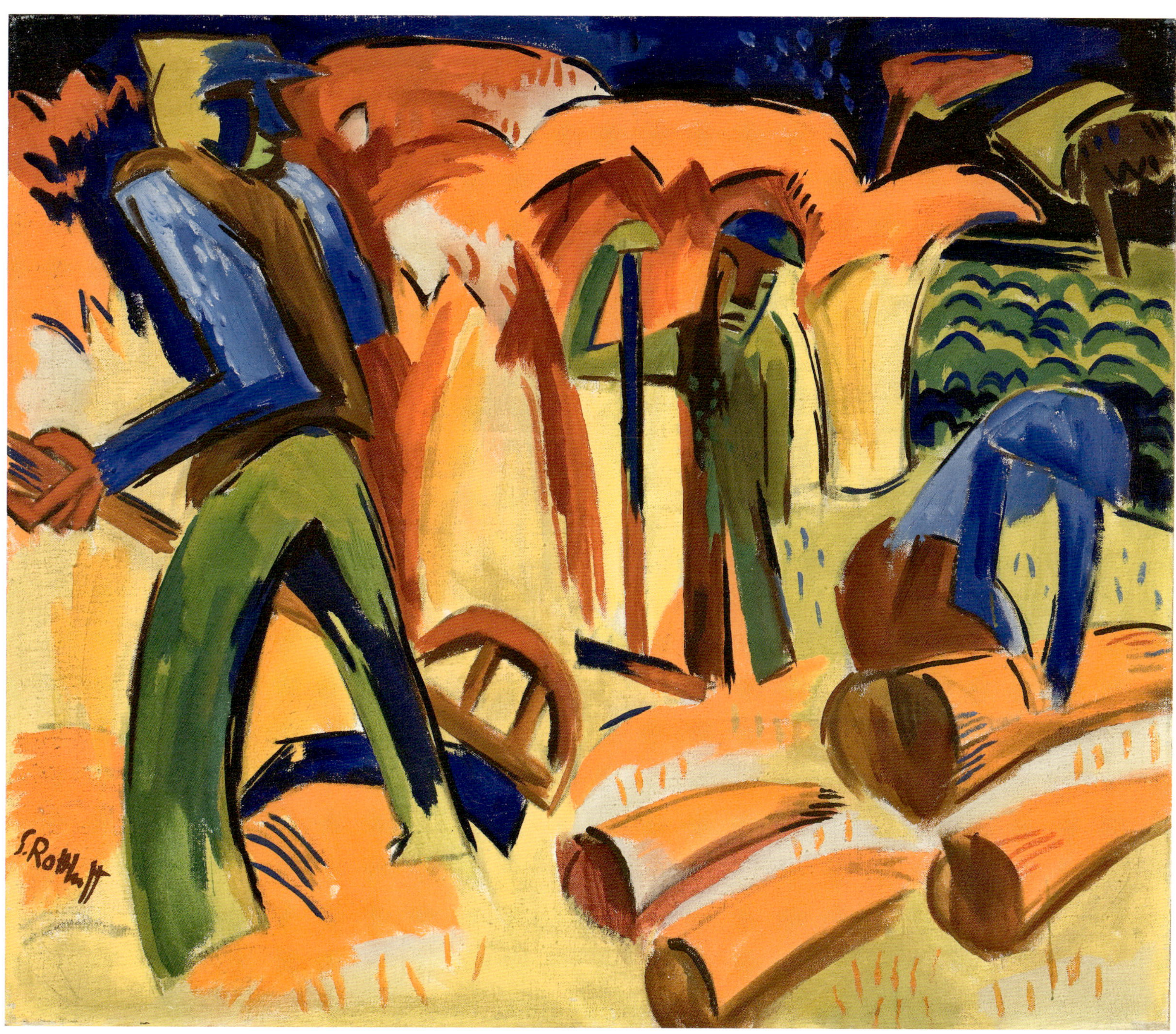

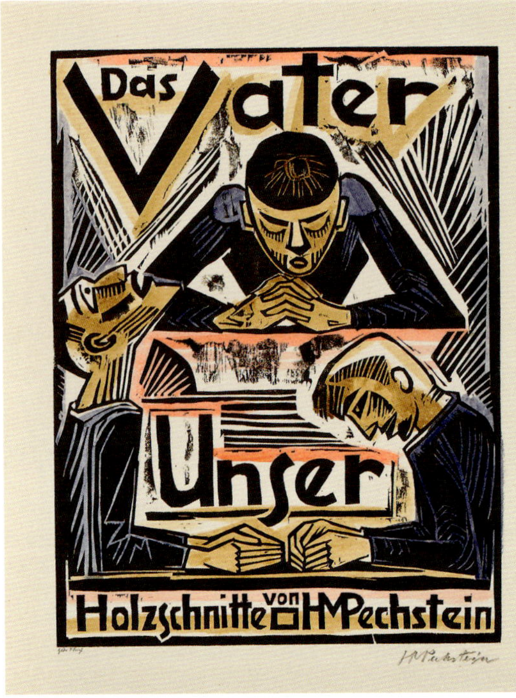

Das Vater
Unser
Holzschnitte von H Pechstein

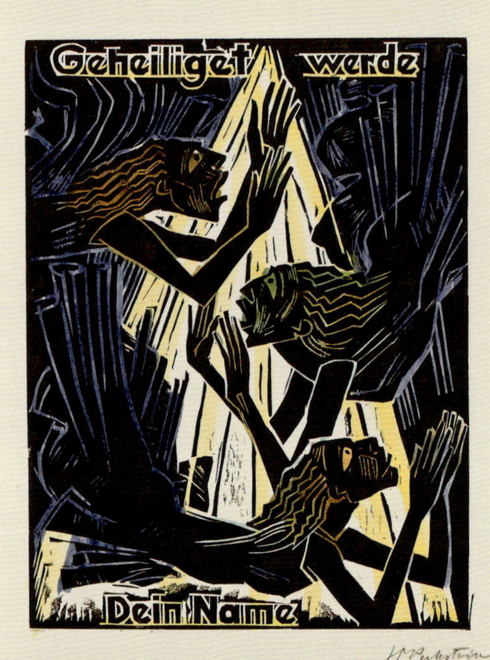

Geheiliget werde
Dein Name

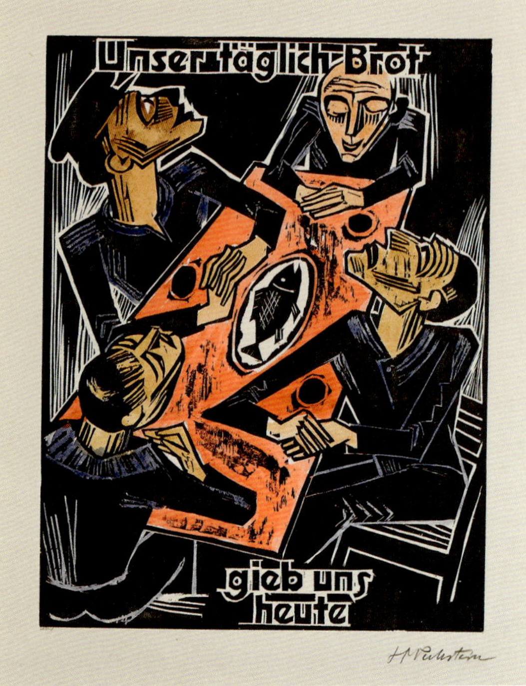

Unser täglich Brot
gieb uns
heute

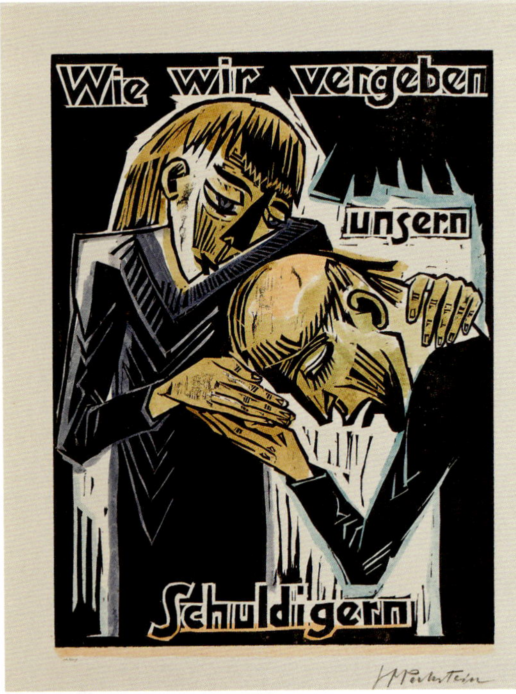

Wie wir vergeben
unsern
Schuldigern

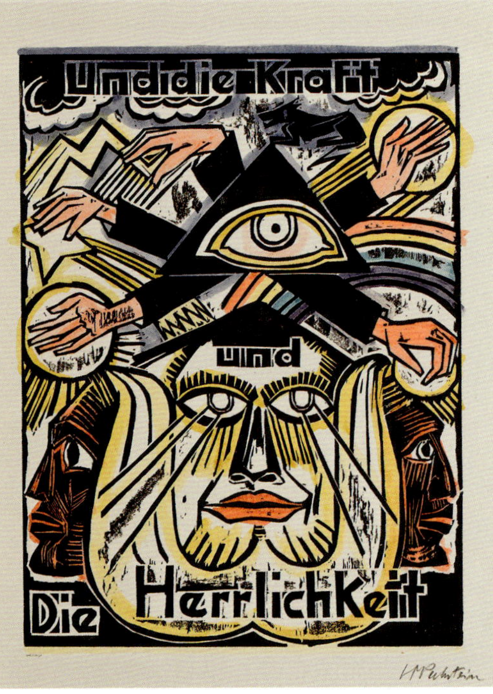

Und die Kraft
und
Die Herrlichkeit

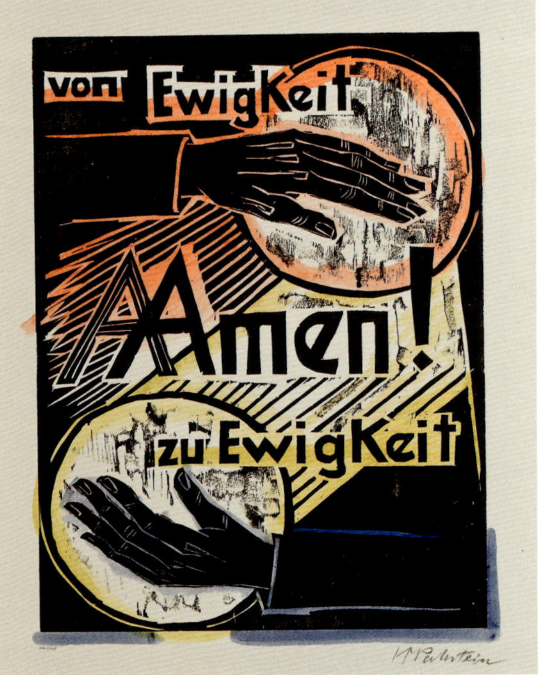

von Ewigkeit
Amen!
zu Ewigkeit

Max Pechstein

German, 1881–1955

Das Vater Unser is one of Max Pechstein's most celebrated works and a landmark in the history of twentieth-century religious art. For the twelve woodcuts that compose this portfolio, Pechstein turned to the archetypal prayer of Christianity drawn from the Books of Matthew and Luke. He selected Martin Luther's German translation rather than the Latin. Pechstein's choice of Biblical version stresses the popular or private devotions of Protestantism rather than the organized religious rites of Roman Catholicism. The artist's every-day imagery of humble and pious North Sea fishermen and their families caught in prayer reflects his choice of text.

Stylistically, *Das Vater Unser* is marked by a graphic vocabulary of flattened shapes and broad black planes, with regularly patterned incisions and manipulations of forms derived from medieval and South Seas sculpture. Pechstein's choice of strong color to embellish the black-ink woodcuts further emotionalizes the artist's fervent and deeply felt illustrations of the Lord's Prayer.

In 1970, Bishop Dr. Hermann Kunst D. D. gifted this portfolio to State Minister Dr. Gerhard Schroeder in the city of Bonn, then the capital of West Germany. It is from Dr. Schroeder's collection that it comes to the Grand Rapids Art Museum.

Das Vater Unser was published in an edition of 250: the first 50 portfolios were hand colored and individually signed; the remaining 200 sets were unsigned and printed in black ink. Complete color sets of *Das Vater Unser* in pristine condition are extremely rare.   RHA

Max Pechstein
German, 1881–1955

Max Pechstein was an important member of the Brücke group that was founded in Dresden, Germany, in 1905 by Fritz Bleyl, Erick Heckel, Ernst Ludwig Kirchner, and Karl Schmidt-Rottluff. With the addition of Emil Nolde and Otto Mueller, Brücke marked the beginnings of German Expressionism, the first modern art movement of the twentieth century that would continue in force through the early 1930s.

Pechstein painted *Reflection* at Nidden in East Prussia, a small fishing village on the coast of the Baltic Sea. It was a frequent summer retreat for Pechstein beginning in 1909. Pechstein and his fellow members of the Brücke group of expressionist artists sought refuge from city life during the summers, particularly in the lake district outside of Dresden and on the shores of the North and Baltic Seas.

In *Reflection*, the sky is ablaze in broad brushstrokes of green and cobalt blue, agitated toward the center to suggest a parting of clouds. The sun or moon that breaks through is reflected off the surface of the water in a dazzling play of radiant light. Pechstein, like other Brücke artists, took comfort in nature as a counterbalance to industrialized society and to the troubled times that followed the disasters of World War I. **RHA**

Spiegelung (Reflection) 1922
Oil on canvas
31 × 39 inches
Gift of John L. Booth
1961.1.1

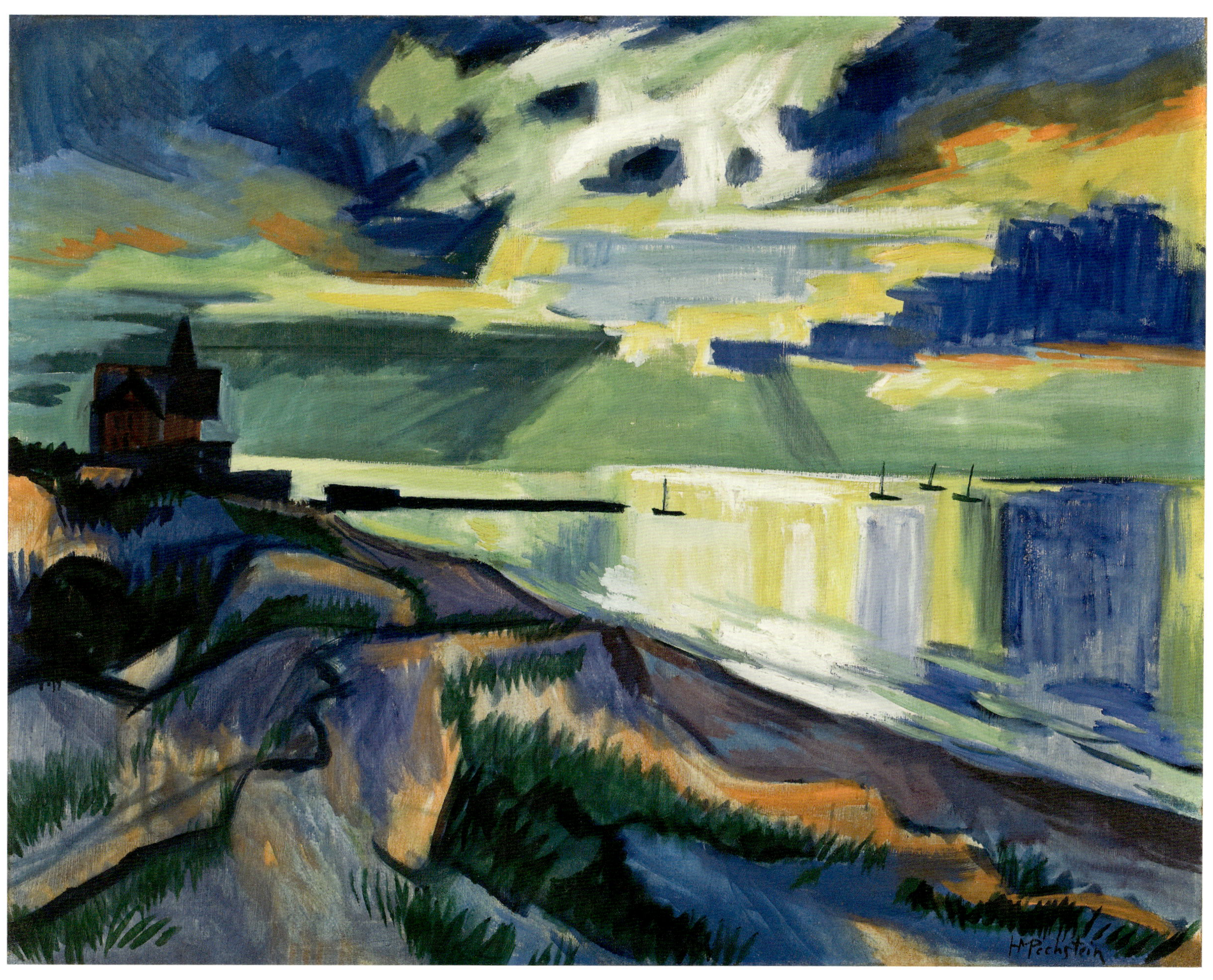

HMPechstein

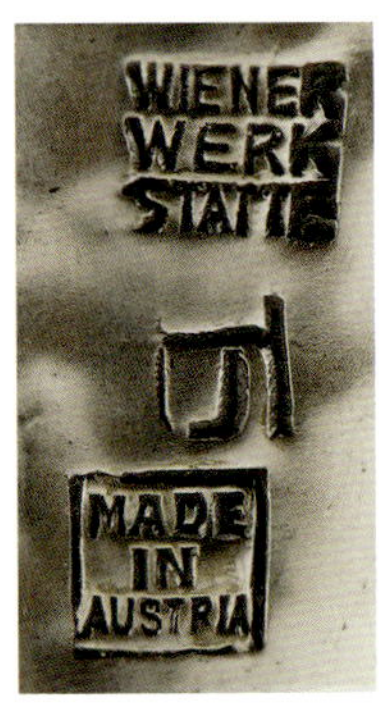

Josef Hoffmann

Austrian, 1870–1956

Josef Hoffmann was the cofounder of the Wiener Werkstätte (Vienna Workshop) established in 1903. The goal of this modern crafts guild, with strong ties to the Art Nouveau movement and the Vienna Secession, was to restore the values of hand-craftsmanship and break down the distinction between fine art and decorative art. In the same tradition as the British Arts and Crafts Movement, the Wiener Werkstätte sought to create new forms that would bring quality in everyday design to a modern audience.

This two-handled stem bowl, designed by Hoffmann in 1920 and in production for six years, is a signature example of the elegance of Hoffmann's decorative style. Closer to the Art Nouveau style than some of his other more concisely functional works, this hammered bowl with its graceful ribbon handles was produced in both a gilt and silver version. Although over one hundred were produced in gilt, only twenty-five were made in silver. **RHA**

Two-handled Stem Bowl 1925

Silver over white metal alloy
7¾ × 11¾ × 7¼ inches
Produced by Wiener Werkstätte 1925–31
Museum Purchase
2007.10

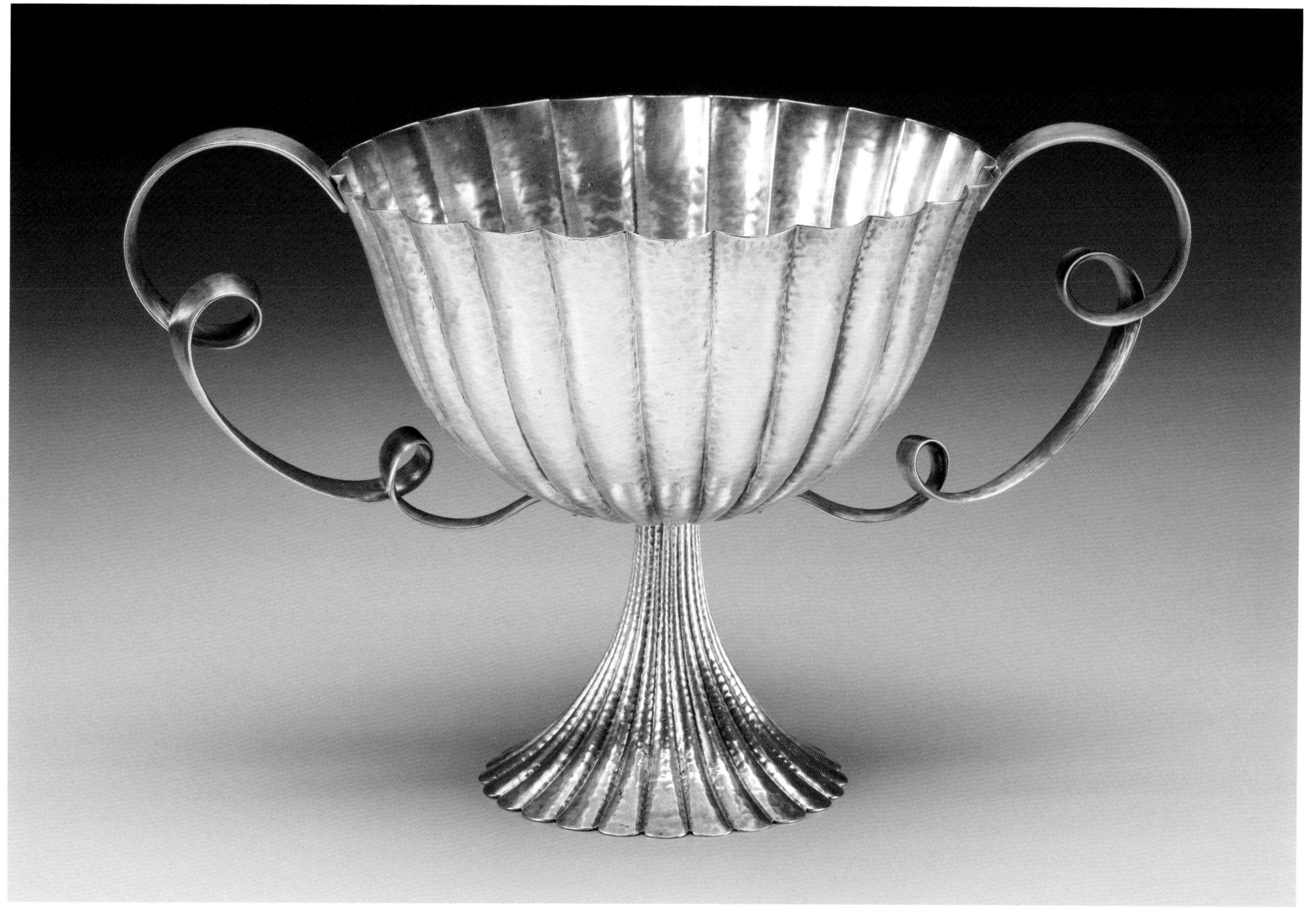

Ernst Barlach presents a winged being with a raised sword, standing on the back of a wolf-like beast. In a letter written in 1928, he described the meaning of the title. The figure represents the individual overcoming adversity. In an upward separation from the "earthly horizontal," the human spirit is "exalted above suffering." Having experienced the horrors of World War I, Barlach became a dedicated pacifist. He conceived many of his sculptures, like *Der Geistkämpter*, as war memorials.

Barlach created wood and bronze sculptures that recall the boldness and simplicity of early Gothic art. His powerful and expressive figures, often wrapped in heavy robes, evoke spiritual redemption. In addition to his sculptures, which made him the most prominent German sculptor of the early twentieth century, Barlach created a large and significant body of woodcuts and lithographs. He was also a noted playwright and novelist, esteemed as highly for his writings as for his accomplishments in the visual arts.

This bronze is one of at least three known casts of *Der Geistkämpter*. Monumental versions of it were also produced and installed in Germany in the cities of Kiel and Berlin. One casting was hidden during World War II to avoid its destruction by the Nazi regime, which condemned modern art. **RHA**

Der Geistkämpter (Champion of the Spirit) 1928
Bronze
45⅝ × 21½ × 6¾ inches
Museum Purchase
1960.4.6

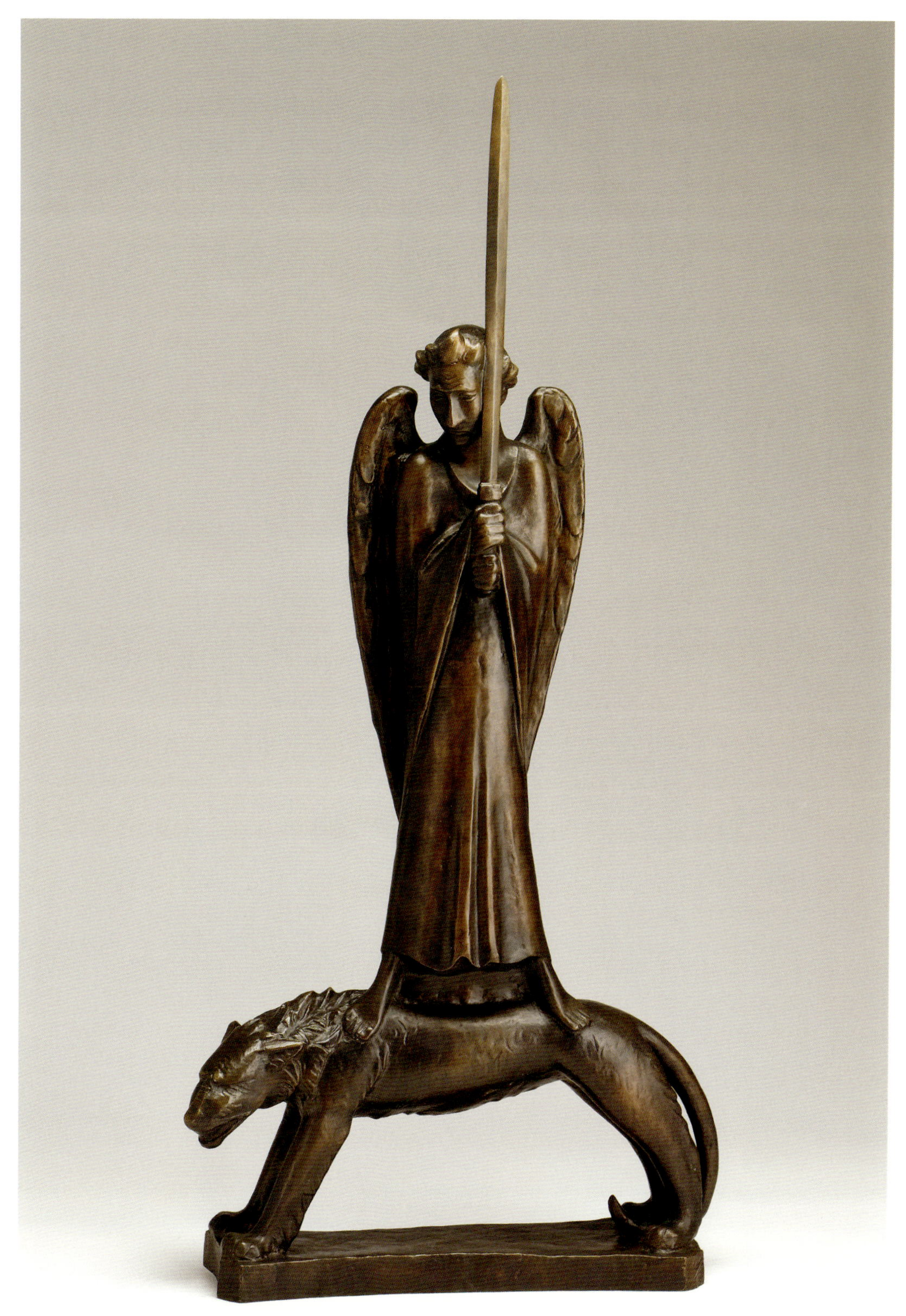

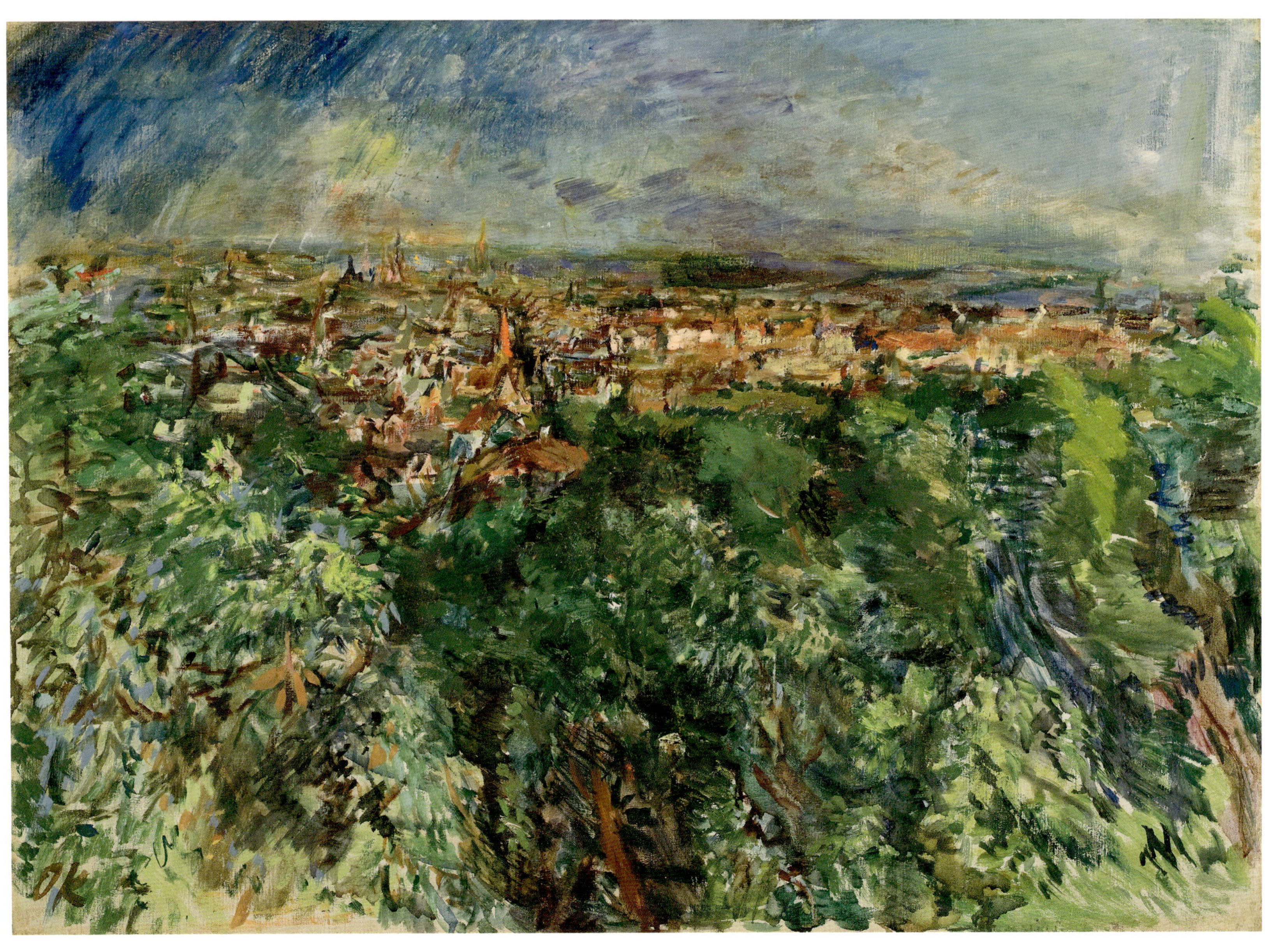

Oskar Kokoschka
Austrian, 1886–1980

*Vienna, View from
Liebharstal I* 1933
Oil on canvas
21 × 29 inches
Gift of Marguerite Inslee
1955.1.4

Settling in Berlin in 1910, Oskar Kokoschka came into contact with the artists of Brücke and Der Blaue Reiter and entered a larger world of modern art to become one of the international figures of German Expressionism. The primary focus of Kokoschka's early paintings was portraiture. By the mid-1920s, though, he began exploring landscape painting in an extended period of travel, creating panoramic vistas that combined brilliant Impressionist color with traditional perspective.

In 1933, after nine years of continuous travel and painting, Kokoschka returned to Vienna. There he painted this view of his native city. In this portrait of Vienna, Kokoschka adopted an aerial view over the city from a hilly, wooded area on the outskirts of the worldly capital. The scene is what the artist saw from his residence at Liebharstal. Abundant green foliage, the buildings of Vienna (with the Danube in the far distance), and the sky are stacked in three horizontal registers. All three elements are unified and energized by feverish brushwork and radiant color—the great city of Vienna immersed in the greater scheme of nature.   **RHA**

Lyonel Feininger

American, 1871–1956

Built on the ruins of a ninth-century monastery, the Church of Locmaria was begun in the early eleventh century and added to over the centuries. It is located in Locmaria, a historical quarter in Quimper, a small town in Brittany in northwestern France.

In 1936, Lyonel Feininger began to draw this small Romanesque church with pen and ink, to which he added washes of blue watercolor. Under the influence of German Expressionist and French Cubist styles, he exaggerated the acute angles of the rooflines and the turret roof of the steeple. He even up-angled the flat ground on which the church stands. The lyrical effect of these manipulations is to lift the building skyward toward a radiant and mysterious cross floating above.

Born to parents of German descent and growing up in New York City, Feininger moved to Berlin in 1887 at the age of sixteen. He took part in various avant-garde art movements, and in the early years of the new century attached himself to Der Blaue Reiter, one of the first German Expressionist groups. Teaching at the Bauhaus in Germany for several years in the early 1920s, he and his wife fled Nazi Europe for America in the late 1930s. After resettling in New York City, Feininger completed this watercolor. **RHA**

Church of Locmaria, Quimper 1936–1939

Pen and ink and watercolor on paper
10⅜ × 15½ inches
Museum Purchase, R. H. Booth Fund
1946.1.3

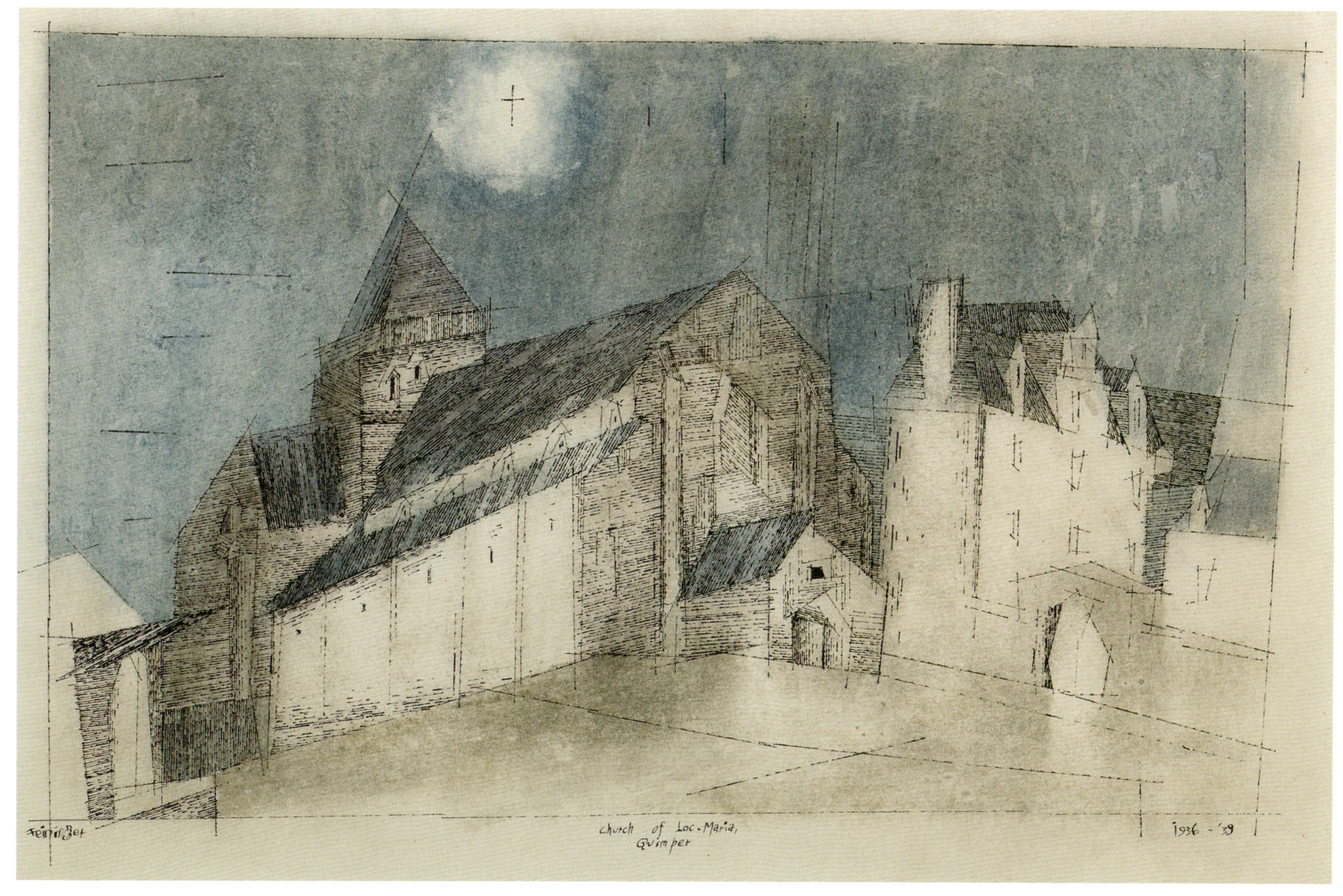

Feininger
Church of Loc-Maria,
Quimper
1936 - '39

. **Edward Hopper**
American, 1882–1967

Before he was recognized as an important American painter in the late 1920s and 1930s, Edward Hopper earned a critical reputation with prints and watercolors. In 1915 he made his first etching. Over the next decade he devoted himself almost exclusively to printmaking. He produced over one hundred etchings, of which *Night in the Park* is one of the most sought after. Although he later painted small towns and rural scenes in his watercolors, Hopper reserved urban subjects for his etchings.

In *Night in the Park*, most likely Central Park in New York City, a solitary man reads a newspaper on a park bench, lit by an overhead street lamp. The distant focus on the individual and the abrupt cropping of the park path suggest someone watching the reader. Engrossed in his reading, he does not notice. The isolated figure illuminated in darkness is one of the great themes in Hopper's art. Here, the person is vulnerable, not only to the implied onlooker but also to the darkness that surrounds him and the possible danger lurking there. Influenced by Rembrandt's nocturnal prints and the Dutch master's handling of strong dark-light contrasts, Hopper used the whitest paper he could buy locally and sent to London for intense black ink not found in the United States.   **RHA**

Night in the Park 1921
Etching on white wove paper
6⅞ × 8¾ inches (plate)
Museum Purchase in memory
of Miss Mabel H. Perkins
1975.2.27

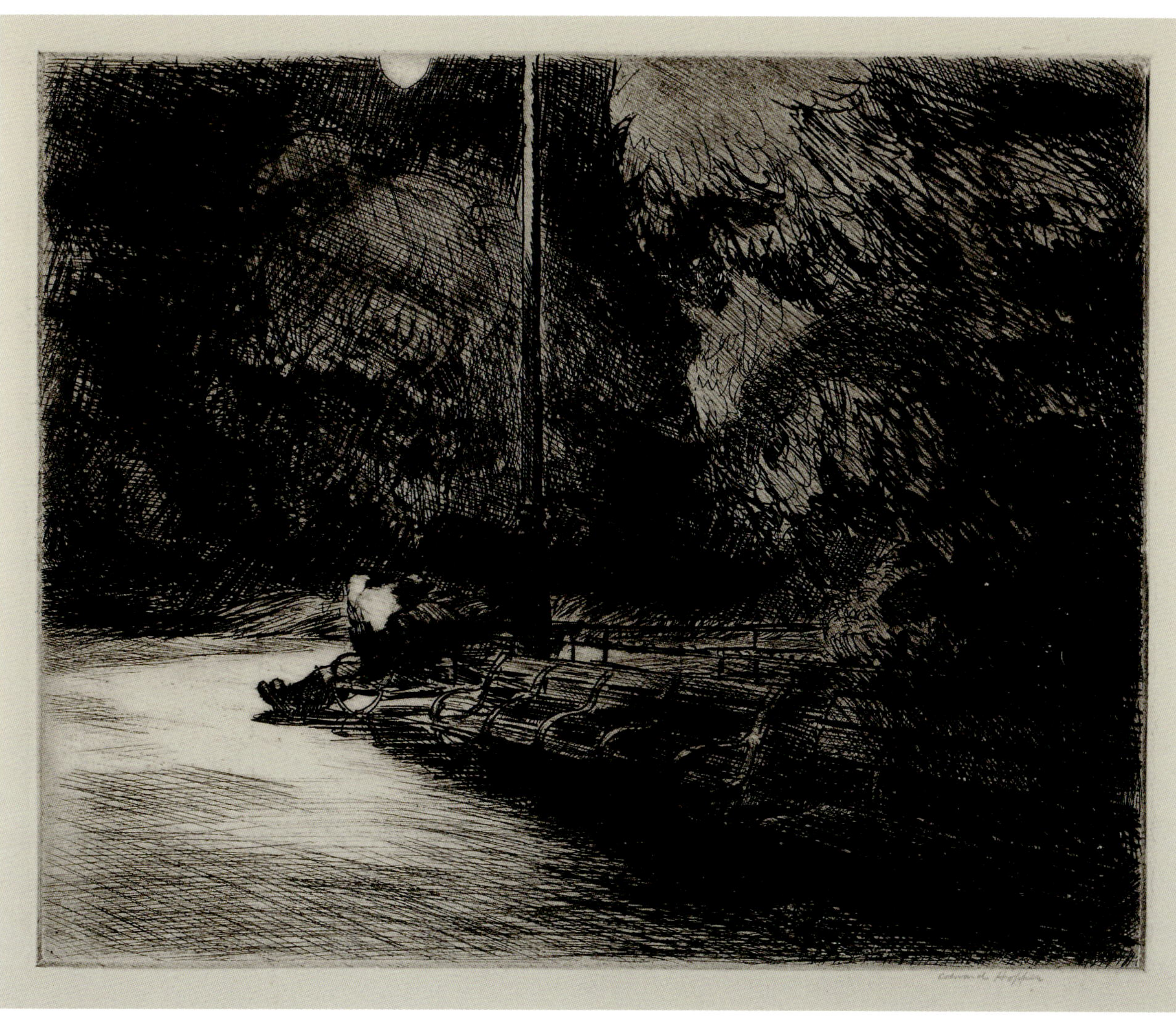

John Marin was both a distinguished painter and watercolorist. He spent the better part of his life dividing his time between New York City and the coast of Maine, the great sources of his cityscapes and seascapes, respectively. Stonington is an old seaport on the south tip of Deer Isle in the Penobscot Bay. While visiting there, Marin painted the low rise of houses as seen from the water. Seemingly stacked on top of each other from this vantage point, they prompted Marin to capture the syncopated rhythms of their shapes. In rapid brushstrokes, washes of color, and angulated shapes, Marin imbued the small village with the light, coloration, and flux of the sea.

Marin had his first New York exhibition in 1909 at Alfred Stieglitz's Gallery 291, the most progressive art gallery of the time. Marin's work on display revealed his contact with the art of Cézanne and the Fauves while in Paris during the previous four years. Although responding to European Modernism, particularly Cubism, Marin forged an art that was distinctly American in subject and treatment. During his lifetime, he was acknowledged as one of the great trailblazers of modern art in the United States.　**RHA**

Stonington, Deer Isle, Maine 1926

Watercolor on paper
14 × 17 inches
Museum Purchase
1955.1.1

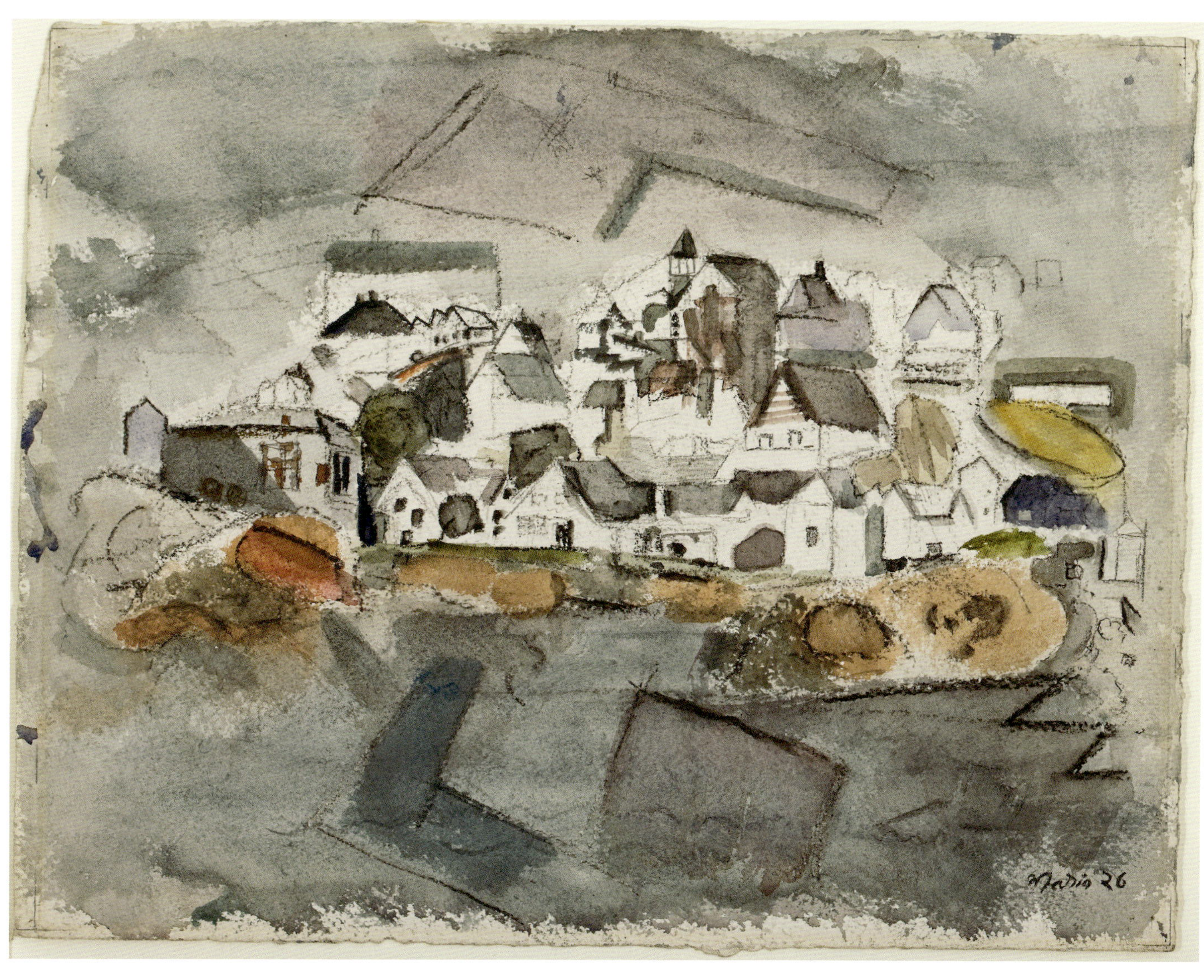

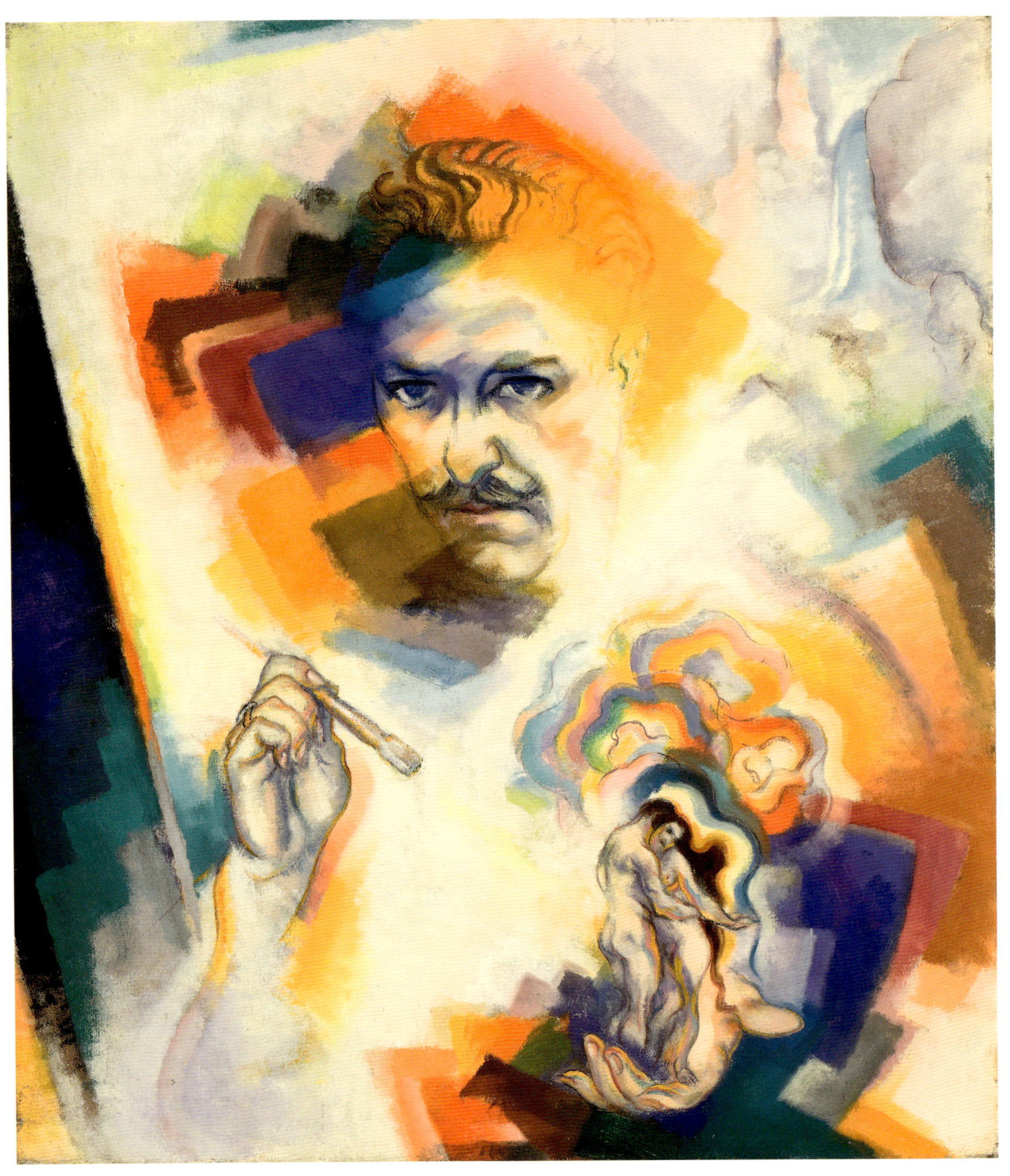

Stanton Macdonald-Wright

American, 1890–1973

Self-Portrait 1926–1927

Oil on canvas
28 × 24 inches
Bequest of Vivian Stringfield
1934.1.3

Stanton Macdonald-Wright is known as the cofounder, with Morgan Russell, of the Synchromist movement. Developed during 1913 in Paris and quickly gaining an international reputation, it was the only early Modernist art movement initiated by Americans. Invented by Russell, the word Synchromism means "with color" and was also a play on the word "symphony." The Synchromists believed that like the pure sounds of music, pure colors could be the basis for visualizing emotions in a work of art.

By 1919, Macdonald-Wright was in search of a new direction for his work and moved to California. He studied Asian art and Zen Buddhism, learning from Japanese culture the idea of "interior realism." During the mid-1920s, when he produced this painting, Macdonald-Wright wrote *A Treatise on Color* and was experimenting with Synchromist stage designs at the Santa Monica Theater Guild. Incorporating realistic passages of his face and of his hand holding an artist's brush, Macdonald-Wright embellished his self-portrait with spectrum-like patches of vibrant color. According to the artist, they represent his inner being as the imaginative artist. In his right hand, he cups the embracing figures of Adam and Eve— representations of the cosmic forces of yin and yang—which, like God, he creates and as an artist gives life to with color.   RHA

. Joseph Stella
American (b. Italy), 1877–1946

Receiving his initial art training in New York at the turn of the century, Joseph Stella was inspired while in Paris in 1911 to follow the example of avant-garde movements in Europe, most especially Cubism and Italian Futurism. Assimilating ideas and motifs from many sources, his work defied specific association with a particular movement or style. Among Stella's Modernist works, his urban landscapes and images of the Brooklyn Bridge are the best known.

Stella's *Still Life* belongs to a smaller group of works in this genre within his oeuvre. In a departure from the more usual depiction of flowers and plants, Stella took as his subject an oversized green squash and lemon. The weighty squash balances precariously, almost impossibly, upon the lemon to echo the classical vase that stands beside the fruits. The simple composition of solid forms fills the picture surface, locking the three elements in balance and creating within a small format a monumental still life with Surrealist overtones. **RHA**

Still Life c. 1925
Oil on canvas
15 × 15 inches
Museum Purchase
1976.1.7

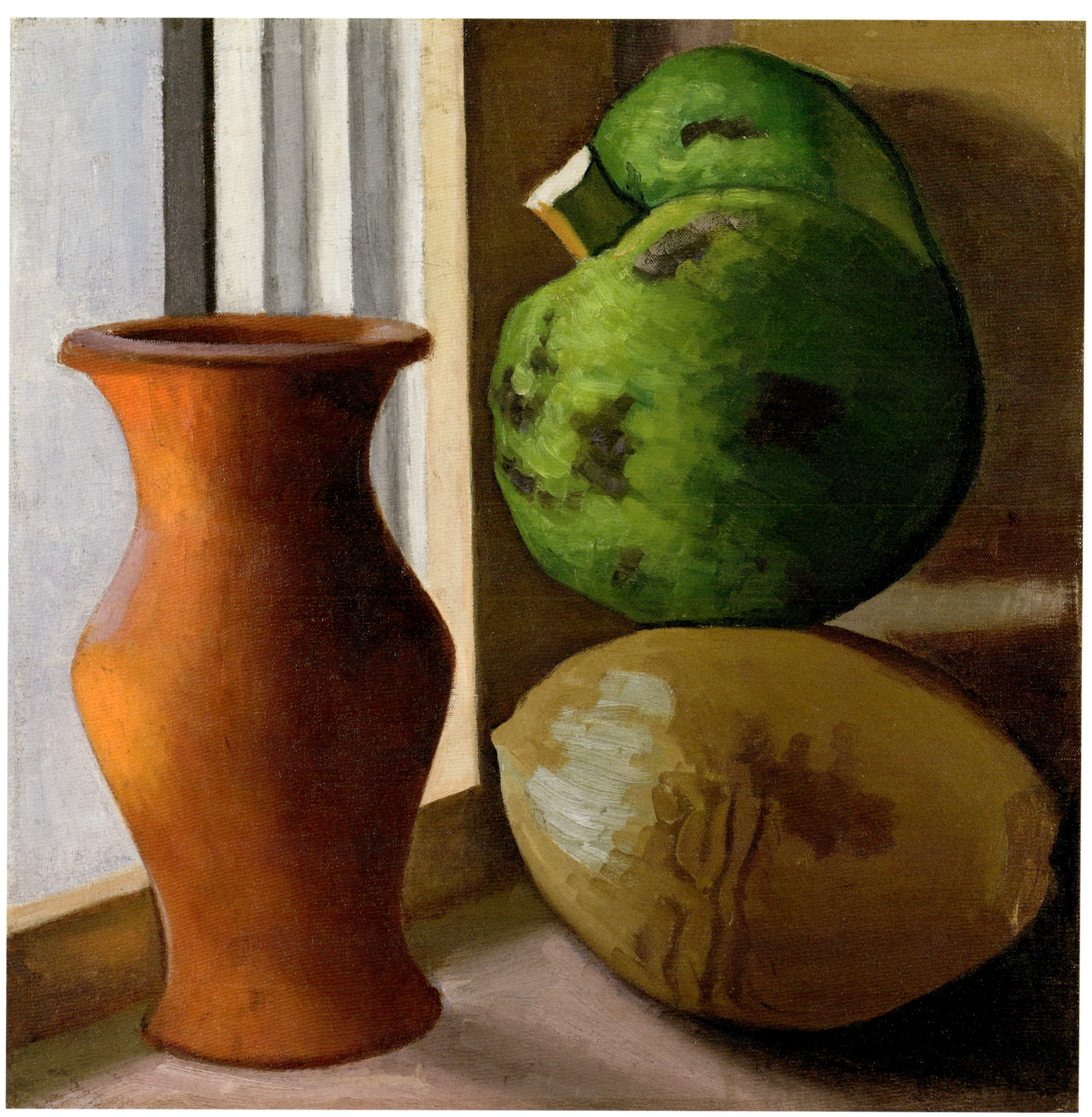

. **Ansel Adams**
American, 1902–1984

Ansel Adams is the great photographer of the American West. His celebrated photographs are epic documents of nature's spectacles, defined by clarity of focus and a rich tonal range—from deep blacks to subtle grays to pure whites. Born in San Francisco, Adams was first trained for a career as a concert pianist. During his early twenties, however, he began making photographs. Photography became his life's mainstay after a transformative experience while climbing with friends in Yosemite National Park to photograph Half Dome. Half Dome is Yosemite's majestic centerpiece, an extraordinary sheer granite shape rising abruptly from the valley's floor—three-quarters of a mile tall and almost half a mile wide.

Carrying his view camera and twelve unexposed glass plates, Adams realized that when he reached the desired vantage point, he had only two plates left. Directing his camera to Half Dome, he composed his view on the ground glass of his viewfinder. As soon as Adams snapped the shutter, he knew he wasn't going to get the right image. He then exposed his last glass plate to the very same view, but this time he attached a red filter to his lens to get what he knew would be missing in the first exposure. The sky is darkened almost to black in the final print; the white accents of snow much more pronounced. In the final print, he felt he had caught the sense of the enormity and terror he felt in the presence of Half Dome.

With this print, Adams realized he could make photographs that were, in his own words: ". . . an austere and blazing poetry of the real" and, more telling in terms of his maturing aesthetic, Adams felt this photograph was a turning point because he was able "to make a mountain look how it feels." **RHA**

Monolith: Face of Half Dome, Yosemite 1927
Gelatin silver print (printed after 1970)
19½ × 14¾ inches
Gift of Varnum, Riddering, Schmidt and Howlett
in honor of the museum's 100th anniversary
1988.14.34

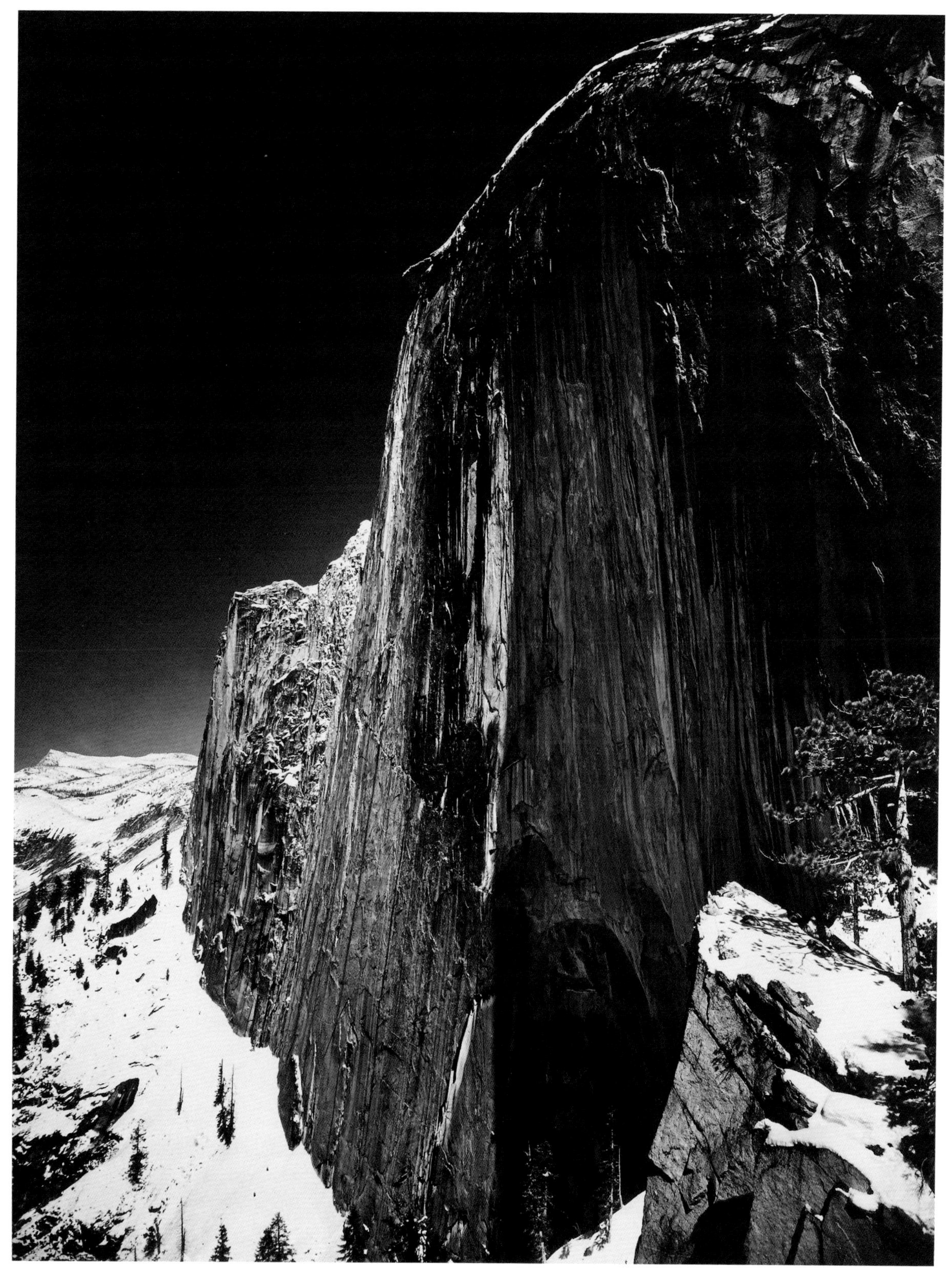

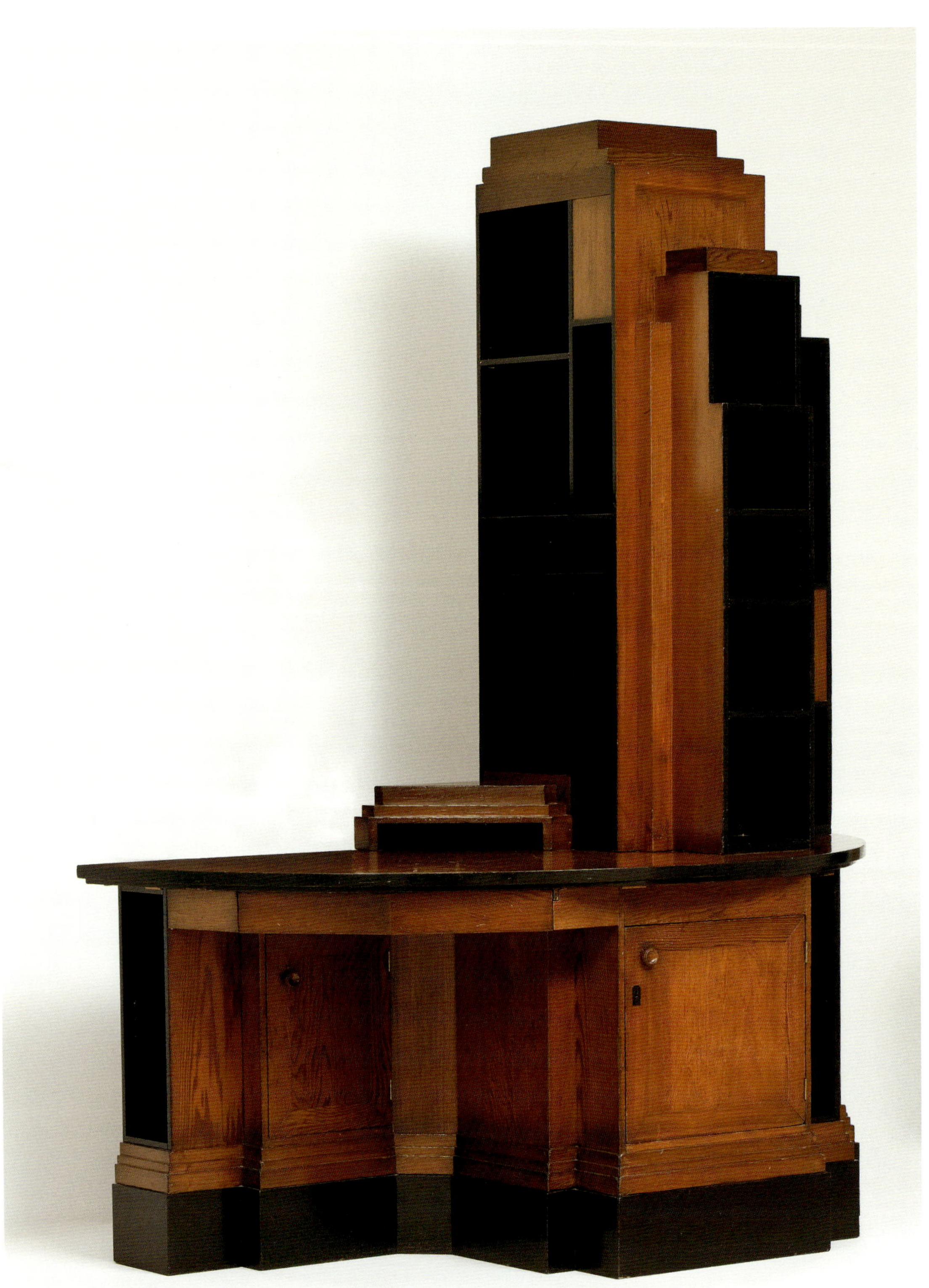

 Paul T. Frankl
American (b. Austria) 1887–1958

Skyscraper Bookcase Desk

C. 1928

California redwood and black lacquer
86½ × 64½ × 33½ inches
Gift of Dr. and Mrs. John Halick
1984.7.2

Viennese-born Paul T. Frankl, furniture designer and maker, arrived in the United States in 1914. He brought with him an outsider's fresh perspective and an enthusiasm for forging a uniquely American design aesthetic. By the 1920s, he had established Frankl Galleries in midtown Manhattan and became a spokesman for Modernist design inspired by the American scene. In the years between World Wars I and II, Frankl, more than any other designer, helped shape the distinctive look of American Art Deco.

In 1925, Frankl offered for sale in his New York gallery the first of his "skyscraper" furniture—wooden cabinetry with flat surfaces, sharp angles, and stepped silhouettes. In 1916, New York City had passed the first zoning law in America that mandated terracing and setbacks for the upper stories of tall office buildings. The new ordinance allowed greater amounts of light and air to reach the sidewalk. The impact on the new stepped-back skyscraper design is reflected in the geometric style of the Skyscraper Bookcase Desk. Frankl considered his "skyscraper" furniture thoroughly modern and purely American. One critic wrote that it was "as New Yorkish as Fifth Avenue itself."

Although an adherent of modern architectural engineering, Frankl rejected the idea that contemporary furniture should be standardized and mass-produced. It should not be "just another factory-made machine product." Frankl's notion of good design, as exemplified in the choice of wood and craftsmanship of the Skyscraper Bookcase Desk, promoted the same ideals of honesty, simplicity, and beauty in natural materials expounded in the writings of the Arts and Crafts Movement and Frank Lloyd Wright.

A publishing firm in New York City commissioned this particular Skyscraper Bookcase Desk in the late 1920s. One of its officials, Joseph H. Brewer of Grand Rapids, Michigan, later gifted it to Dr. and Mrs. John Halick.   RHA

. **Berenice Abbott**
American, 1898–1991

Berenice Abbott was an American photographer who spent her formative years in Paris from 1921 to 1929. There she met Marcel Duchamp and worked as Man Ray's assistant from 1924 to 1926, developing a passion for photography. Ray introduced her to Eugène Atget, the celebrated French photographer whose work influenced her for the remainder of her career and for whom she became a tireless and staunch advocate.

During her years in Paris, Abbott turned exclusively to portraiture, taking her subjects from the avant-garde worlds of the visual and literary arts. By the early 1920s, James Joyce had settled in Paris where in 1922 he finished *Ulysses*, one of the landmark novels of the twentieth century. Abbott photographed Joyce during two sessions: in 1926 in the author's apartment in Paris and in 1928 in the photographer's studio.

In this photograph of the author, the most famous of the set, Abbott presents a seated Joyce in a fedora hat and holding a walking cane. With his sight severely compromised by chronic iritis and glaucoma, which often left him in unbearable pain, he wears thick-lensed glasses, temporarily removing his eye patch. Looking pensively off camera, Abbott catches the writer in a relaxed moment of introspection. This portrait is one of the most famous photographs of the celebrated writer.   **RHA**

James Joyce, Paris 1928
Signed gelatin silver print (printed 1985)
14 × 11 inches
Gift of Frederick Currier, Jr.
1987.14.42

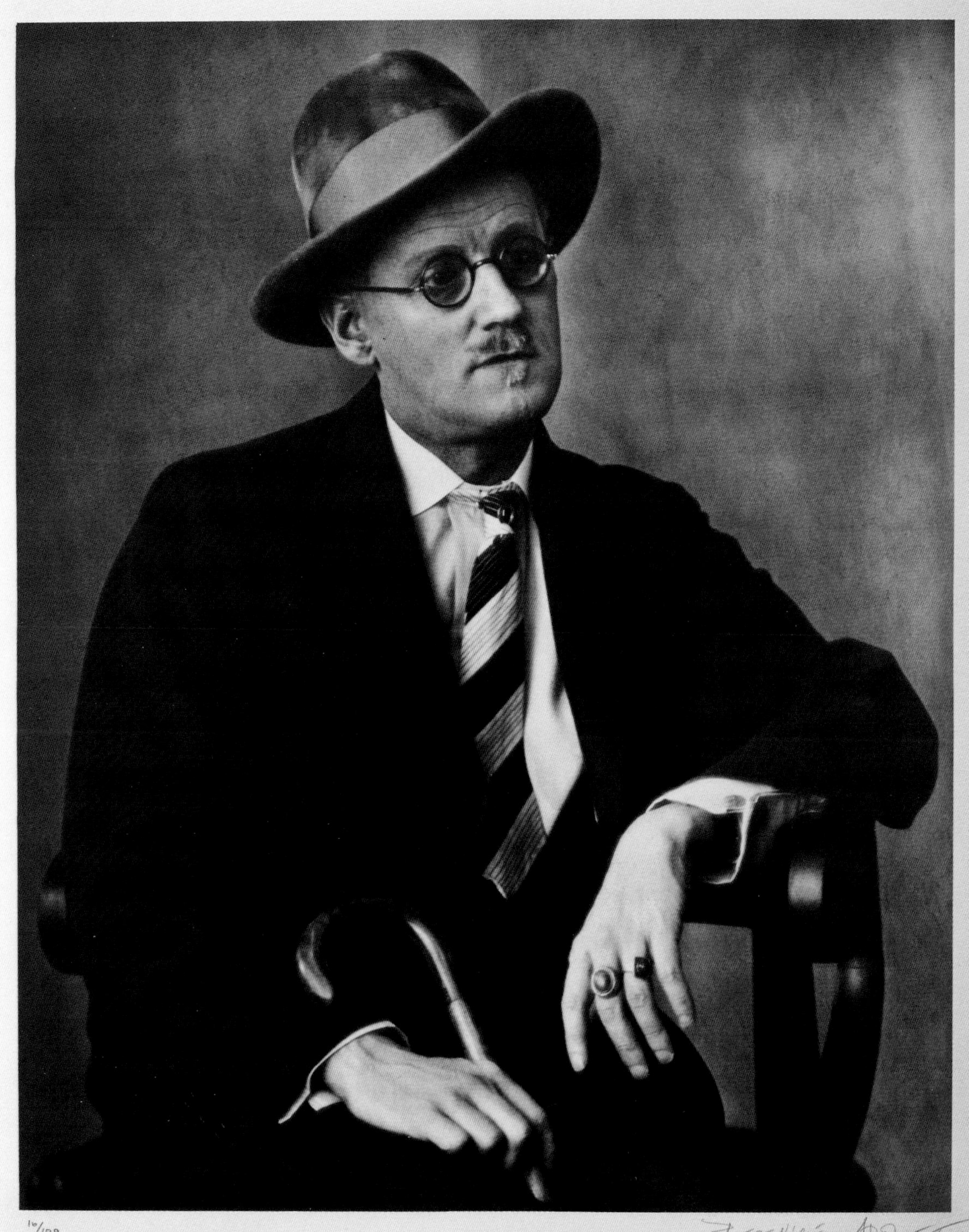
10/100
BERENICE ABBOTT

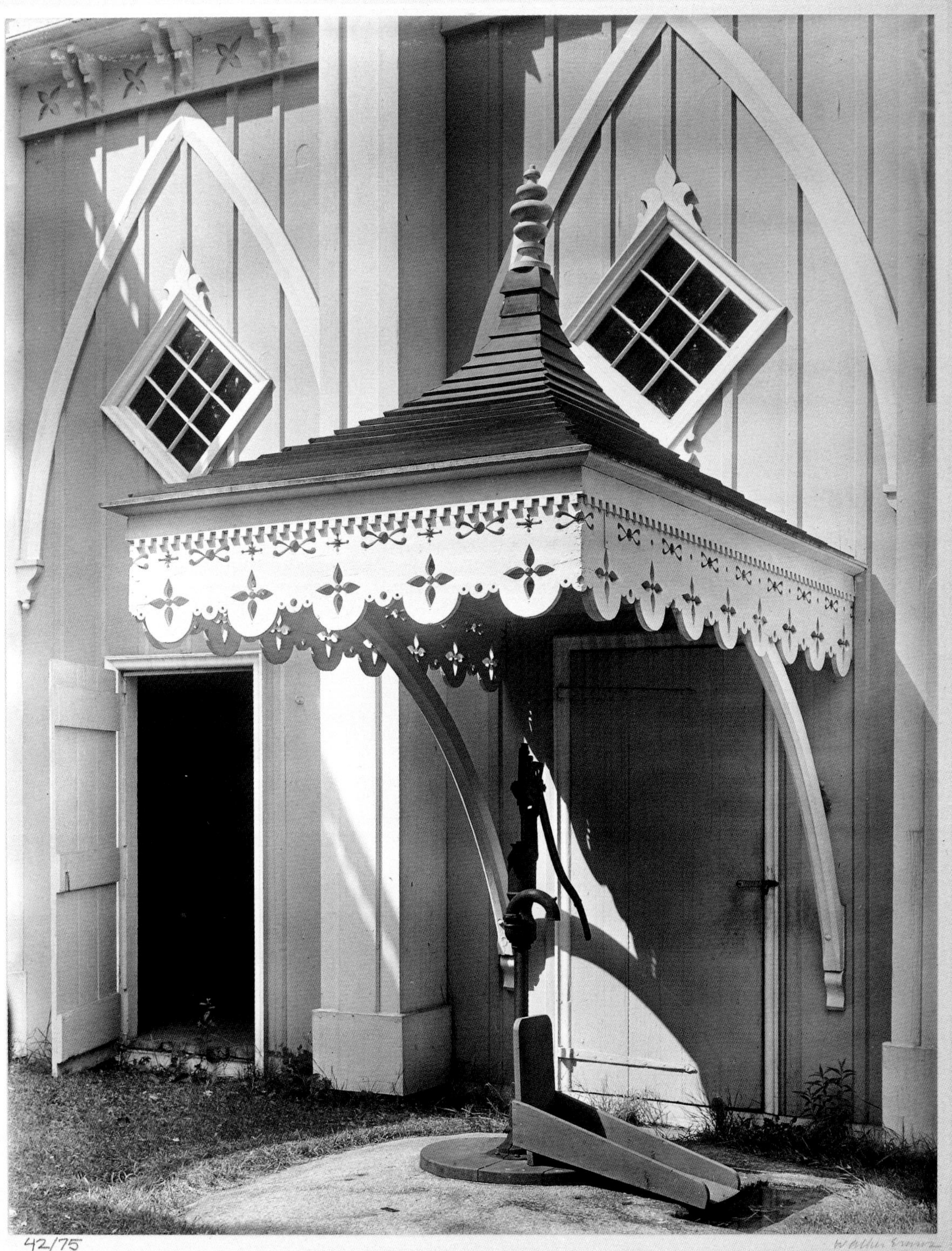
42/75
Walker Evans

 Walker Evans
American, 1903–1975

Maine Pump 1933

Signed gelatin silver print (printed 1974)
11¼ × 8½ inches
From the portfolio *Walker Evans:
Selected Photographs,* published by
Double Elephant Press, New York, 1974
Edition: 42/75
Gift of Frederick P. Currier
1990.14.35

Walker Evans is primarily known for his work under the auspices of the Farm Security Administration during the Great Depression. In the memorable photographs he took in 1936 documenting rural poverty in southern Alabama, he immortalized three disenfranchised white families with great compassion. Evans, however, also turned to other subjects with equal success.

In 1931, Evans toured New England in search of vernacular American architecture of the nineteenth century. One of the most famous buildings in the Carpenter Gothic style is the Wedding Cake House in Kennebunk, Maine (1825). Evans documented it from various angles, one of which captured the canopied water pump along the wing façade of the house. A wood awning shelters a slender black water pump with its wooden sluice. The awning and wall are embellished with the characteristic gingerbread detail of Revival Gothic architecture: the scalloped and cutout bargeboard of the canopy, its pointed roof topped by a finial, and pointed arches applied as trim to the board and batten siding.

Between 1931 and 1934, Evans refined his mature "palette" with a rich range of whites, grays, and blacks epitomized in *Maine Pump*. The gray raking shadows spill across the white trim on off-white wall; the black interior silhouettes the white crisscross mullions of the diamond-shaped windows; the open door to the left and darkness inside contrast with the adjacent closed painted door catching both the shadow of the canopy and the sunlight. Evans' passion for detail is expressed in his choice of subject and its sharp focus; his complex composition is a masterful play of light and form.   RHA

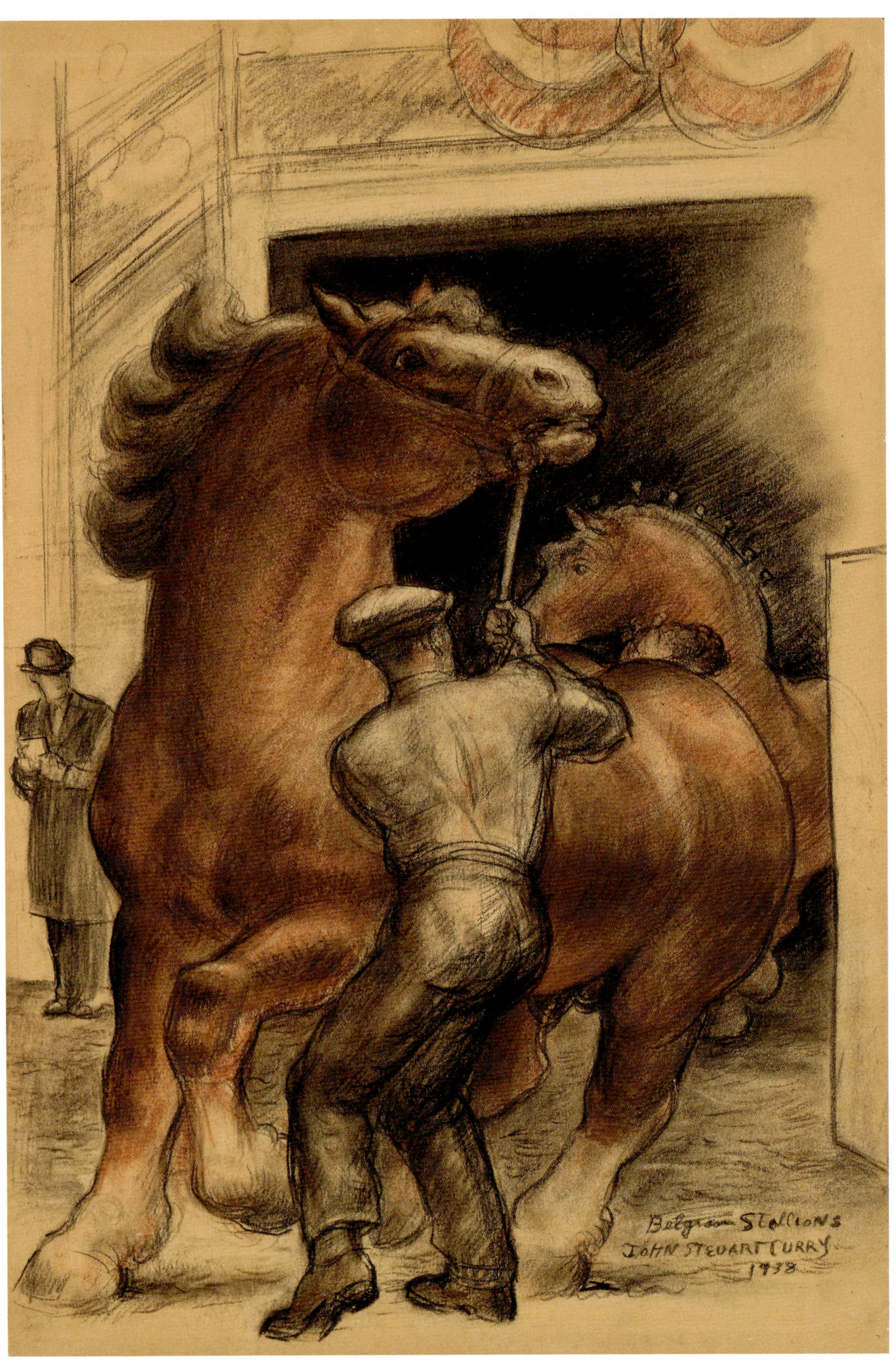

Belgian Stallions
John Steuart Curry
1938

John Steuart Curry

American, 1897–1946

Belgian Stallions 1938

Red and black chalk on paper
17¾ × 11¾ inches
Gift of Peter M. Wege
2007.18

Curry's chalk drawing *Belgian Stallions* portrays a powerful horse brought out into the ring for auction, with a stable boy barely keeping control. Curry monumentalizes the horse by exaggerating its proportions, revealing the important influence of Michelangelo. The Belgian horse was introduced into the United States in the mid-nineteenth century, a breed of heavy draft horse that was put to work across the American countryside. The horse was a recurring subject in Curry's art and functioned as a symbol of American freedom and power. Its symbolism is echoed here by the presence of the stars-and-stripes bunting above.

This drawing was the basis for a lithograph, also included in the Museum's collection, that Curry created for Associated American Artists in New York. Entitled *Prize Stallions*, the print was published the same year the drawing was executed. Although the subject and composition are the same, the lithograph is not a literal reproduction of the drawing. Each technique provides its own distinct qualities of line and texture.

Born in Kansas, Curry studied at the School of the Art Institute of Chicago and in Paris. He taught at the Art Students League of New York but returned to the Midwest in 1936 to teach as artist-in-residence in the College of Agriculture at the University of Wisconsin–Madison. He continued to teach and paint there until his early death in 1946 at the age of forty-nine. Curry, along with Thomas Hart Benton and Grant Wood were the Regionalist painters who defined American Scene Painting of the 1930s. This art movement sought to portray American life in traditional Realist styles and to celebrate the life of the rural Midwest.   CMB

A Realist painter and illustrator, Newell Convers Wyeth declared himself an authentic American artist. He is considered one of the great American illustrators. His illustrations for Robert Louis Stevenson's *Treasure Island* and *Kidnapped* captured the mystery and adventure of these great stories as told by one of America's beloved authors. Wyeth regarded his paintings, however, as distinct from his illustrations. In them he depicted broader American subjects and scenes more resonant in meaning than the more literal images of narrative storytelling. In *Checking the Traps*, a sole fisherman confidently checks his traps for lobsters. The simplicity of detail in the artist's rendering of the setting—the sea, sky, and sharply rising rock formations suggesting deep water—imbues the scene with an eerie silence and lends dignity to the fisherman's quiet labors.

N.C. Wyeth is the patriarch of the Chadds Ford, Pennsylvania, family of painters that boasts his son, the well-known Andrew Wyeth, and grandson Jamie Wyeth. **RHA**

The Red Dory 1938
Oil on canvas
25 × 40 inches
Gift of Peter M. Wege
2007.7

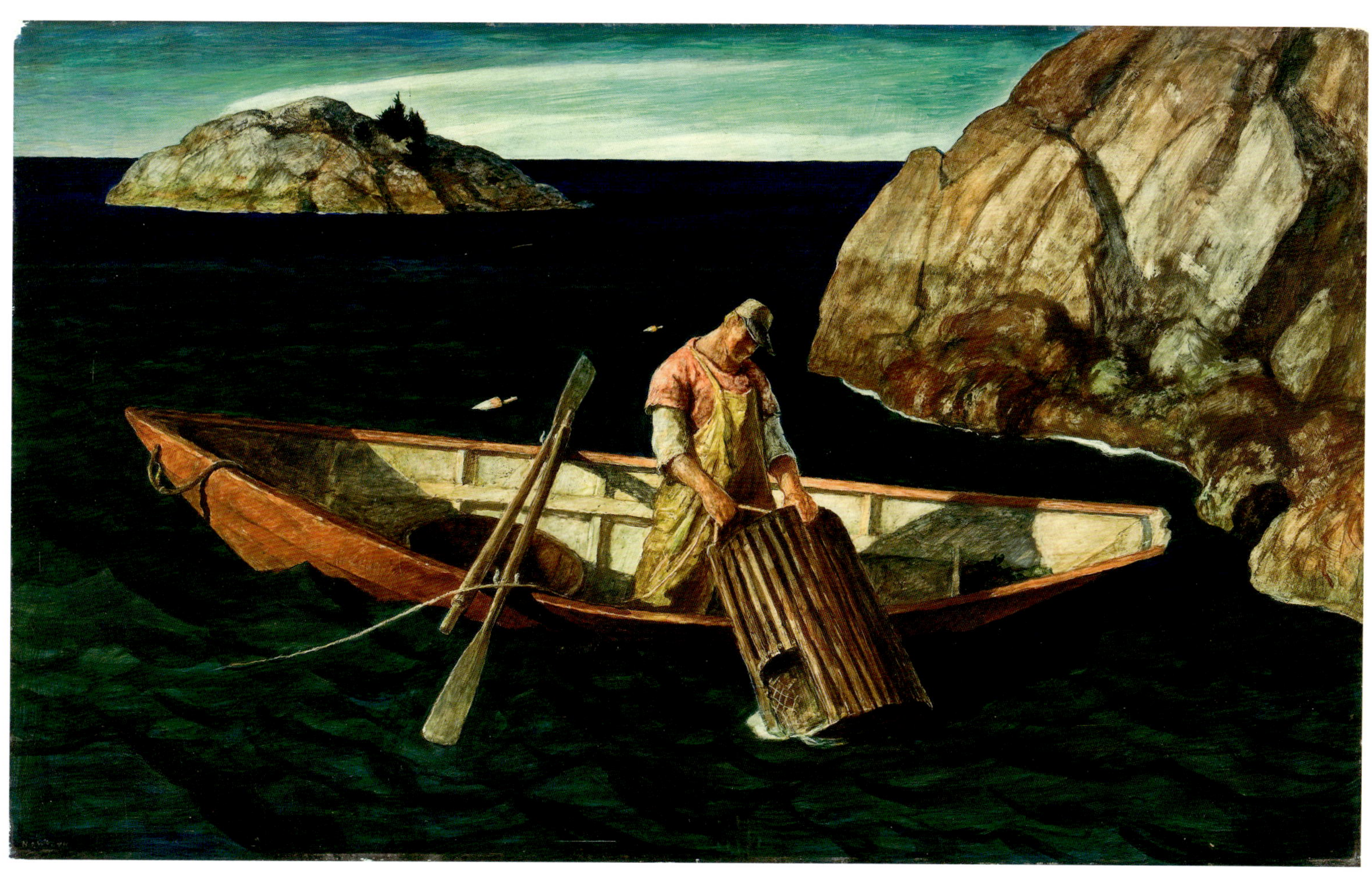

. **Ben Nicholson**
English, 1894–1982

Ben Nicholson was the first important abstract painter in England. Committing to painting in 1920, his early figurative and landscape work became increasingly influenced by Modernist developments in Paris. In 1933, after coming to know Constantin Brancusi, Georges Braque, and Piet Mondrian, their example, as well as Pablo Picasso's synthetic Cubism, prompted him to convert to abstraction. As a member of Abstraction-Création, a loose association of artists in Paris that promoted geometric abstraction, Nicholson became an important spokesperson for the style in England.

16 December 1939 clearly shows the influence of Mondrian yet is original in its own right. On a squared, deep-gray ground, Nicholson places a slightly smaller, squared system of interlocking blocks of color. Without a distinct line separating shapes, as is true in Mondrian's compositions, the painting displays a broader tonal range of color, including pale blue, and a modulation of color, especially of the white rectangles. The blue and red shapes accent and hold the system of blacks, grays, brown, and white in balance. The addition of earth tones, a move away from Mondrian's primary colors, adds a suggestion of landscape. Painted in December of 1939, with World War II begun the late summer before, the painting's subdued palette and irregular pattern calls to mind the Atlantic coastline around St. Ives in southwest England.

In 1939, the year of the painting, Nicholson and his second wife, Barbara Hepworth, the distinguished British sculptor, settled there. They wished to escape the increasing turmoils of war. Attracted by the solitude of the place and its reputation as an artists' colony, they were furthermore influenced in their art by the natural beauty of the ocean site. **RHA**

16 December 1939 (painting) 1939
Oil on canvas
27⁵⁄₁₆ × 30⁵⁄₁₆ inches
Gift of Hollis S. Baker
1959.1.4

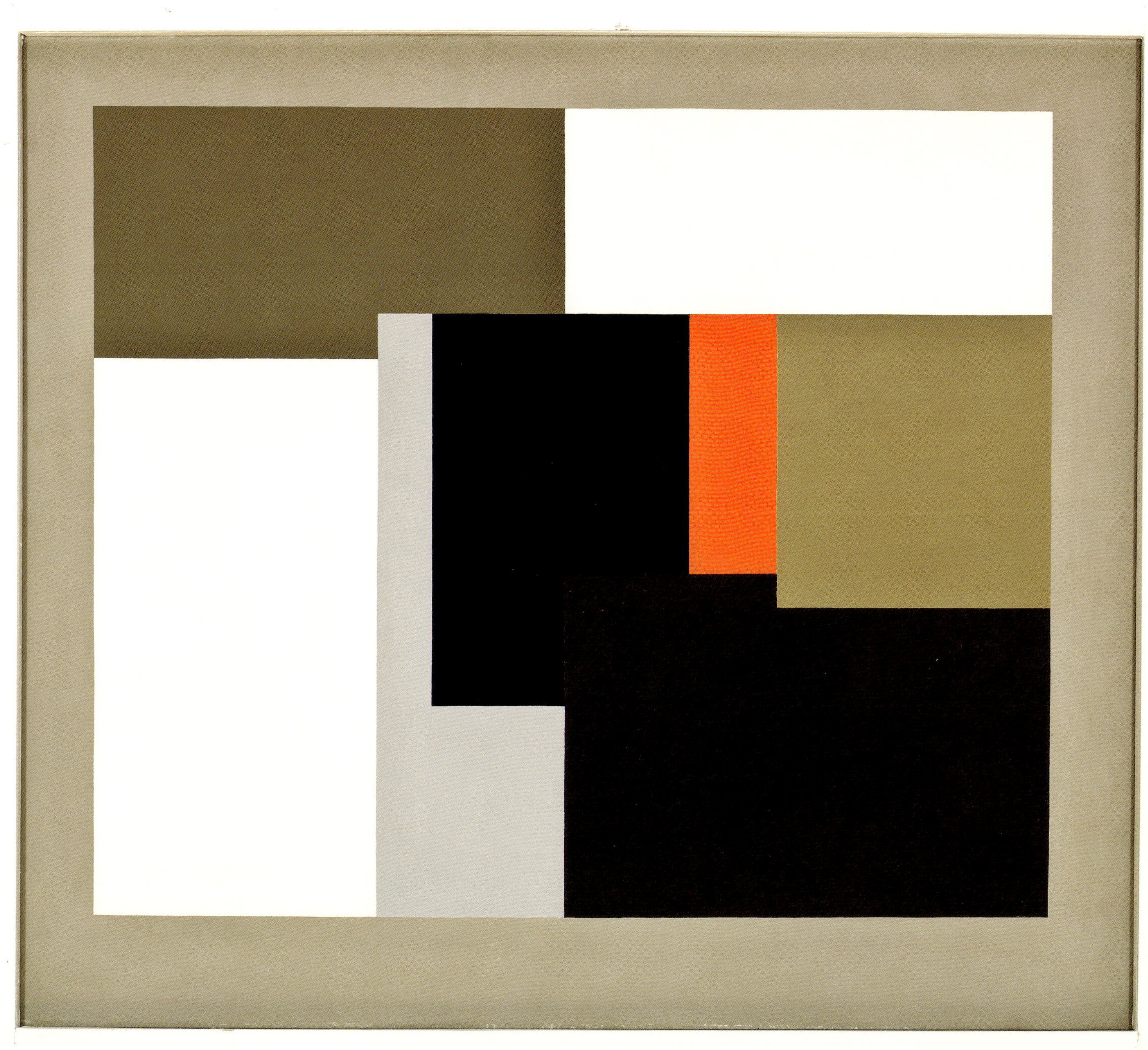

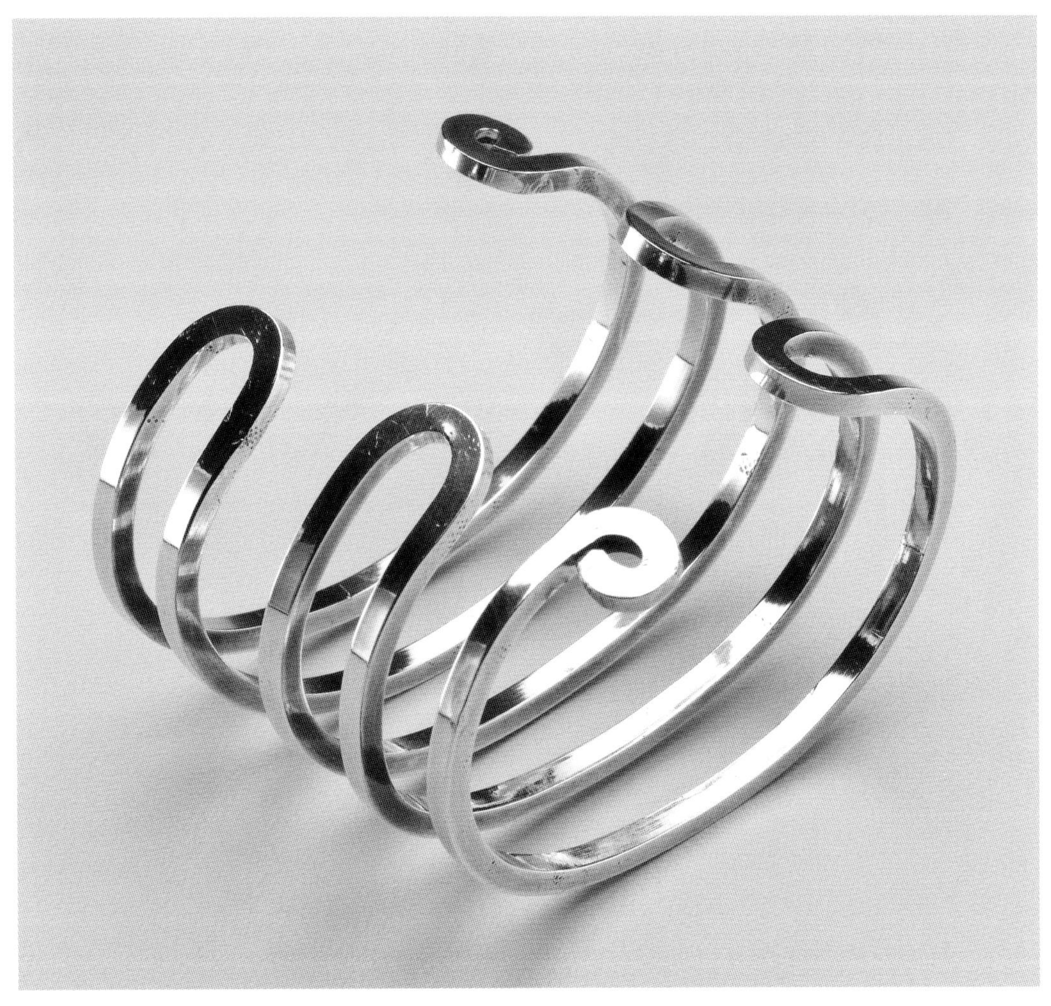

. **Alexander Calder**
American, 1898–1976

Bracelet c. 1940

Silver wire
3 × 3⅜ inches
Museum Purchase, Hollis Baker Fund
2009.130

In addition to his well-known sculptures and works on paper, Alexander Calder produced more than 1,800 works of jewelry. Avoiding precious materials, he typically worked in silver and brass, usually hammering metal wire into flattened shapes for brooches, necklaces, earrings, and bracelets. Conceived as wearable art, the three-dimensional forms of Calder's jewelry suggest his larger kinetic sculptures and were inspired by the artist's interest in Surrealism and primitive art.

This bracelet dates to a period of Calder's emergence as a leading American artist. Here the silver wire defines a concise triple spiral with elegant simplicity. It echoes the characteristic spirals of the artist's wire sculptures, gouaches, and prints. More classical than eccentric, the bracelet is a pure linear form that reflects Calder's fascination with line in space.　**RHA**

. **Barbara Morgan**
American, 1900–1992

Barbara Morgan is best known for her dance photography, especially that body of work documenting Merce Cunningham, Martha Graham, Doris Humphrey, and José Limon.

Martha Graham—Letter to the World is one of Morgan's most famous photographs of a twentieth-century American dancer. She wrote, "My first pictures of Martha Graham were taken in 1936. I worked for pictures which contain the essential emotion of that dance . . . that communicate the intense reality of movement. My pictures are designed to arrest time and to capture the dance at its visual peak." *Martha Graham—Letter to the World*, alternatively titled *The Kick*, was made in 1940 with a 4×5 Speed Graphic camera. Morgan required Graham to repeat a single kicking sequence until she had captured the image she wanted. The movement depicted is part of Graham's dramatic ballet "Letter to the World," based on the love life of American poet Emily Dickinson. Morgan's photograph is one of the most widely published images of Martha Graham.

Martha Graham has often been compared to Pablo Picasso because of her long dominance of her chosen art. She made the single greatest contribution to dance in the last century and is recognized for her contribution to poetic drama. Her collaborations with Isamu Noguchi and other artists and musicians made her work a universal influence on the arts. In October 1976, President Gerald R. Ford awarded Martha Graham the Medal of Freedom, making her the first dancer-choreographer to receive this honor. Ford's wife, First Lady Betty Ford, was for a time a member of the Graham company. **RHA**

Martha Graham—Letter to the World 1940
Gelatin silver print, printed c. 1960
13¾ × 17¾ inches
Museum Purchase in honor of
First Lady Betty Ford
2002.14.1

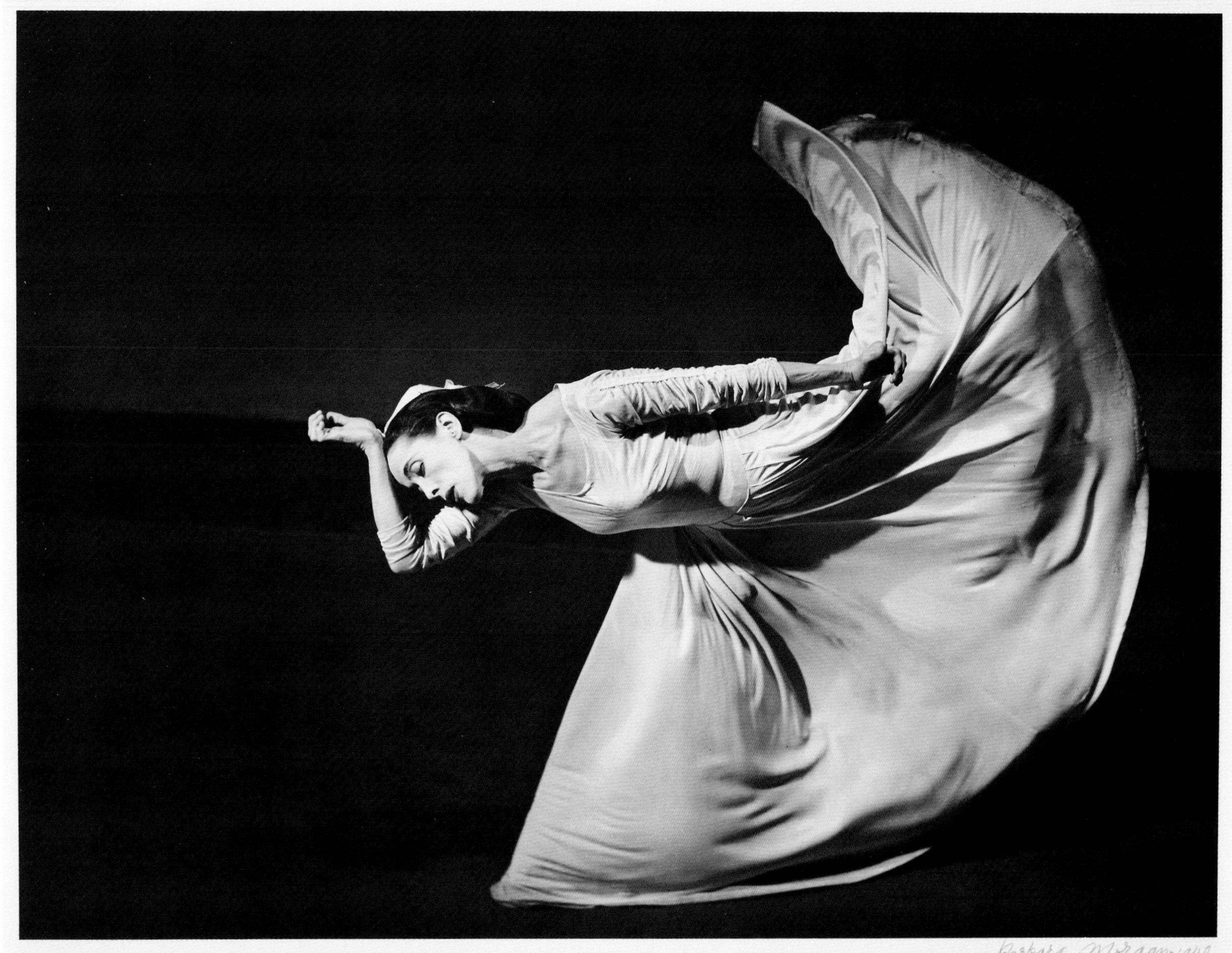

Barbara Morgan - 1940

. **Gordon Parks**
American, 1912–2006

Gordon Parks, filmmaker, musician, poet, novelist, journalist, and activist, was the first African American photographer to gain an international reputation in the twentieth century. Parks opened the field for African American photographers with his accomplishments in documentary and fashion photography. His distinguished work for *Life* magazine was a pivotal influence on a new generation of black photographers who recorded the events of the Civil Rights Movement in the 1950s and 1960s.

Parks first began working as a photographer in Chicago. He then received a fellowship that took him to the Farm Security Administration in Washington, D.C., where he made the photograph *American Gothic*—ironically named after Grant Wood's famous painting of a Midwest farmer and his wife. The photograph is a portrait of Ella Watson who was on the cleaning crew for the FSA building. It became one of many banner images for the emerging Civil Rights Movement after World War II, and possibly Gordon Parks' best-known image.

Parks later said of it, in reference to his arrival in Washington, D.C., and to his subject:

> I had experienced a kind of bigotry and discrimination here that I never expected to experience. . . . I felt that I must photograph this woman in a way that would make me feel or make the public feel about what Washington, D.C., was in 1942. So I put her before the American flag with a broom in one hand and a mop in another. And I said, "American Gothic"—that's how I felt at the moment. . . . That's what I felt about America and Ella Watson's position inside America. **RHA**

American Gothic, Washington, D.C. 1942
Signed gelatin silver print (printed later)
11¾ × 8⅜ inches
Museum Purchase
2006.60

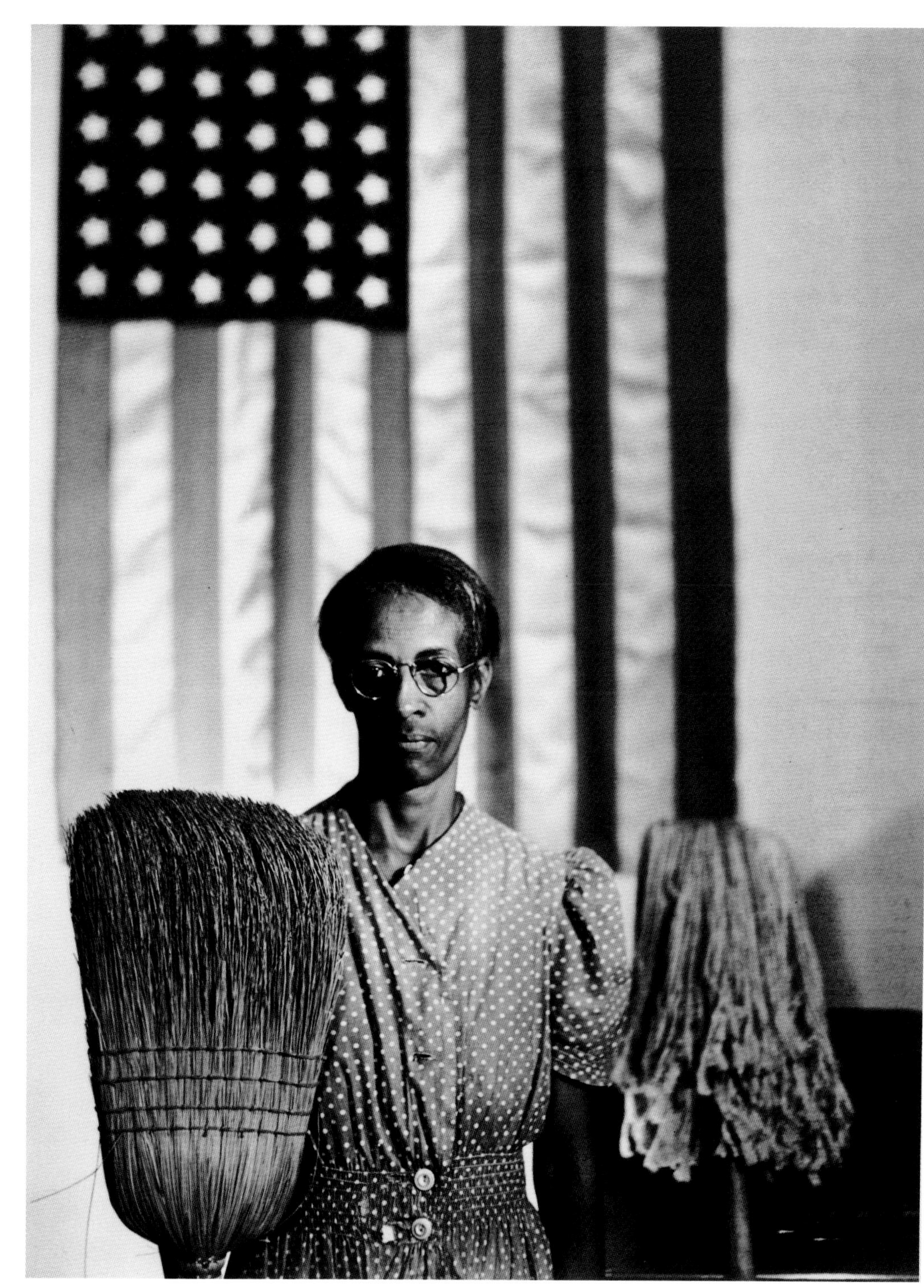

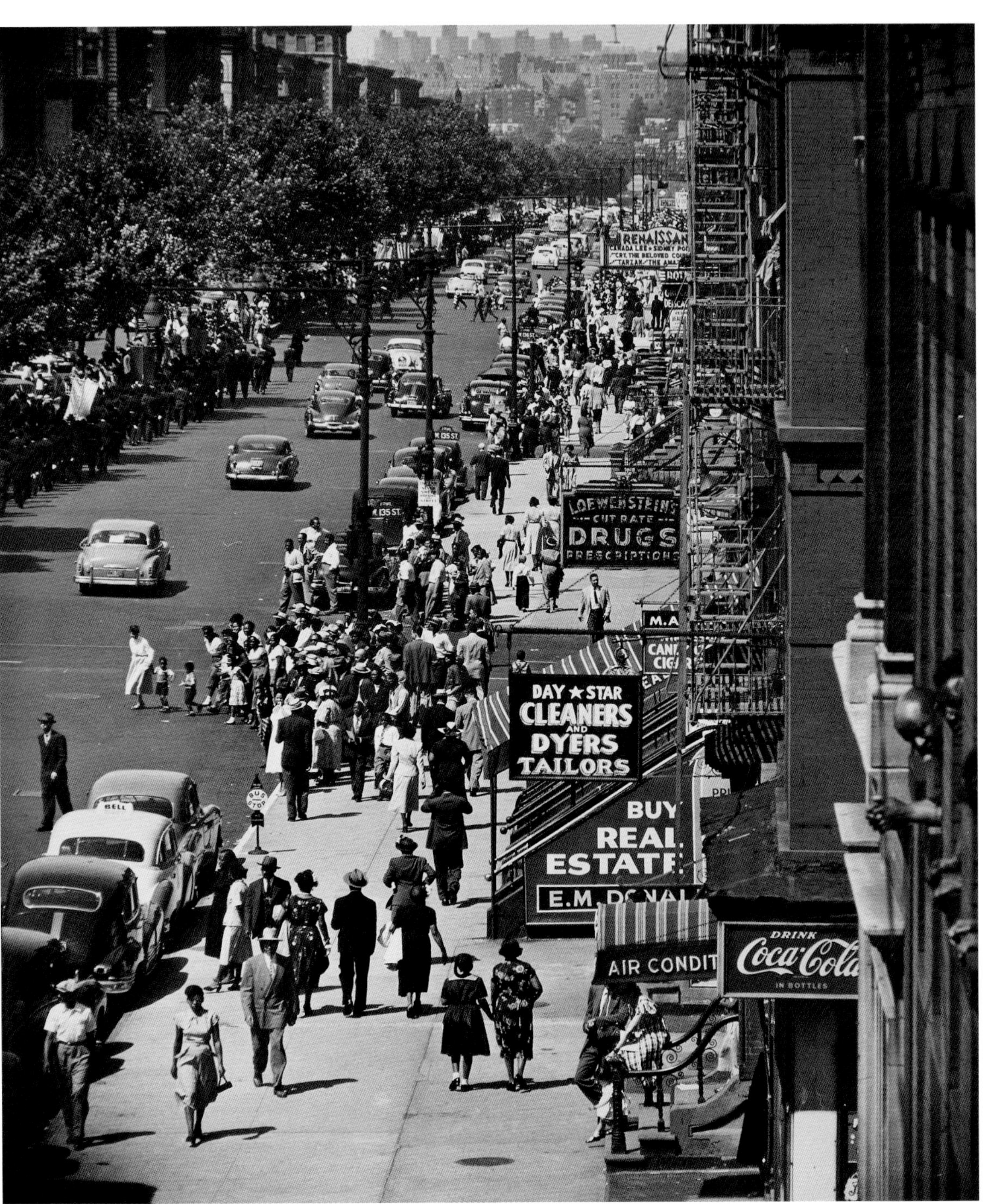
RENAISSAN
CANADA LEE • SIDNEY PO
CRY THE BELOVED COU
TARZAN THE AMA
LOEWENSTEIN'S
CUT RATE
DRUGS
PRESCRIPTIONS
N. 135 ST.
M. A
CAN
CIGAR
DAY ★ STAR
CLEANERS
AND
DYERS
TAILORS
BUY
REAL
ESTATE
E. M. DONAL
AIR CONDIT
DRINK
Coca-Cola
IN BOTTLES
BELL

Gordon Parks

American, 1912–2006

Untitled (Harlem 135th Street at 7th Avenue) 1948

Vintage gelatin silver print
12½ × 10¼ inches
Museum Purchase
2006.49

In 1944, Gordon Parks moved from Washington, D.C., to Harlem on the Upper West Side in New York City. In New York, Parks became a freelance photographer for *Vogue* magazine and continued his documentary photography. A 1948 essay on a young Harlem gang leader, Red Jackson, won Parks a staff job as photographer and writer for *Life* magazine, where he worked for the next twenty years.

Harlem has a long history as one of the most important black communities in the United States. During the 1920s and 1930s, it was the center of the Harlem Renaissance—a cultural outpouring in the visual, literary and performing arts. Parks captures the continuing vitality of the neighborhood in this shot looking down 7th Avenue at West 135th Street. It was taken from a fire escape that allowed Parks a generous view of car and pedestrian traffic. At this time, Parks was living at the Harlem Branch YMCA that was built in the early 1930s specifically for African American men. As both an athletic and residential facility, it was a temporary home over the years to a distinguished roster of black Americans.

Parks' view of Harlem is one of the finest examples of American street photography in the history of the genre. It takes a distinguished place in the museum's permanent collection, which includes fourteen signed works by Parks.   RHA

Rockwell Kent
American, 1882–1971

Rockwell Kent created works in a wide variety of media, including painting, prints, and graphic design. He also worked as an illustrator. In 1930, he finished the illustrations for the Herman Melville classic, *Moby Dick*, his greatest achievement in this genre. Kent earned a great reputation for his travels, which included then-exotic locales such as Alaska, Greenland, and Tierra del Fuego. He often painted scenes of the rocky, rugged landscape of these barren lands, which along with his images of upstate New York and Maine, are among his most memorable works.

Typical of Kent's painted landscapes, *From Palmer Hill* depicts a remote expanse of mountain range. Palmer Hill is near Asgaard, the family dairy farm in the Adirondack Mountains, where Kent made his home and kept his studio, a few miles from the town of Au Sable Forks, New York. In a series of carefully composed horizontal registers, the distant landscape, shadowed by dark overhead clouds, is still and silent as the evening light softly reflects on the softened, blue mountains in the distance. The clarity and sharp focus in this work, and in much of Kent's art, finds its source in his interest in the graphic arts. **RHA**

From Palmer Hill c. 1946
Oil on canvas
28 × 44 inches
Gift of Peter M. Wege
2007.4

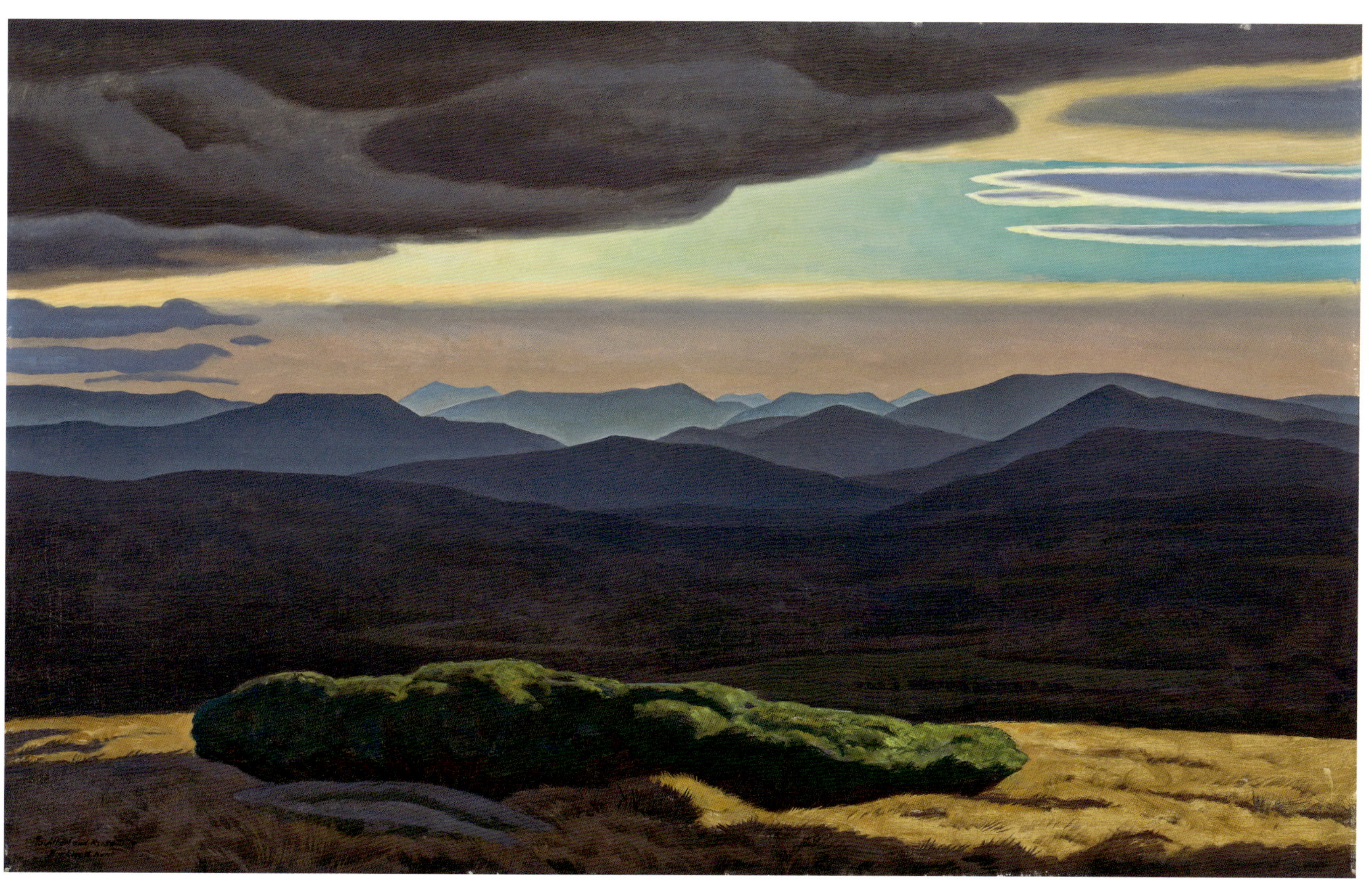

Stuart Davis went to Paris in 1928 to study the works of the European Modernist painters, particularly the Cubist artists and Henri Matisse. Upon his return to New York, where he spent his adult life, Stuart was inspired to paint a series of abstracted cityscapes. They combined abstract forms and suggestive shapes and words to establish a recurring visual theme in the artist's work.

The small-scale *Configuration* reflects Davis' skill as a bold abstractionist and colorist. Inspired by jazz and modern music, Davis painted a vibrant composition using strong color and flat graphic imagery. The jagged, sharp-edged shapes recall his early and continued interest in developing European Cubism into an American idiomatic expression. The incorporation of crisscrosses, grids, notational arrows, and other linear markings are reminiscent of his use of words in other works. Davis was a highly original and complex artist. He is considered to be one of the most important figures in the American Modernist movement of the early twentieth century. **RHA**

Configuration 1946
Oil on canvas
12 × 8 inches
Museum Purchase
1979.1.5

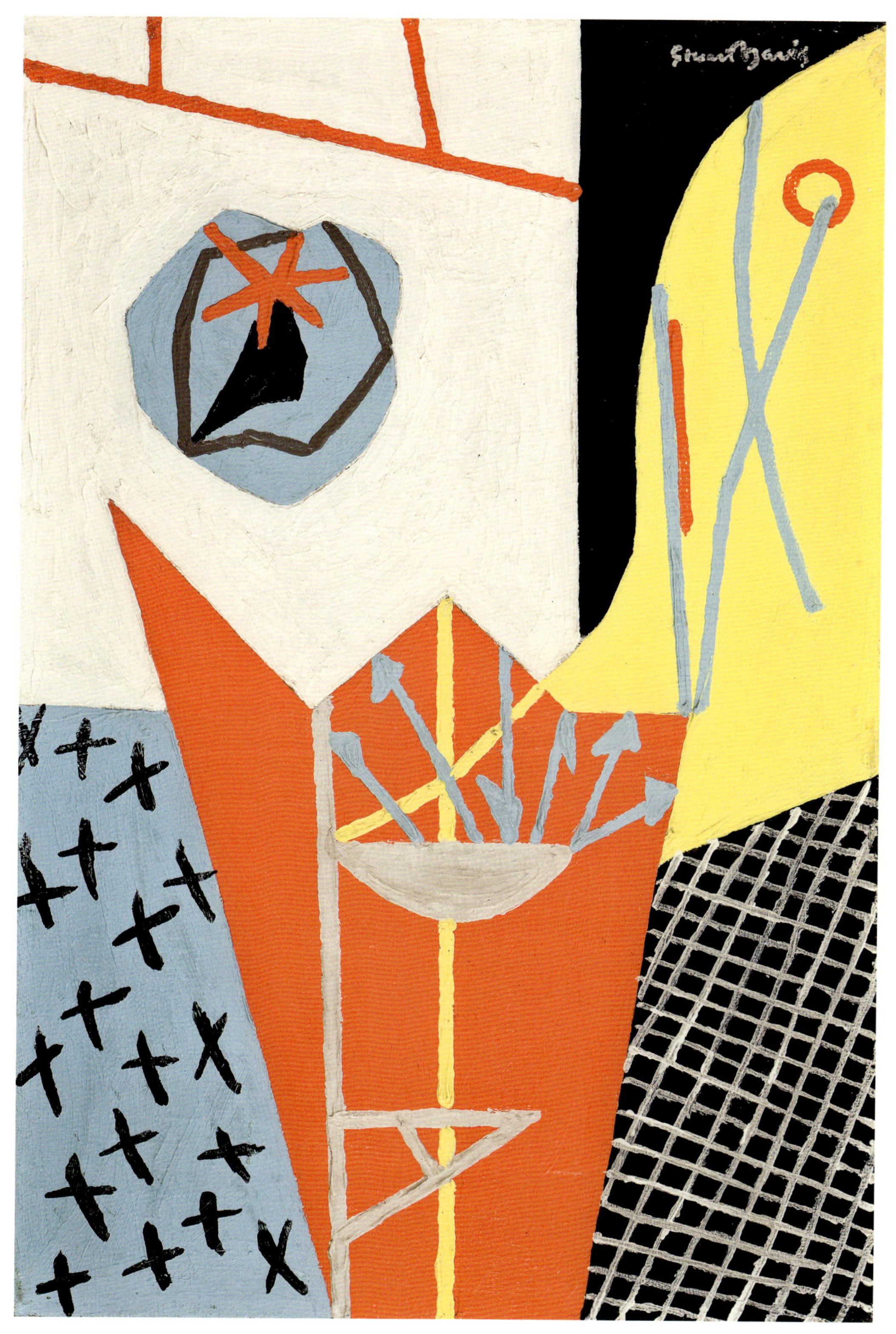

. Charles Eames
American, 1907–1978

. Ray Eames
American, 1912–1988

The LCW (Low Chair Wood), also referred to as the "potato chip" chair, was the original design that connected Charles and Ray Eames to Herman Miller, Inc. The chairs resolved the Eameses' quest for practical, low cost seating that could be easily mass-produced. Each component of the chair was streamlined into a minimal organic shape and produced separately, thereby eliminating the need to replace an entire chair if one component cracked during the assembly process. The chairs were initially produced in ash, birch, rosewood, and walnut and could also be aniline-dyed red and black, or covered in a wide variety of fabrics. An affordable and beautiful chair produced by the thousands, the LCW was awarded the distinction, "Best Design of the Century" in 1999 by *Time* magazine.

The husband-and-wife design team of Charles and Ray Eames ranks among the most influential designers of the twentieth century. Their design philosophy of "the-way-it-should-be-ness" continues to influence generations of students and designers, and their work exemplifies American design ingenuity in the modern era. Charles met Ray (born Bernice Alexandra Kaiser) at the Cranbrook Academy in Bloomfield Hills, Michigan, where he was teaching industrial design and Ray was studying textile design. They married in 1941 and moved to Pacific Palisades, California, where they established the Eames Office, a studio dedicated to solving problems through design.   CMB

LCW (Low Chair Wood) 1945–1946

Molded birch plywood with red aniline stain
First produced by Evans Products Company and
distributed by Herman Miller Furniture Company
22 × 25 × 27 inches
Museum Purchase
2006.24

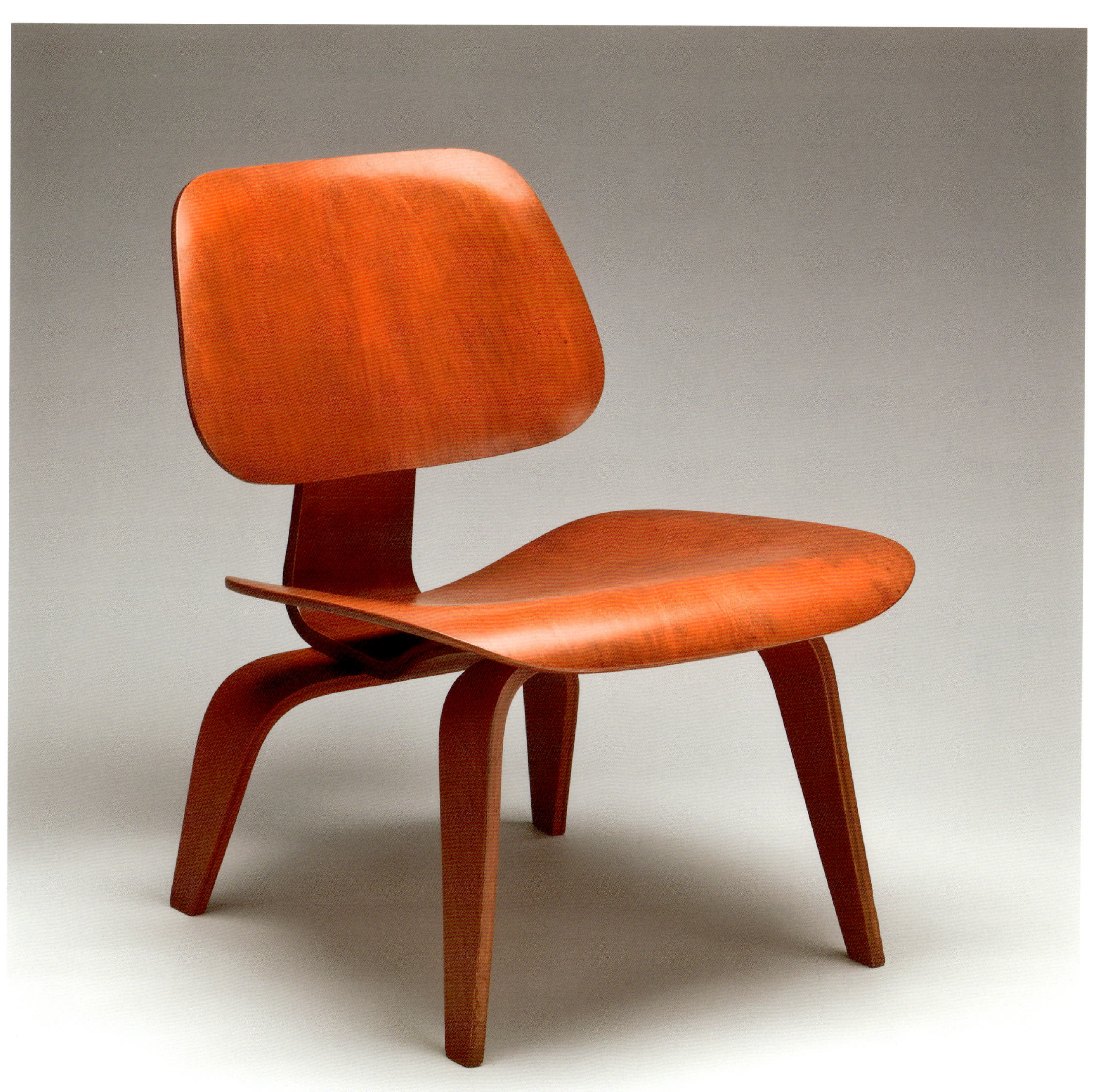

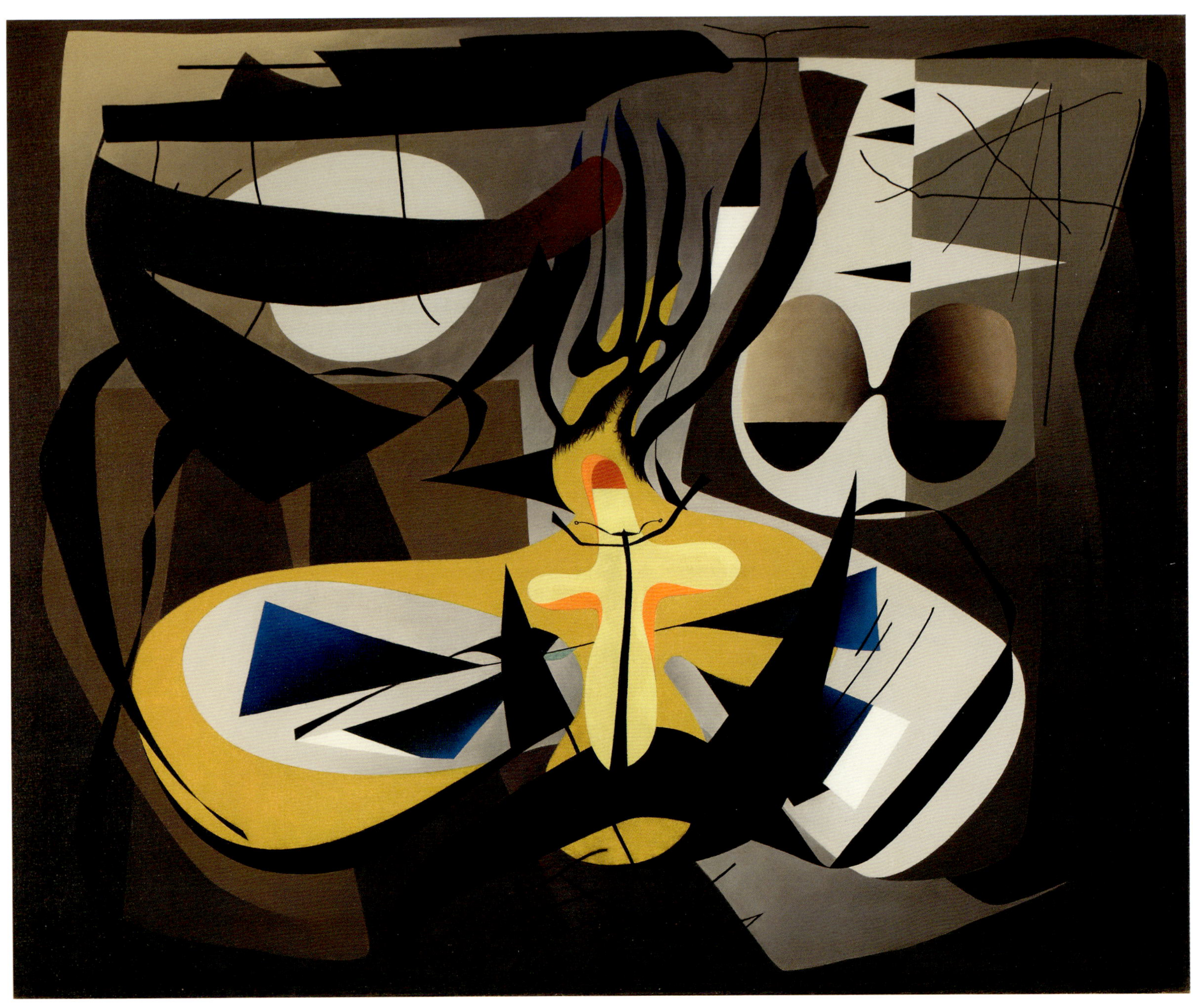

. **Charles Howard**

American, 1899–1978

The Independent Source 1950

Oil on canvas
25 × 30 inches
Museum Purchase, James Pingree and
Mary G. Nelson
2004.9

In New York and London during the 1930s, Charles Howard embraced European Surrealism. Its influence remained lasting in his work. In 1941, Howard settled in the San Francisco Bay area and was soon recognized as one of the Bay area's major abstract painters. His most important works were executed in the years from 1938 to 1952.

Often described as an Abstract Surrealist, Howard navigated between European and American Surrealism. His canvases are meticulous and concise in technique and incorporate the shapes and spatial concepts of biomorphic abstraction and automatic drawing taken from the art of Joan Miró and Alexander Calder. *The Independent Source* is characteristic of Howard's style in its use of primary colors against black, delicate forms that flip and reverse in the composition, and in a glowing center against a neutral ground. Its title declares that art's subject matter is conceived purely in the subconscious mind of the artist without reference to the natural world. Despite the irrationality it ascribes to, the painting is rationally balanced. Its immaculate and magical forms are in pleasing balance—like the undulating shapes of a Calder mobile. **RHA**

The year 1950 was the emerging moment for the Abstract Expressionists in New York. At this time, Robert Motherwell, who worked as an artist in the city during the 1940s, had become closely associated with key members of the group, including special ties to Adolph Gottlieb, Willem de Kooning, Mark Rothko, and David Smith. *Black Figuration on Blue*, a critically important early work, was first shown in a 1950 exhibition at the Kootz Gallery under the title *Black Plant and Window*. It was one of fourteen paintings that were listed as part of a series called "capriccios." Motherwell described "capriccio" as a word used by musicians to mean a "composition in a more or less free form." The painting compresses its subject in such a fashion that we still see elements of the plant/figure and the window, without them becoming a literal representation of the subject. This kind of equilibrium between real experience and abstraction lies at the heart of Motherwell's achievement.

Though at the center of a new American art movement, Abstract Expressionism, Motherwell remained deeply connected to French writers and artists. He considered Henri Matisse the greatest painter of the twentieth century. *Black Figuration on Blue* reflects Motherwell's admiration for Matisse and looks toward his future *Open* paintings, inspired by the squared image of a window or door of the artist's studio. Motherwell kept *Black Figuration on Blue* as one of what he called his "seed" works that provided him with ongoing inspiration for the rest of his life. The painting was in Motherwell's estate at the time of his death and acquired by the Grand Rapids Art Museum, its second owner, from his Foundation. **RHA**

Black Figuration on Blue 1950
Oil on Masonite
25½ × 47½ inches
Kate P. Wolters Family in memory of Richard Wolters,
Museum Purchase and Gift of Dedalus Foundation
2006.1

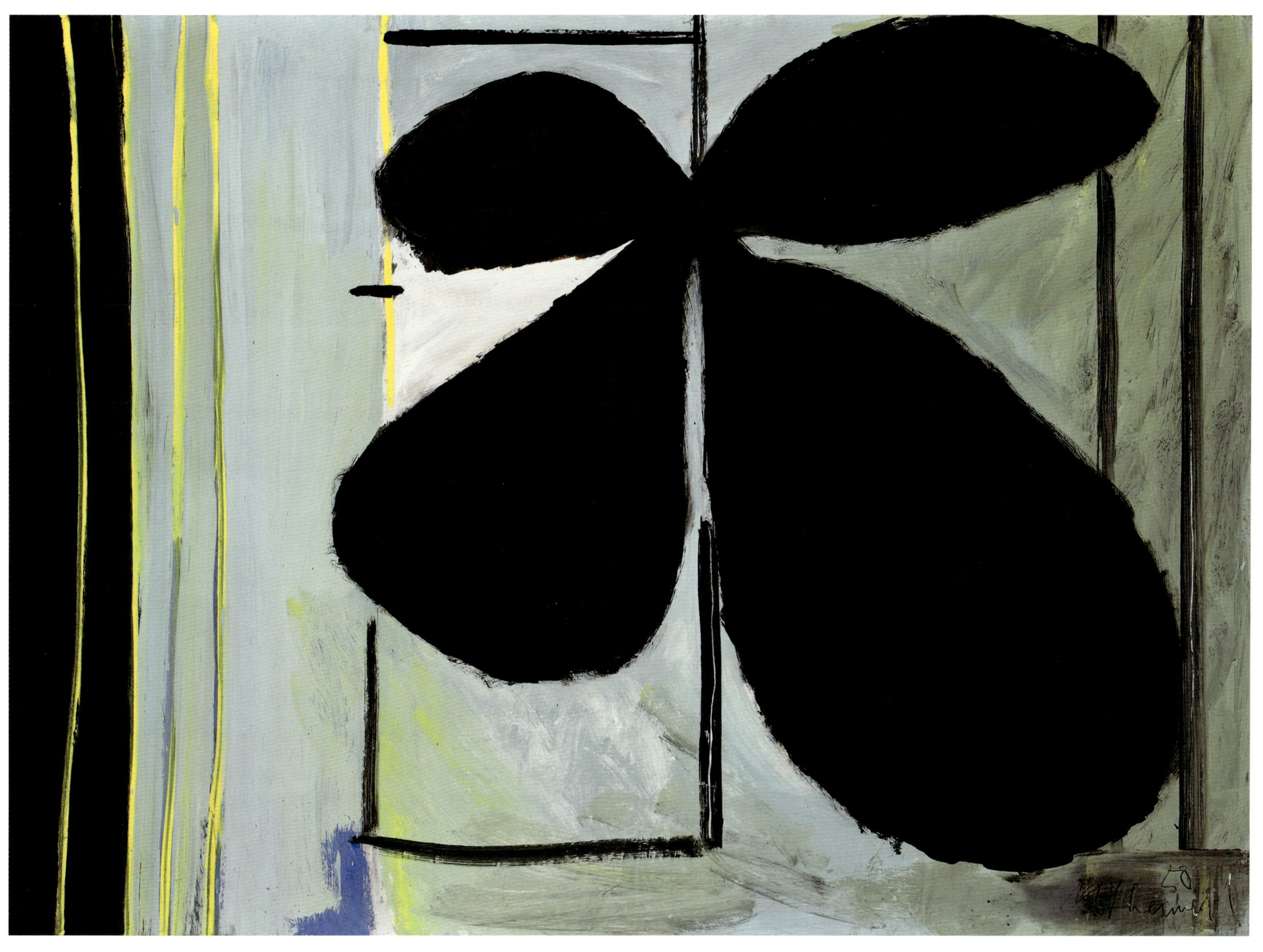

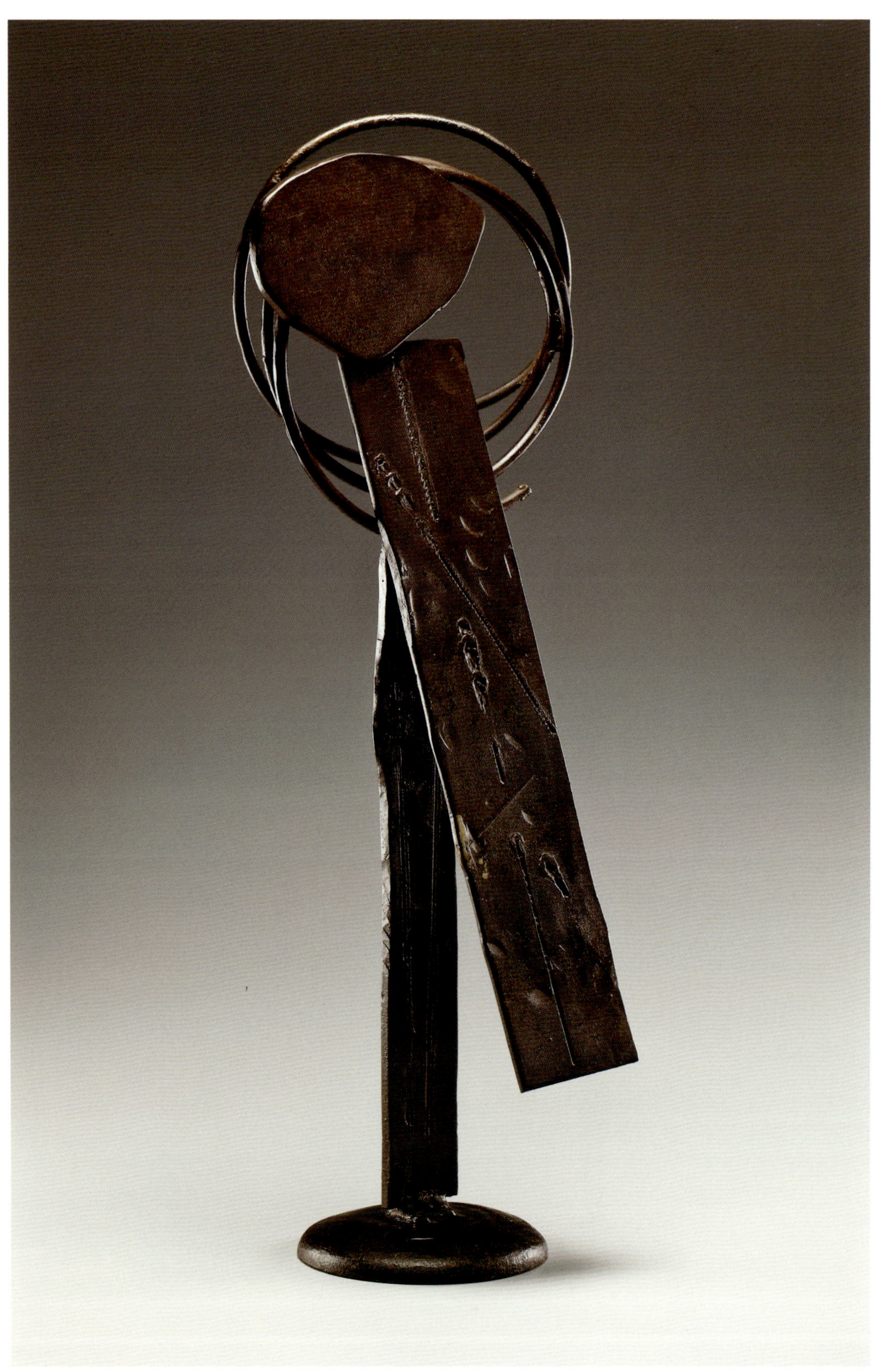

David Smith
American, 1906–1965

Welded metal sculpture, as opposed to cast bronze or carved stone sculpture, was an important new direction in American art after World War II. David Smith, influenced by the welded sculptures of Pablo Picasso and Julio González, was in the forefront of these developments. His life work—from the early welded pieces to the monumental late work in burnished stainless steel—marks him as one of the twentieth century's greatest American sculptors.

Born in Indiana and schooled in the Midwest, Smith moved to New York City in 1926 to pursue a career as a sculptor. During the 1930s, he created welded constructions using found objects, scrap material, and forged metal. At the end of the decade he began to focus on welded iron, a format that would define the majority of his sculpture during the 1940s. In this context of interests, he produced *Coil Spring* in 1953. Welding together separate pieces of iron, he fashioned the abstract semblance of a figure, spinning about its head a halo of iron wire—construed by the artist to resemble a coil spring. Patinated with a rich dark-brown finish, the sculpture has the mysterious quality of a totem, a primal symbol of a venerated guardian.   **RHA**

Charles Burchfield
American, 1893–1967

Song of the Bobolink is a large-scale painting that represents Charles Burchfield's later work of the 1950s and 1960s. The transcendental images of nature from this period are acknowledged as marking his most enduring achievements. Here he chooses a bobolink, a songbird found in open habitats and nesting only in meadows. The bird is depicted flying over an open field that seems to reverberate visually with the sound of the bird's call. The image is alive with undulating colors as the waving grasses merge with the waves of sound that fill the air.

Burchfield was born in Ashtabula Harbor, Ohio. He studied at the Cleveland School of Art (now Cleveland Institute of Art) and briefly at the National Academy of Design in New York. Burchfield is an American Regionalist and Modernist who created a completely orig-inal style imbued with mystery and lyricism. His chosen medium was watercolor and his contributions to it are equal to those of Winslow Homer. He stated: "An artist must paint not what he sees in nature, but what is there. To do so he must invent symbols, which, if properly used, make his work seem even more real than what is in front of him." **RHA**

Song of the Bobolink 1952–1959
Watercolor on paper
27½ × 40⁵⁄₁₆ inches
Gift of Mr. and Mrs. David Hunting
1962.1.3

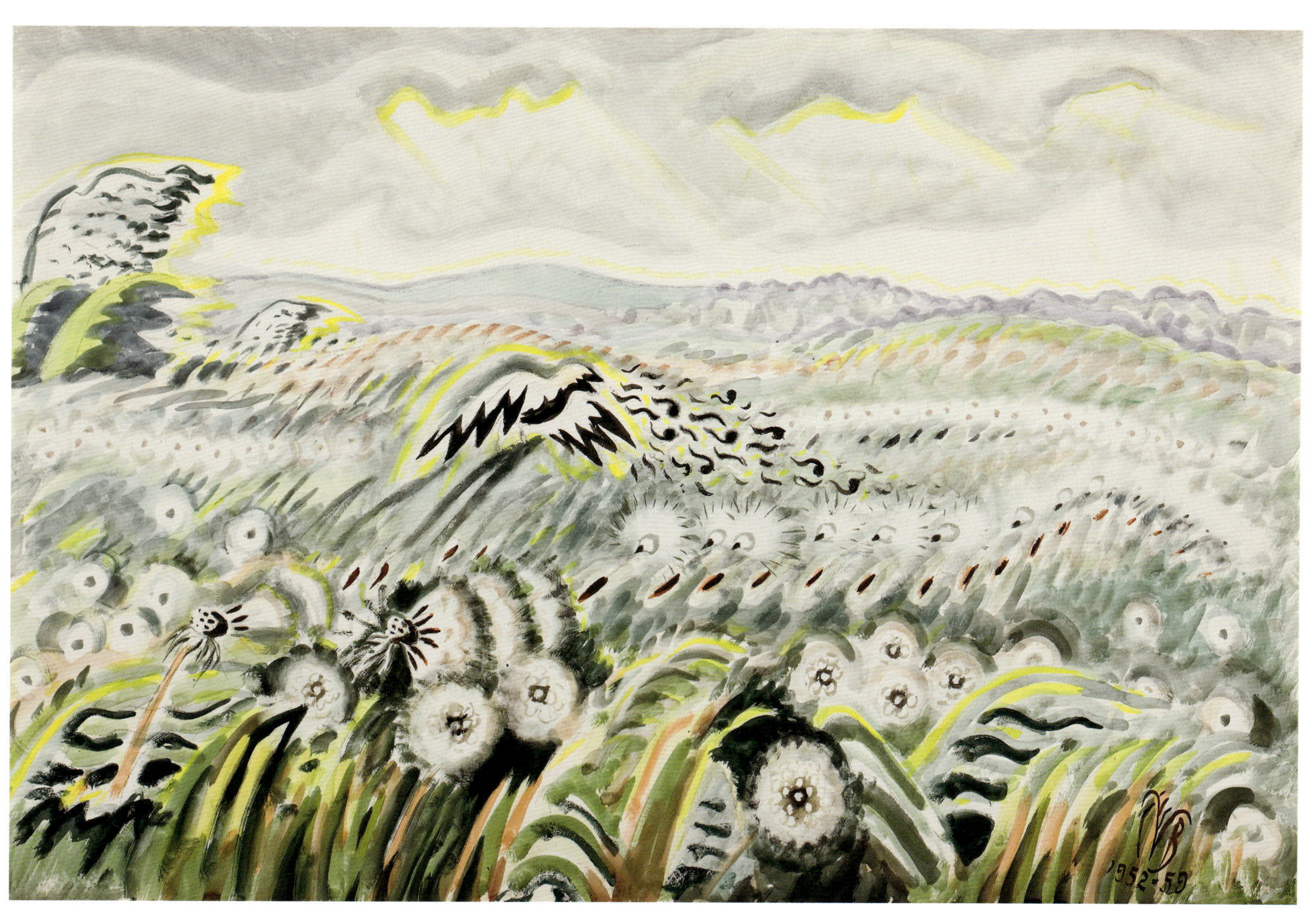

Tapio Wirkkala
Finnish, 1915–1985

Declared "The Most Beautiful Object of 1951," Tapio Wirkkala's laminated wood platter was designed to suggest the form of a leaf. It was chosen by *House Beautiful* magazine from all works exhibited by eleven countries at the 1951 International Exposition of Decorative and Industrial Art in Milan. Praised for its simplicity and organic form, it was described as a symphony of movement, effortlessly flowing and perfectly balanced. As pure in form as an abstract sculpture, Wirkkala's platter was also humble and utilitarian. It embodied the highest virtues of modern design. Regarding his core principle of design, elegantly applied to the *Leaf Platter*, Wirkkala wrote: "All materials have their own unwritten laws. You should never be violent with a material you are working on. The designer should aim at being in harmony with his material."

Inspiration from nature and truth to materials were primary characteristics of Finnish design, which had gained distinction by the 1940s through the work of Eliel Saarinen and Alvar Aalto. During the 1950s, Scandinavian design gained ascendancy in the United States through an exhibition conceived by Elizabeth Gordon, editor of *House Beautiful*, and organized by the American Federation of the Arts. Titled "Design in Scandinavia," the exhibition toured twenty-four museums in the United States and Canada from 1954 to 1957. Wirkkala designed the cover of the exhibition catalogue. The Museum of Modern Art was also a champion of Finnish design, featuring Wirkkala's work in both wood and glass in a series of exhibitions from 1950 to 1954 titled "Good Design," organized by Edgar Kaufmann, Jr., department store magnate and patron of Frank Lloyd Wright. **RHA**

Leaf Platter 1951

Laminated birch wood
¾ × 18¼ × 9½ inches
Produced by Marti Lindqvist, Helsinki
Museum Purchase, Frank and Ann Battistella Fund
2008.1

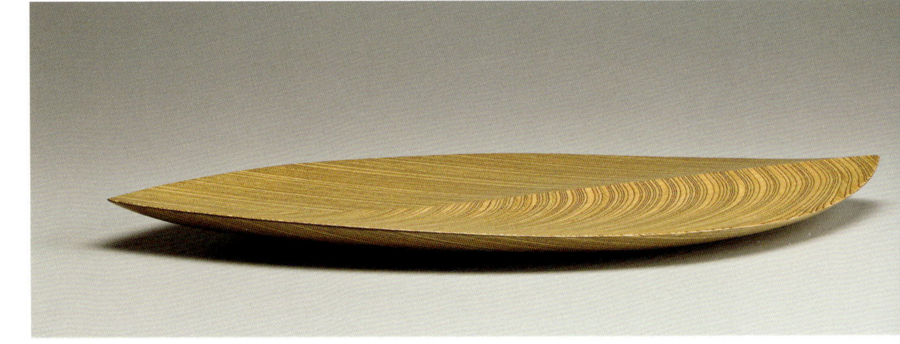

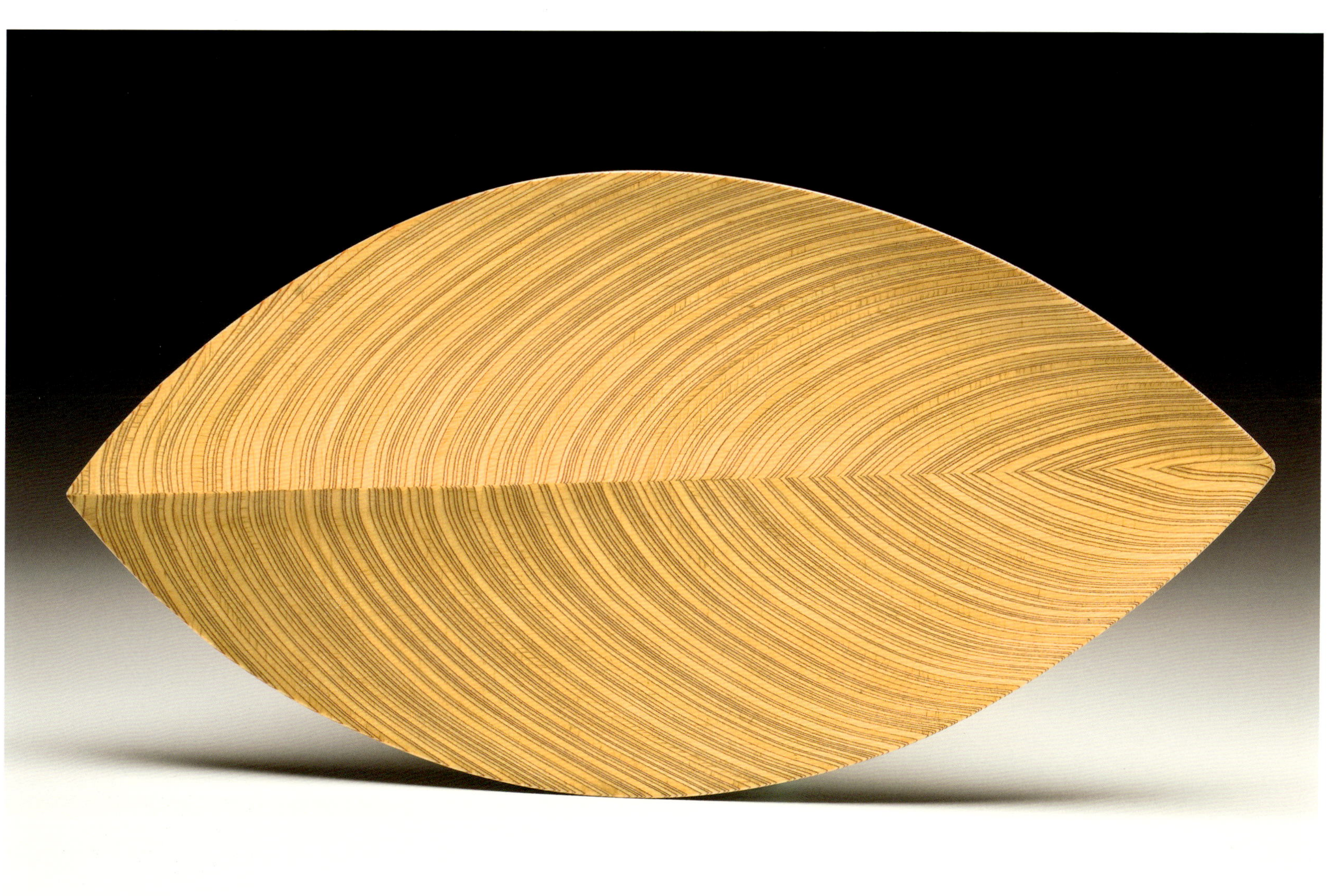

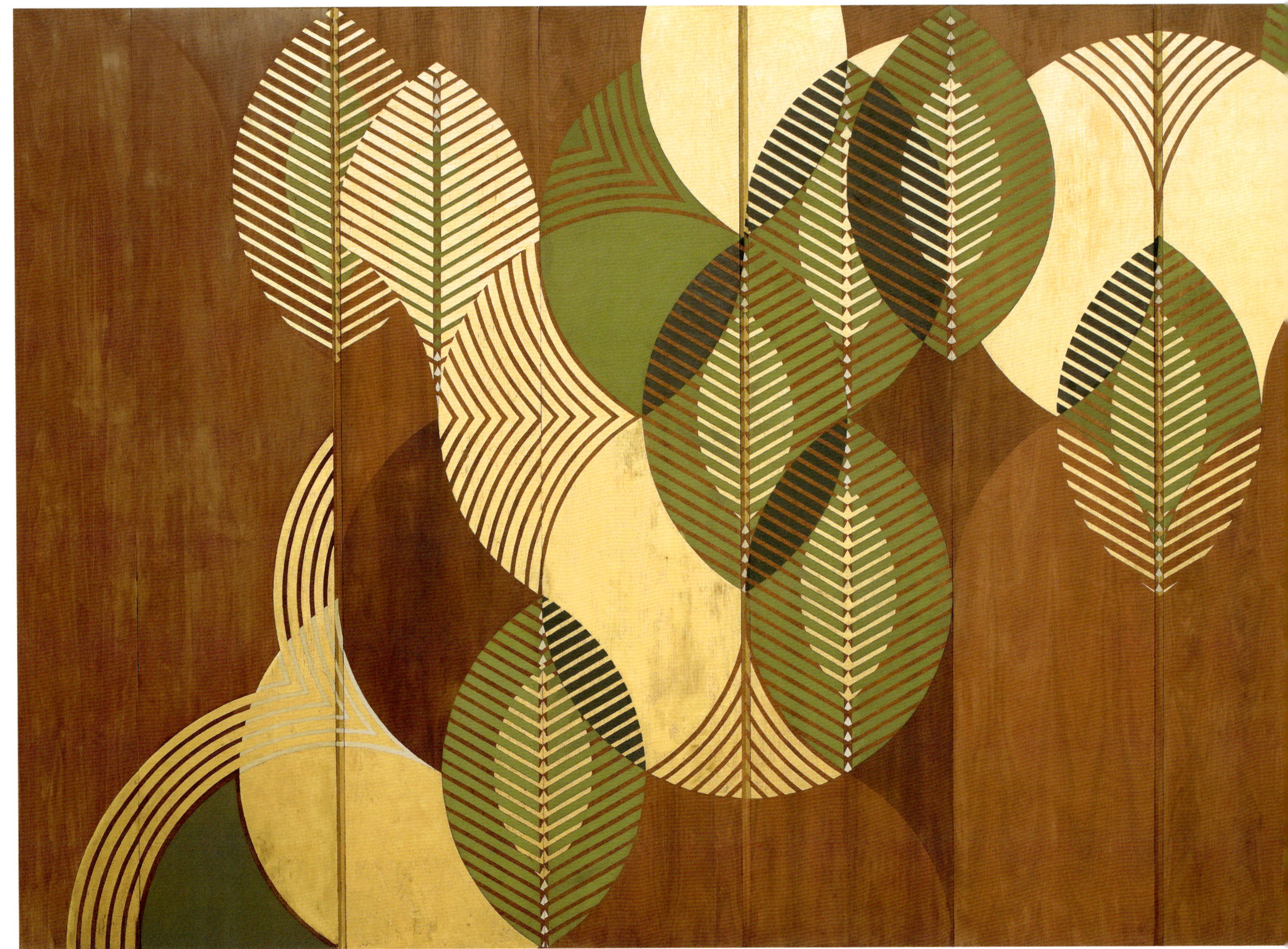

Eugene Masselink

American (b. South Africa), 1910–1962

Eight-fold Screen 1956

Stained walnut with paint and gilt
93 × 149 inches
Museum Purchase
2006.28

Born in Capetown, South Africa, Eugene Masselink moved with his family to Grand Rapids where he attended Central High School. In 1933, after receiving a degree in architecture from Ohio State University, Masselink was invited to join Frank Lloyd Wright's Taliesin Fellowship in Spring Green, Wisconsin. He served as Wright's personal assistant and became a highly respected graphic designer for the office, eventually working with Wright on decorative elements for the interiors of houses.

In 1956, Elizabeth Gordon, editor of *House Beautiful*, commissioned Frank Lloyd Wright to redesign portions of the interior of her home in Dobbs Ferry, New York. Masselink designed this screen for the master bedroom. Wright's passion for Japanese art, shared by Masselink, inspired the use of decorative screens and wall panels in many commissions. Masselink painted this screen by hand and utilized gold leaf to create a highly decorative and dynamically modern pattern of leaves and other organic forms that epitomizes mid-century American Modernist design. He created only about a dozen screens and often used Wright's floor plans for inspiration. At the time Masselink produced this screen, Wright was completing his design for the Solomon R. Guggenheim Museum in New York. The unique *Eight-fold Screen* is the centerpiece of the Museum's Gallery of Design and Modern Craft. **RHA**

Yousuf Karsh, of Armenian heritage, traveled to North America in 1924 and settled in Canada. He numbers among the most important portrait photographers of the twentieth century, notable for his portraits of celebrities, political figures, and artists.

In 1956, Karsh traveled to New Mexico to photograph the famous American painter Georgia O'Keeffe. He posed the artist in the entryway of her house in Abiquiu. She sits under an elk's skull hung on the wall behind her—a recurring motif in O'Keeffe's paintings and for Karsh's portrait of the sixty-nine-year-old artist a reminder of death's inevitability. Karsh was known as a master of lighting, particularly highlighting his sitters' hands. O'Keeffe sits in meditation with her eyes drawn to the doorway, yet the photographer embellished the play of light from it with additional lighting to emphasize not only the artist's hands, but also her face, the elk's magnificent rack of antlers, and the arranged still life objects.

Karsh's dedication to capturing the inner soul of his sitters is best characterized in the photographer's own words: "Within every man and woman a secret is hidden, and as a photographer it is my task to reveal it if I can. The revelation, if it comes at all, will come in a small fraction of a second with an unconscious gesture, a gleam of the eye, a brief lifting of the mask that all humans wear to conceal their innermost selves from the world. In that fleeting interval of opportunity the photographer must act or lose his prize." **RHA**

Georgia O'Keeffe 1956
Signed gelatin silver print (printed later)
12⁷⁄₁₆ × 10 inches
Gift of the Artist
1972.14.3

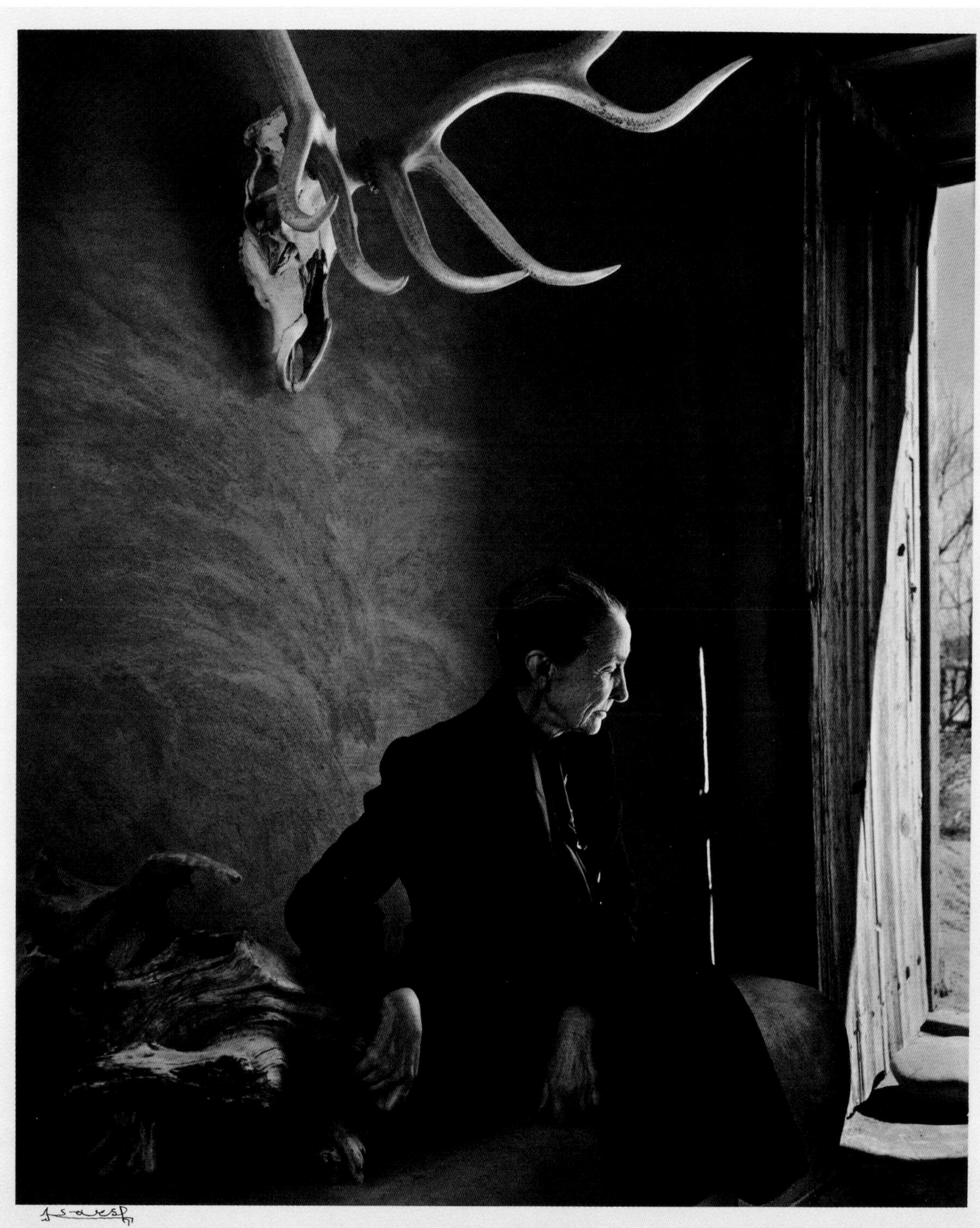

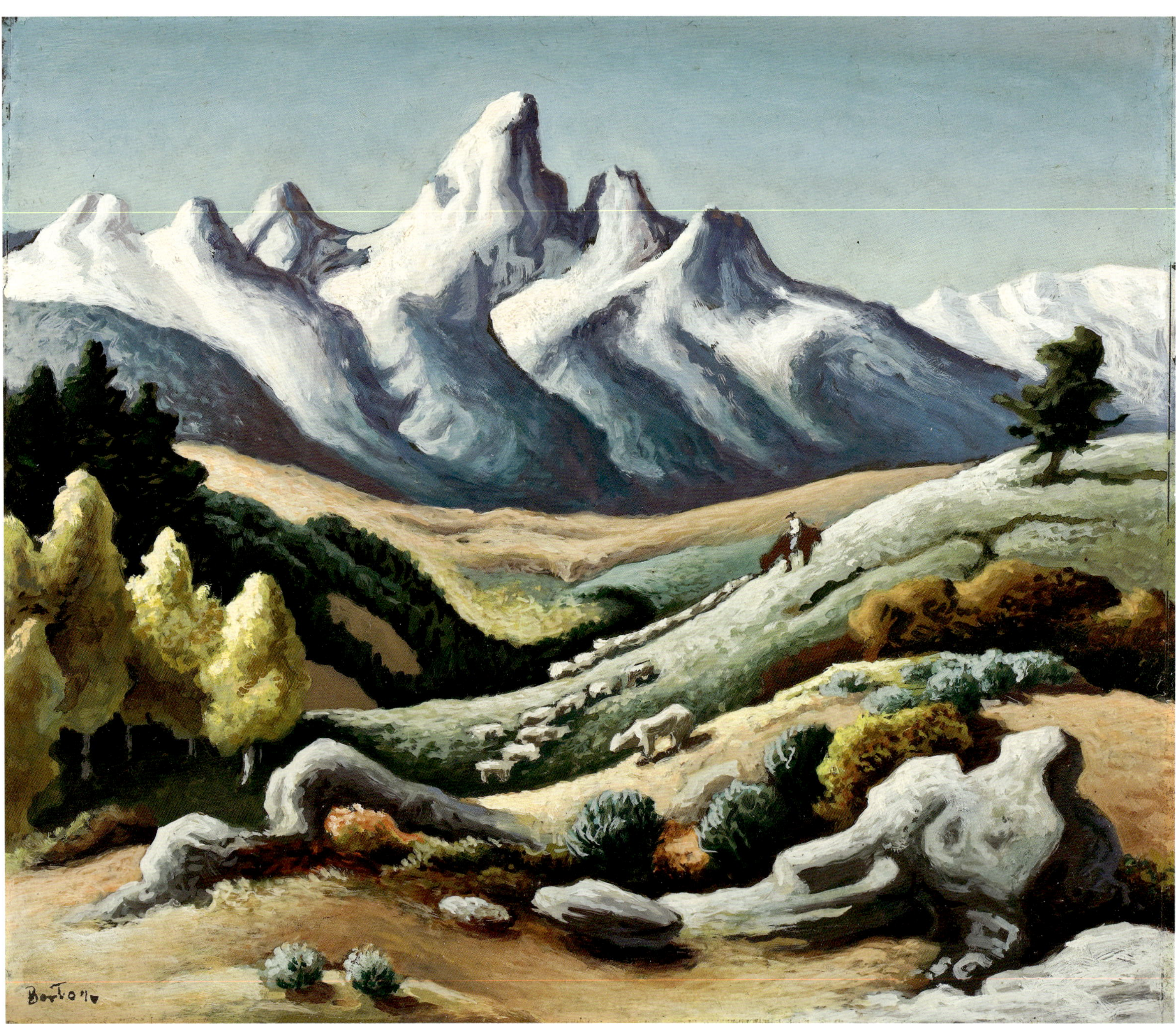
Benton

Thomas Hart Benton

American, 1889–1975

The Grand Tetons 1955–1960

Oil on tin
10 × 11¾ inches
Gift of Peter M. Wege
2007.3

As one of the American Scene painters emerging for recognition during the later 1920s and 1930s, Thomas Hart Benton, along with John Steuart Curry and Grant Wood, sought to capture the many aspects of national identity as reflected in diverse locales. These three artists, numbering among an important group of American Regionalists, were drawn to nostalgic and heroic depictions of everyday life in small towns and open landscapes both agricultural and natural.

Although turning his artist's eye to the Eastern seaboard from New York to Martha's Vineyard and to the South, Benton is best known for his paintings and prints of the Midwest and western portions of the United States. In *The Grand Tetons*, an oil study for a larger oil painting, *The Sheepherder* (1956), Benton presents a mounted herder shepherding his flock of sheep against a majestic mountain range dominated by Grand Teton, its tallest peak at 13,000 feet above sea level. Located in Wyoming, south of Yellowstone National Park, the Teton Range is part of the Rocky Mountains. Famous for their dramatic elevations, the Tetons lack foothills that might obscure their view and rise sharply from 5,000 to 7,000 feet above the Jackson Hole valley floor.   **RHA**

Pablo Picasso
Spanish, 1881–1973

During the late 1950s and early 1960s, Pablo Picasso reinvented the linoleum cut, which had been a commercial and craft medium. One of the one hundred linoleum cuts the artist created is the magical *Nature morte à la pastèque*. Animated slices of watermelon and a bunch of cherries dance with each other under the sway of a hanging fixture, whose sun-like bulb charges the scene with yellow zigzags of light. Even the frame that Picasso wittily includes in the composition is energized, electrified it seems by the overhead lamp.

The color brilliance of *Nature morte à la pastèque* results from Picasso's color choices and the thickness of inks characteristic of linoleum-cut printing. Rather than using different blocks for each color, which is common practice in color printing, Picasso devised an inventive process of cutting one or two blocks for a print of multiple colors. His innovative "reductive method" consisted of cutting away additional portions of a single block for each new color, avoiding the problem of over-registration that weakens color.

The eight stages or "states" reveal Picasso's development of the print from initial idea to its final resolution. Each state discloses the gradual reduction of the original blocks of linoleum for new colors and shapes. These states are not simply the progressive stages of the print, revealing the cumulative additions of colors and shapes, but eight independent images, each with its own aesthetic integrity. This unique set of eight is the only complete set of this work in the world.   RHA

Nature morte à la pastèque (Still Life with Cherries and Watermelon), States I–VIII 1962
Series of eight linoleum cuts on Arches wove paper
23½ × 16¾ inches
Gift of Miner S. and Mary Ann Keeler
2002.7–14

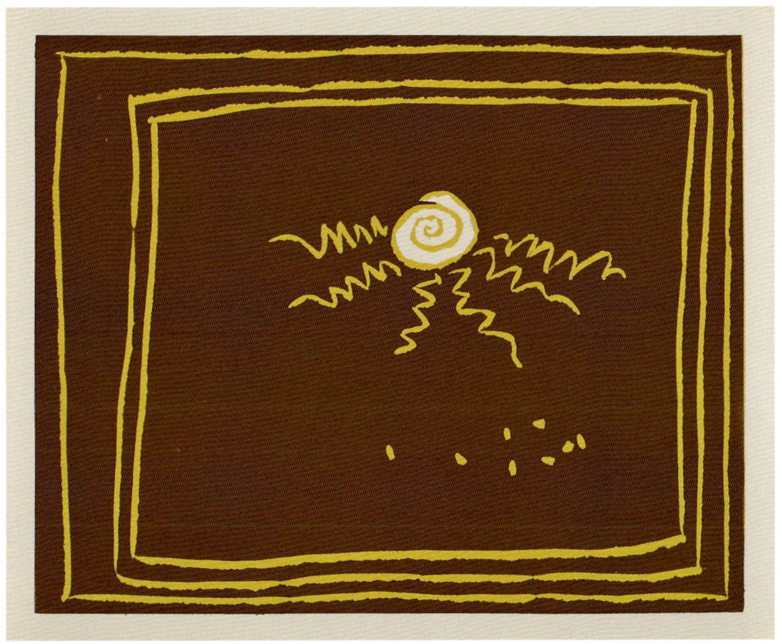
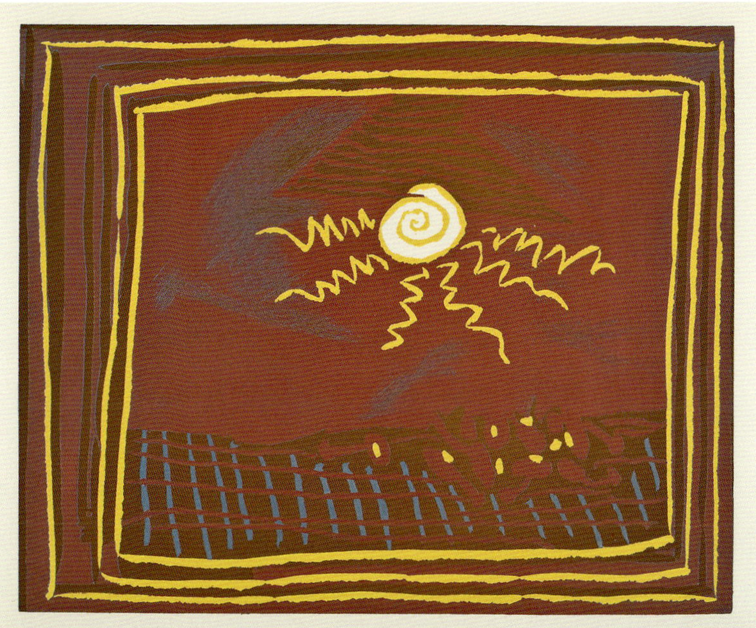
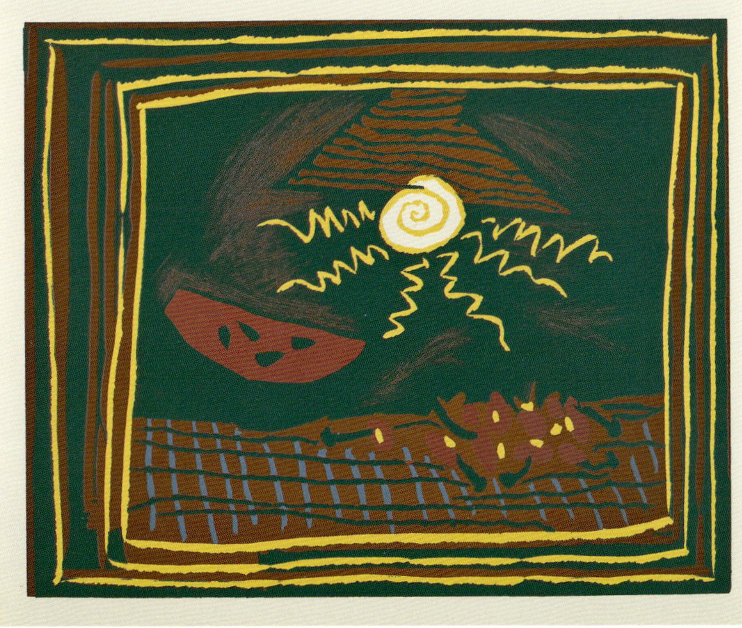
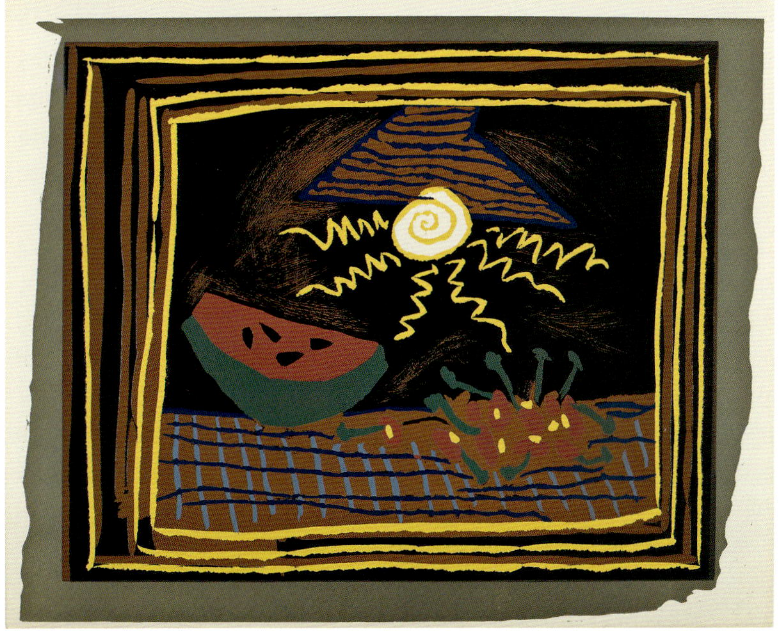

Recognized as one of America's preeminent artists of the twentieth century, Richard Diebenkorn was so closely associated with
California—the Bay area in his youth and later, Los Angeles—that
he was at times considered as only a West Coast regional painter.
His stature as a great master of American painting, however, was
established in a major retrospective *The Art of Richard Diebenkorn,*
organized by the Whitney Museum of American Art, New York, and
touring to leading museums in the United States during 1998–99.

Ingleside is the most important monumental landscape painting of Diebenkorn's early years. This landscape, or more precisely,
cityscape of suburban San Francisco, is an expression of the artist's figurative style, before he turned to pure abstraction. Strongly
influenced in those years by Paul Cézanne, Henri Matisse, and Piet
Mondrian, Diebenkorn organized the undulating planes of green
lawns, gray asphalt streets, and white stucco houses into a structured geometry of colored forms. So solid is the pictorial design
of this painting that the artist's confident progression into pure
abstraction in the *Ocean Park* series is inevitable. One critic wrote
of *Ingleside*: "Never did he {Diebenkorn} achieve a more dramatic
tour de force of light and color, especially in the use of white, than
in this eternally fresh painting."   RHA

Ingleside 1963
Oil on canvas
81¹³⁄₁₆ × 69½ inches
Museum Purchase
1967.1.1

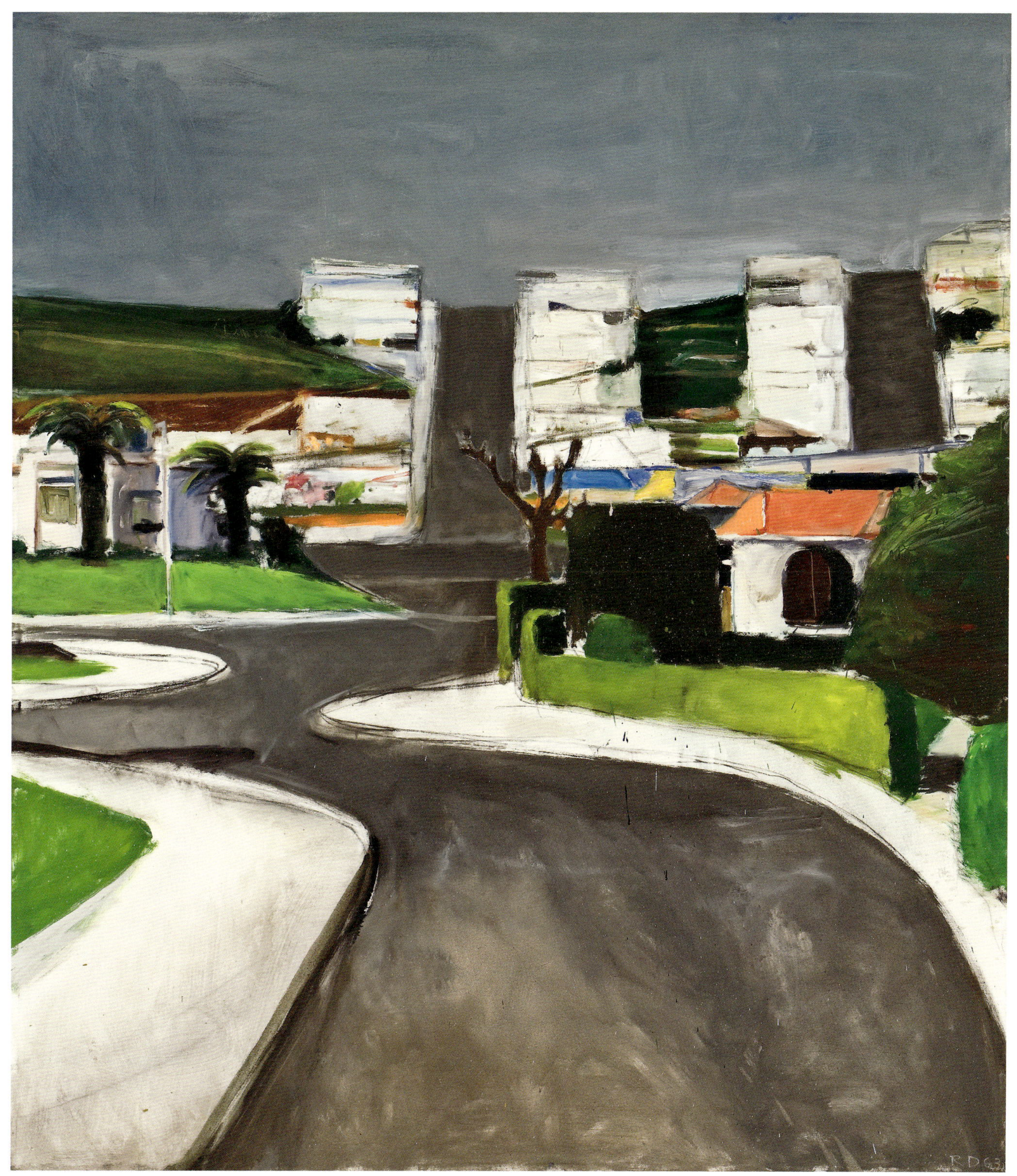

Andy Warhol
American, 1928–1987

Suicide is one of the most important images in Warhol's *Death and Disaster* series of silkscreened paintings and prints executed between 1962 and 1964. In these works, the artist focuses on the wrenching disconnect between the actual horrors of death and its dispassionate coverage by the cool eye of the media.

A reporter's photograph that Warhol retrieved from city files of a man leaping to his death was the basis for a small number of uneditioned silkscreen prints. Each one is unique, a function of varying the angle of the silkscreen over the paper, the strength of inks, and the cropping of the photographic image. Signed and dated, they are exceedingly rare; only five or six are believed to exist. The initial impression from 1962 is in the Menil Collection in Houston, Texas. The remaining prints were produced in 1964 and, with the exception of the promised gift to the Grand Rapids Art Museum, are thought to reside in private collections.   RHA

Suicide 1964
Screenprint on paper
40 × 30 inches
Promised Gift of
Miner S. and Mary Ann Keeler

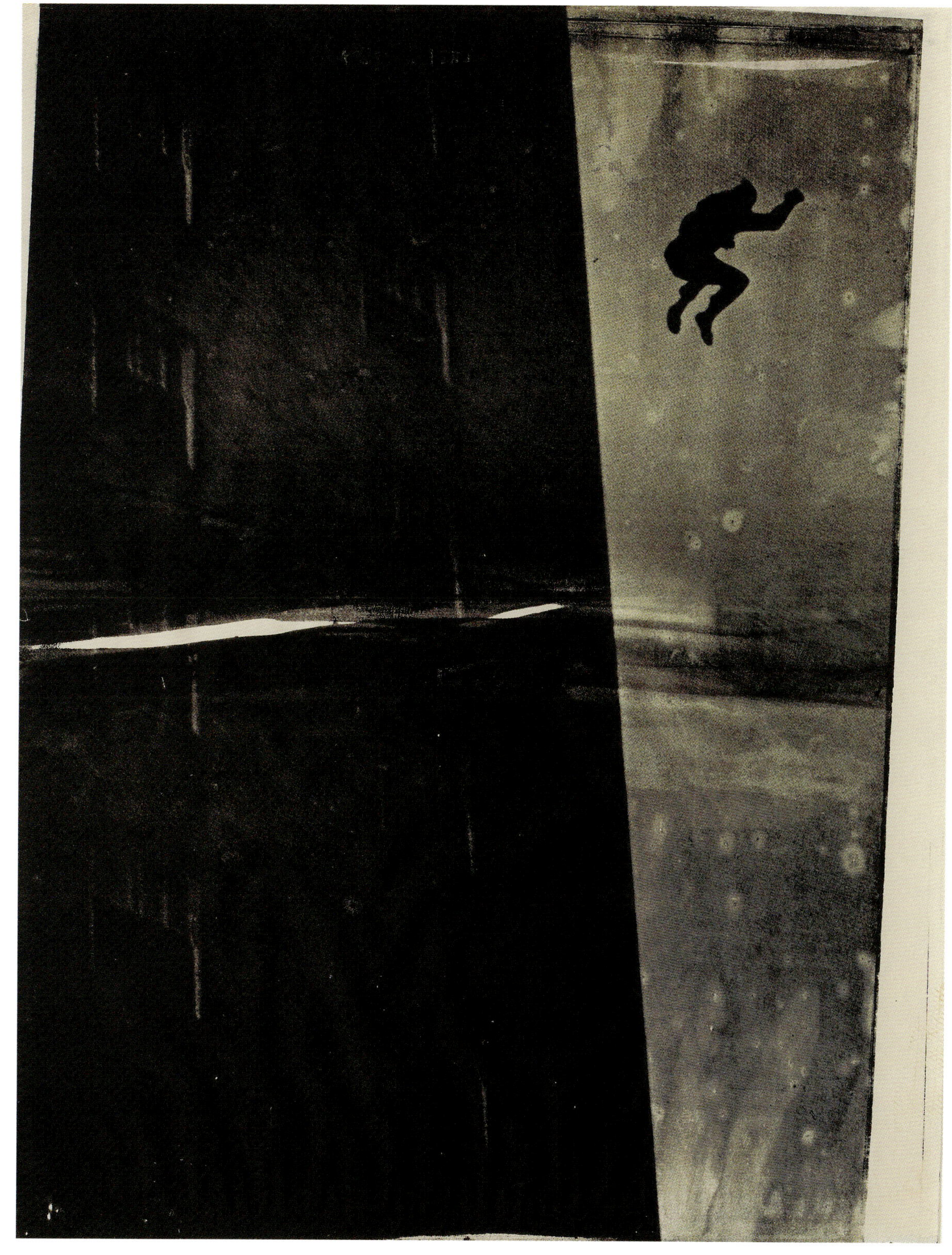

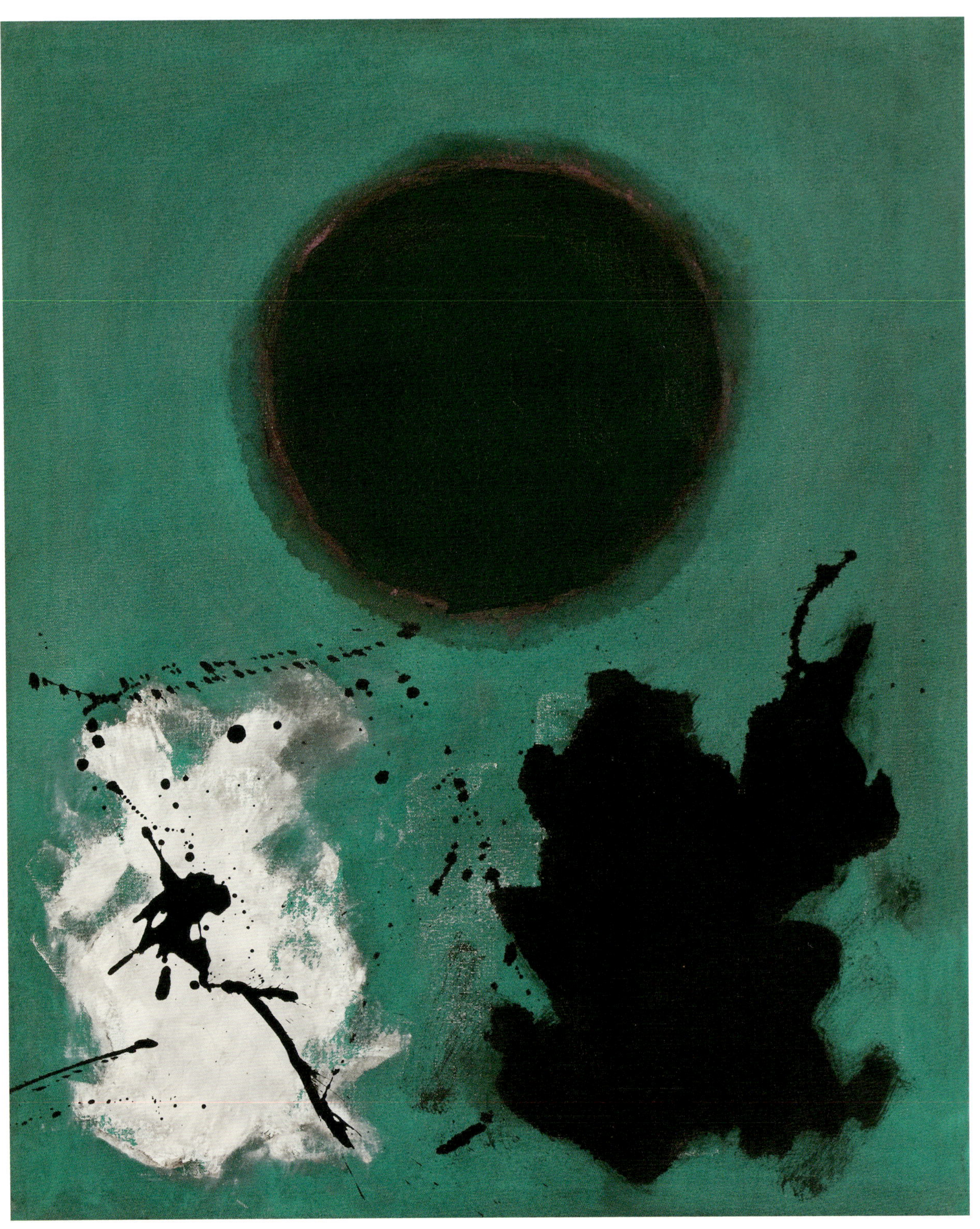

Adolph Gottlieb

American, 1903–1974

Oriental 1965

Oil on canvas
30 × 24 inches
Promised Gift,
Miner S. and Mary Ann Keeler

Adolph Gottlieb was among the important Abstract Expressionists, whose works dominated postwar American art in the later 1940s and 1950s. Centered in New York City, this original American movement held abstraction, spontaneous gesture, and the personal expression of universal ideas as the highest aims of art.

Gottlieb's *Oriental* is from the Burst series that the artist initiated in 1957 and which became his hallmark during the 1960s. In this series, he played variations upon two basic shapes: the disk or sun-like orb and an assertive cluster of freely brushed marks. Always in contrast, they can be read as multiple dualisms of competing forces—new star/dying star, warming/cooling, explosion/implosion. Gottlieb wished to give image to archetypal symbols that expressed fundamental, even mythic forces that could bring the viewer into contact with a greater scheme of things.

In *Oriental*, Gottlieb placed a centered orb over two agitated clusters—one black, the other white. The calligraphic gestures that form them call to mind the spontaneous marks of East Asian script. In the contrast of black and white, their dualism evokes the yin-yang principle of ancient Chinese philosophy, often visualized as a circle divided into black and white halves by an S-shaped line. Yin and yang is a universal concept that sees opposite forces in nature—life/death, male/female, day/night—as complementary and held in balance to express aspects of a single reality.   RHA

. Richard Pousette-Dart
American, 1916–1992

During the later 1930s and 1940s, Richard Pousette-Dart found inspiration for his painting in African, Oceanic, and Native American art, focusing on the latter as a source of archetypal symbols and pictographs. Along with other modern artists, such as Marsden Hartley, Barnett Newman, and Jackson Pollock, he believed that Native American art would be an important source in the definition of an independent and nationalist American art movement. These concerns were a contributing force in the creation of the Abstract Expressionist movement in New York, of which Pousette-Dart was a founding member.

By the later 1960s, Pousette-Dart came into his own as a mature painter of great distinction. The earlier structured compositions of symbols gave way to works like *Transcendent Presence*.

Centered circles of undefined boundaries emerge from a complex field of small color dots. These star-like bursts of radiant color, inspired by the pointillist patterning of the French Neo-Impressionists, transfix the eye. Pousette-Dart's interest in the reconciling and unifying of world philosophies led to paintings such as *Transcendent Presence*, which express the artist's belief in the power of abstract painting to evoke the spirituality of nature. **RHA**

Transcendent Presence 1966–1967
Oil on canvas
61 × 61 inches
Gift of the Estate of Helen Keeler Burke
2005.2

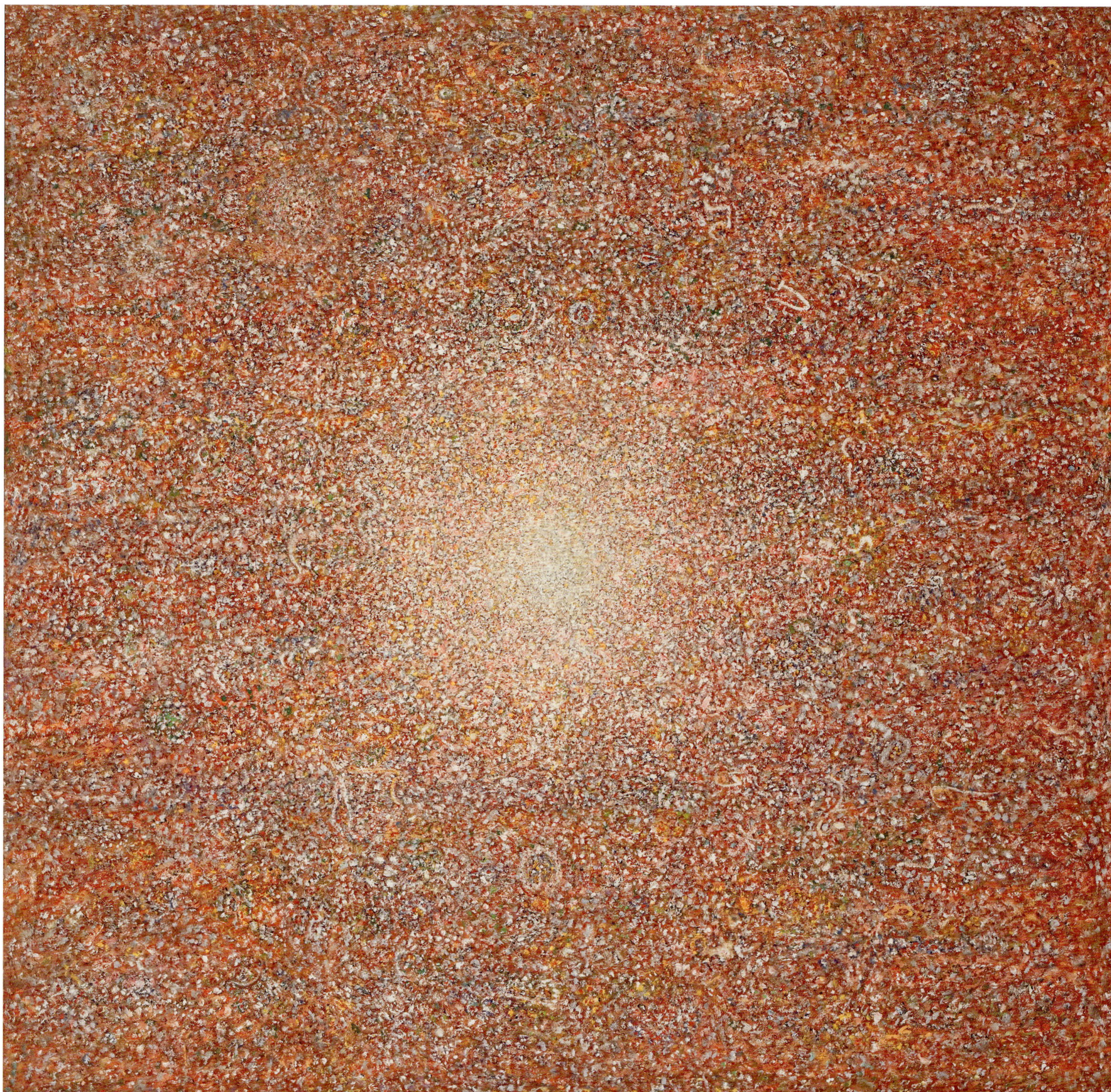

Alexander Calder
American, 1898–1976

White Spearhead is the type of sculpture for which Alexander Calder is best known: the "mobile" or moving suspended sculpture that he invented in the early 1930s and which was named by Marcel Duchamp. In his mobiles, Calder pioneered the introduction of motion into metal sculpture. He was so taken with this form of sculpture that he continued to make mobiles for the remainder of his life. Reflecting on the energy of mobiles, he stated: "A mobile is a feisty thing, and seldom stays tranquilly in one place to be measured. A mobile in motion leaves an invisible wake behind it, or rather, each element leaves an individual wake behind its individual self."

White Spearhead takes its name from the painted white arrowhead shape at the tip end of the mobile. All other shapes are less specifically arrow-shaped and carry associations with the colorful feathers at the back of an arrow's shaft—the fletchers designed to keep the arrow pointed in the right direction. The whimsy of the piece lies, however, in a spear or arrowhead that is forever shifting its aim. **RHA**

White Spearhead 1963
Painted sheet metal and steel wire
38 × 64 inches
Promised Gift of Miner S. and Mary Ann Keeler

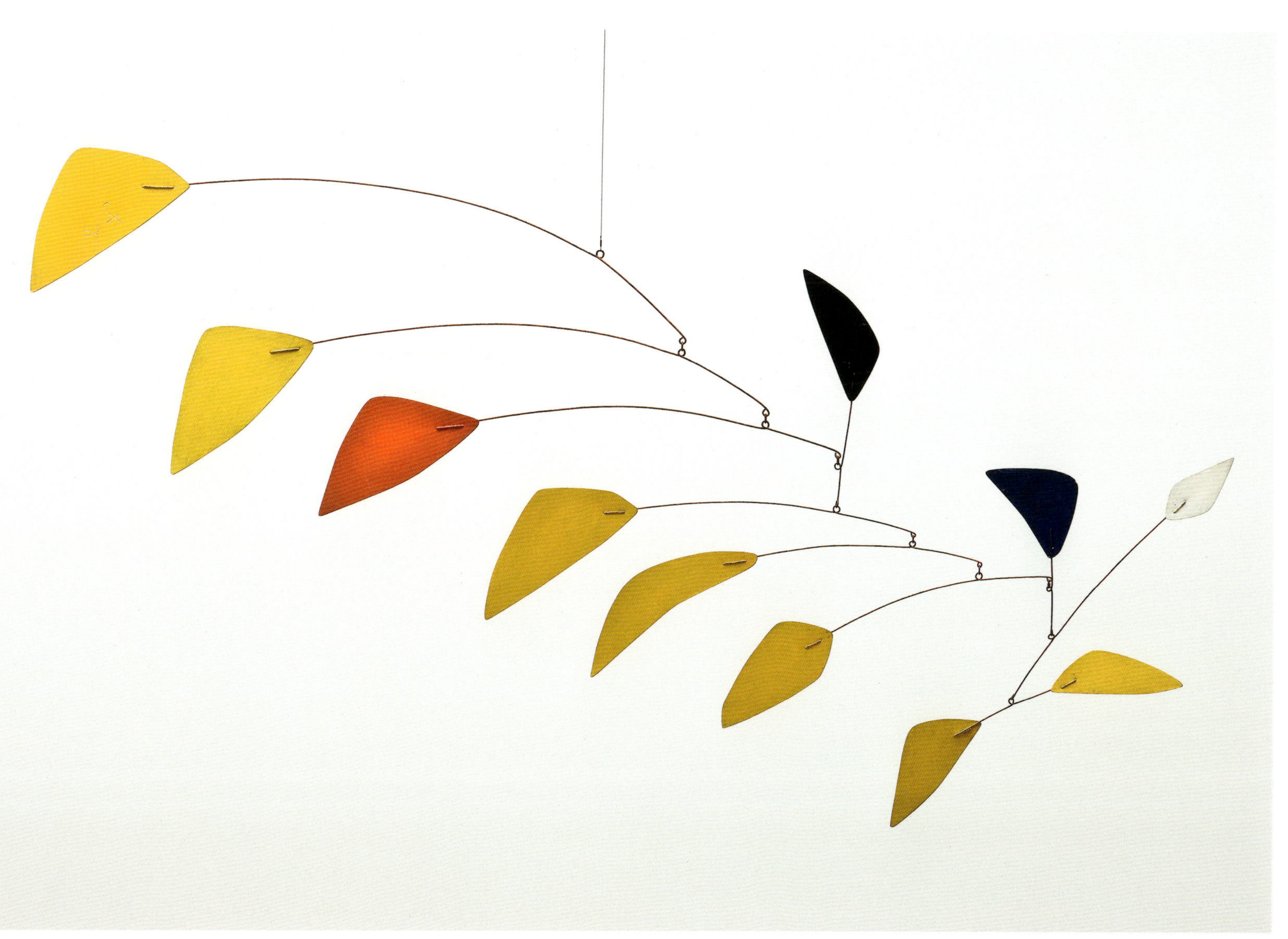

Alexander Calder
American, 1898–1976

Alexander Calder was partial to animal sculpture all his life, at an early age sketching animals he saw at the circus and zoo. Working while an art student in 1925 for the *National Police Gazette* in New York, he made drawings of the Ringling Bros. and Barnum & Bailey Circus. The next year, he began work on his famous *Cirque Calder*, a portable, miniature circus of animals and entertainers made of wire and found objects. In the late 1960s, he returned to animals as subject, creating a new type of sculpture his wife, Louise, named animobile—a blend of the French word *animaux* (animals) and mobile, Calder's earlier format of suspended, kinetic sculptures fashioned of painted metal and wire.

The Blunt-Tailed Dog consists of an unmoving red body, with its "blunt tail," upon which rests a "mobile" of shifting parts that wittily suggest eyes, ears, tongue, and head. Calder's dog is sweet, funny, and endearing—even irreverent in its eccentric shapes.   **RHA**

The Blunt-Tailed Dog 1970
Painted sheet metal and steel wire
33½ × 22 × 36 inches
Promised Gift of Miner S. and Mary Ann Keeler

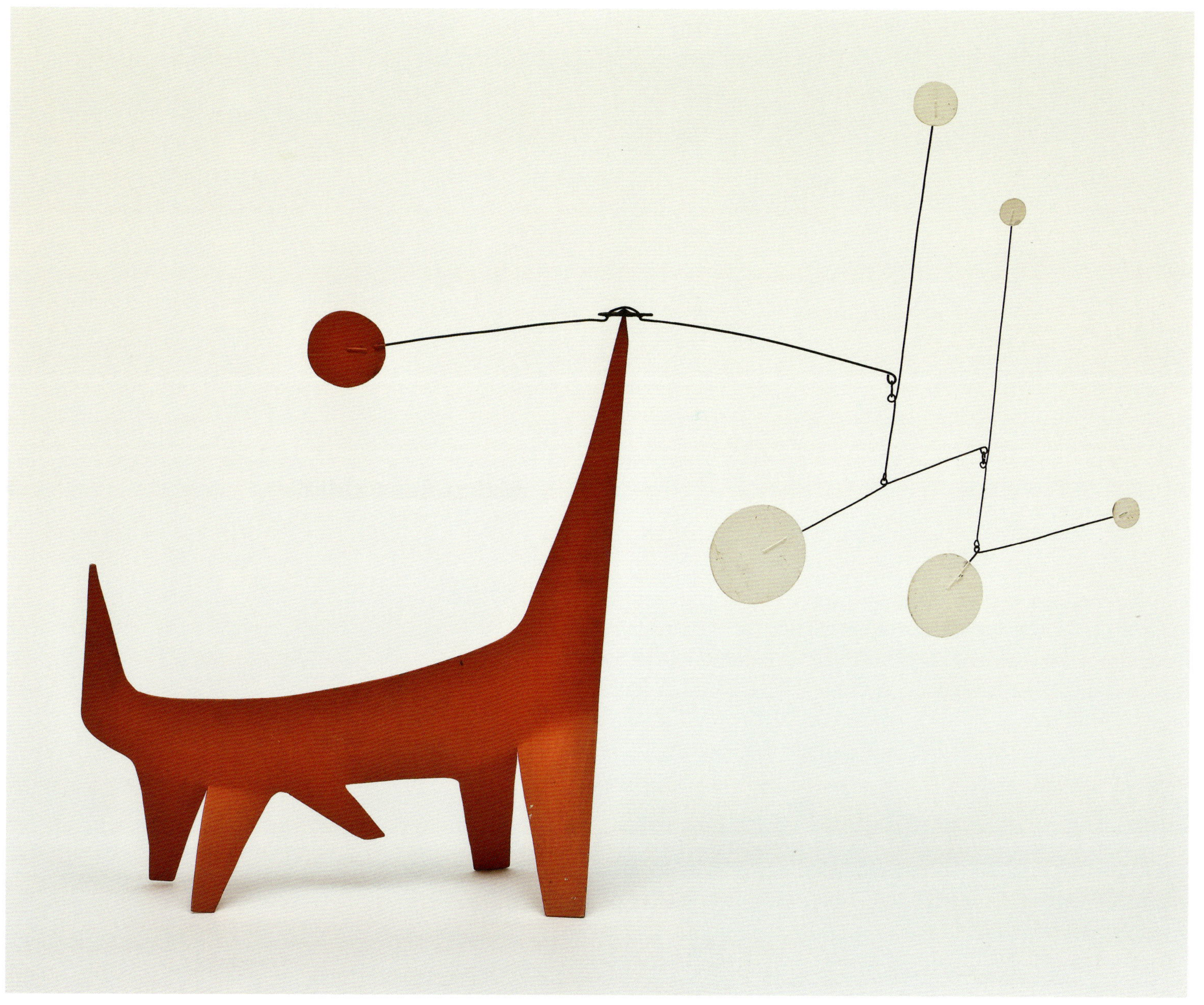

Alexander Calder, one of the great masters of modern sculpture, created *La Grande Vitesse* for Grand Rapids in 1969. Installed in Calder Plaza, the giant red sculpture became in time the city's proud logo. It is prized for being the artist's greatest "stabile," or standing abstract sculpture.

Red: Rudder in the Air is one of Calder's last mobiles. Its sheet metal shapes are painted, like *La Grand Vitesse*, in a shade of red that Calder always favored. They are delicately balanced so that with the slightest current of air they revolve and create different configurations in space. Calder was fascinated by flight. The abstract shapes of his mobiles often allude to forms in nature affected by wind: leaves, trees, and birds in flight. These forms are poetically suggested in *Red: Rudder in the Air*—as well as a rudder, a device used to steer and steady planes through air currents.   **RHA**

Red: Rudder in the Air 1975
Painted sheet metal and steel wire
31 × 68 inches
Gift of Mrs. Isaac S. Keeler and
Miner S. and Mary Ann Keeler
1976.4.1

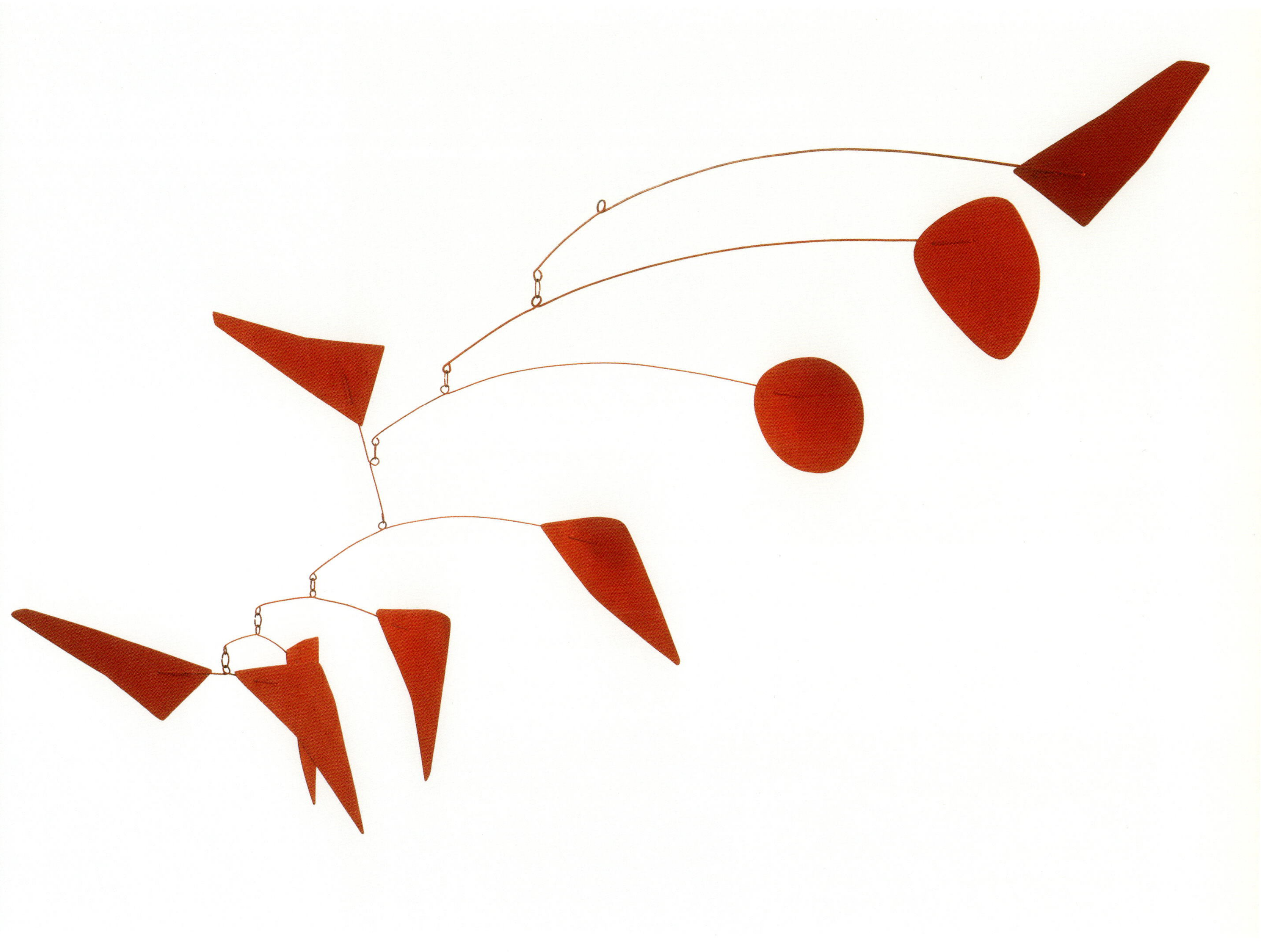

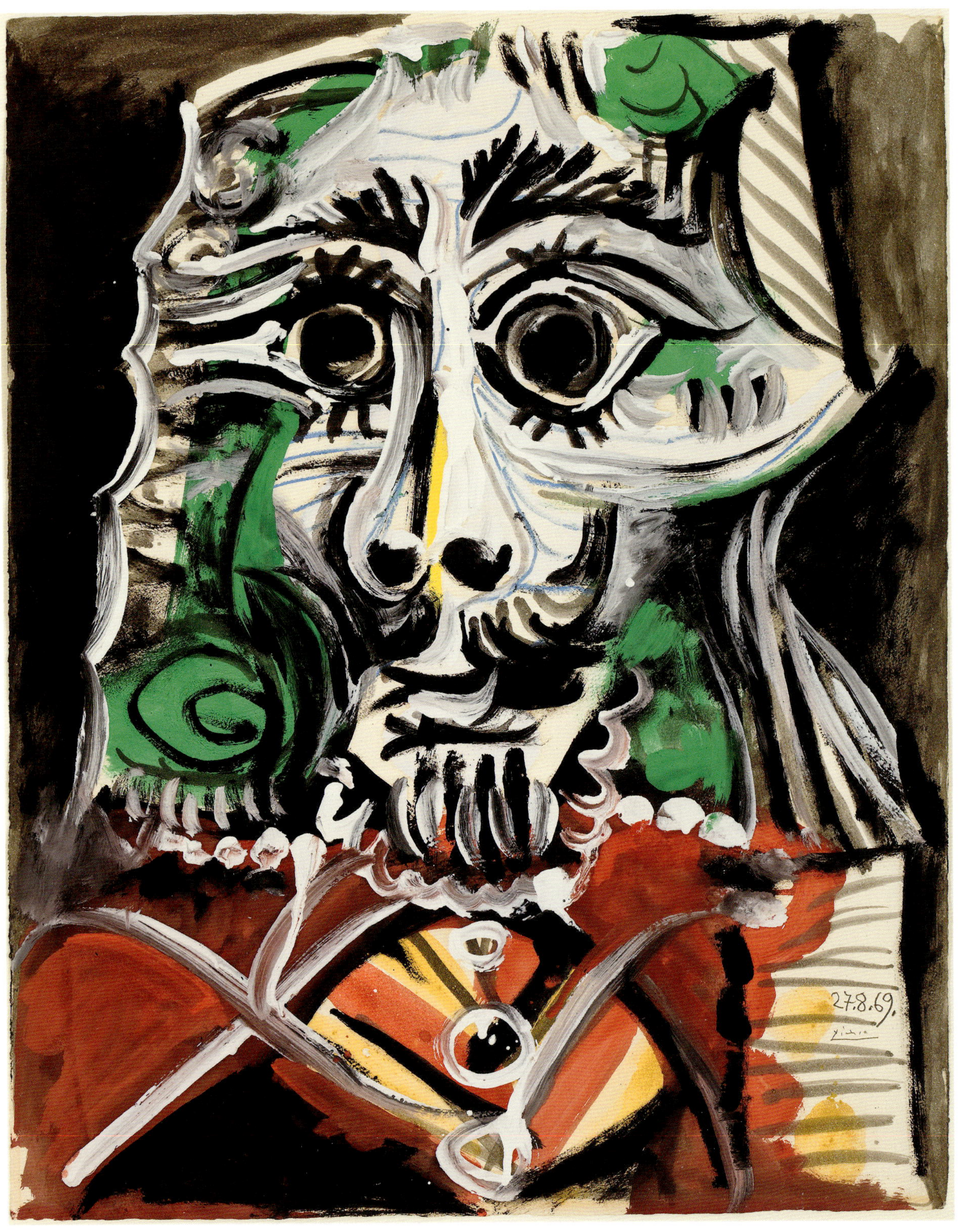
27.8.69.

 Pablo Picasso
Spanish, 1881–1973

Tête d'Homme (Head of
a Man) 1969
Oil, watercolor, and pastel on paper
25¾ × 20 inches
Promised Gift of Miner S. and
Mary Ann Keeler

After Pablo Picasso reread Alexandre Dumas' *The Three Musketeers* in 1966, he introduced a new character to his art—the French musketeer, or armed infantryman who served at the King's pleasure. This seventeenth-century cavalier of the sword, coming from the lower nobility, was known for his can-do spirit, boisterous behavior, and romantic exploits with the ladies. During the later 1960s, the musketeer became Picasso's primary and final alter-ego—preceeded by over fifty years of celebrated stand-ins for the artist, including the Harlequin, the monkey, the Minotaur, and classical sculptor.

In 1966, Picasso began picturing the musketeer in notebook sketches. Later that year, he committed his subject to drawing and then to large ink wash bust-portraits that he followed by renderings of his subject in oil paint in early 1967. A series of heads was next, culminating in full-length seated portraits. Picasso continued to treat his theme over the next several years, including the creation of two major series of etchings from 1968 and 1970–71 in which the musketeer plays a prominent role. He also created a series of mixed-media works on paper similar to *Tête d'Homme*. The musketeer drawings, paintings, and prints were the last major series of variations on a theme that Picasso undertook in his late period.

In this mixed-media drawing, the musketeer's face dominates, with his characteristic long curls of hair, Van Dyke beard, and brocaded jacket. His large, deep-set eyes—wide open and dark as coals—unmistakably identify the figure as the older, vulnerable Picasso in self-portrait.   **RHA**

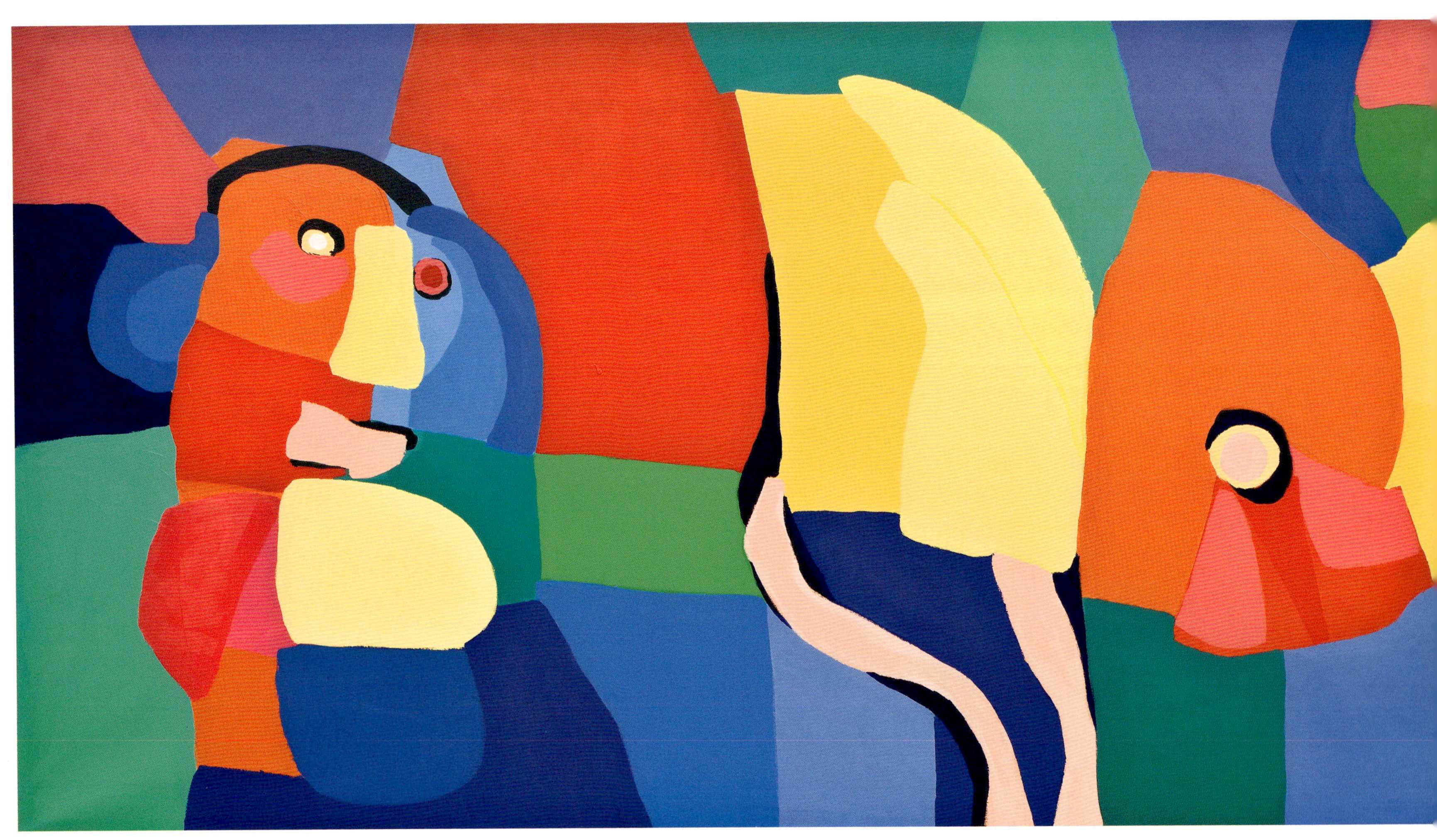

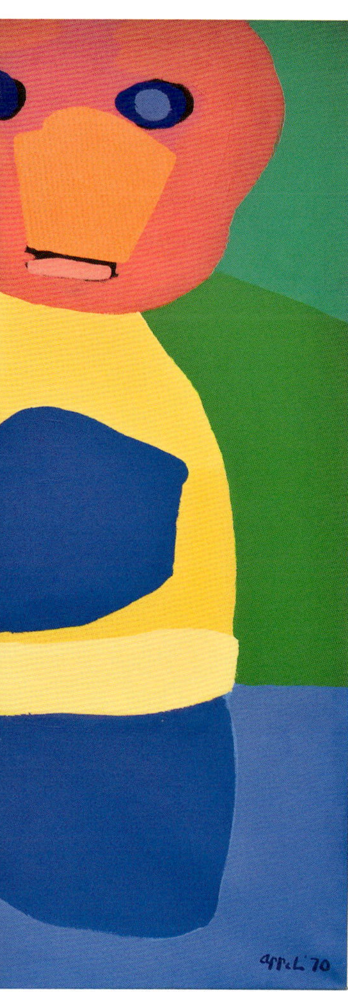

Untitled 1970

Oil on canvas
78 × 174 inches
Gift of La Salle Bank ABN AMRO
2004.1.4

Karel Appel

Dutch, 1921–2006

Karel Appel is considered one of the major Dutch artists of the twentieth century. He is recognized as a leading figure in the postwar European Modernist movement CoBrA, an international group named for the three cities from which the artists originated—Copenhagen, Brussels, and Amsterdam.

Active from 1948 to 1951, CoBrA was dedicated to the free expression of artistic ideas and rejected traditional approaches to art. Affirming the animating power of color, CoBrA artists studied and referenced the art of children and the folklore of developing cultures, which they felt were more directly in touch with essential truths, unaffected by dominant culture and its social restrictions. In 1948, Appel declared, "A painting is no longer a construction of colors and lines, but an animal, a night, a scream, a human being, or all of them at once."

In 1957, Appel established a studio in New York. The large-scale *Untitled*, a classic example of Appel's expressive style, was executed in the artist's mature years while dividing his time between New York and Florence. Vivid areas of red, blue, yellow, and green fill a panoramic canvas in irregular abstract shapes that suggest submerged faces and human or animal forms that playfully interact. **RHA**

. Jan Dibbets
Dutch, b. 1941

Jan Dibbets is a Dutch artist and photographer associated with Post-Minimalist and Conceptual Art. The portfolio *Ten Cupolas* consists of upward views into the ceilings of domed structures, both religious and secular, dating from the first to the twentieth centuries. Each cupola allows natural light into interior spaces. The dome, with roots in the ancient Near East, symbolizes the heavens above, the cosmos in its entirety.

Dibbets has pursued an analytic scrutiny of nature that reflects a Dutch tradition of scientific inquiry dating to the 1600s. Although cupolas and windows are architectural elements, Dibbets explores these forms as refractors of light. Light itself was the subject of the great discoveries made in optics by Dutch scientists during the Renaissance that resulted in Europe's finest telescopes and microscopes. The impact on art is seen in the special use of light in Dutch painting of the period. Dibbets claims an affinity with the seventeenth-century painter Pieter Jansz. Saenredam, whose austere church interiors are filled with a radiant light that illuminates open architectural spaces and design.   RHA

Ten Cupolas 1999

Amsterdam, Round Lutheran Church, 1984
Dublin, Four Courts, 1983
Cortona, Madonna del Calcinaio, 1988
Barcelona, El Born, 1989
New York, Guggenheim, 1986
Oudenbosch, St. Jan, 1996
Montepulciano, San Biagio, 1987
Roma, Pantheon, 1988
Paris, Observatoire, 1995
Barcelona, Palacio Güell, 1989

Portfolio of ten inkjet prints taken from dye-coupler prints
23⅝ × 23⅝ inches
Museum Purchase, Fred and Lena Meijer
2004.54a–j

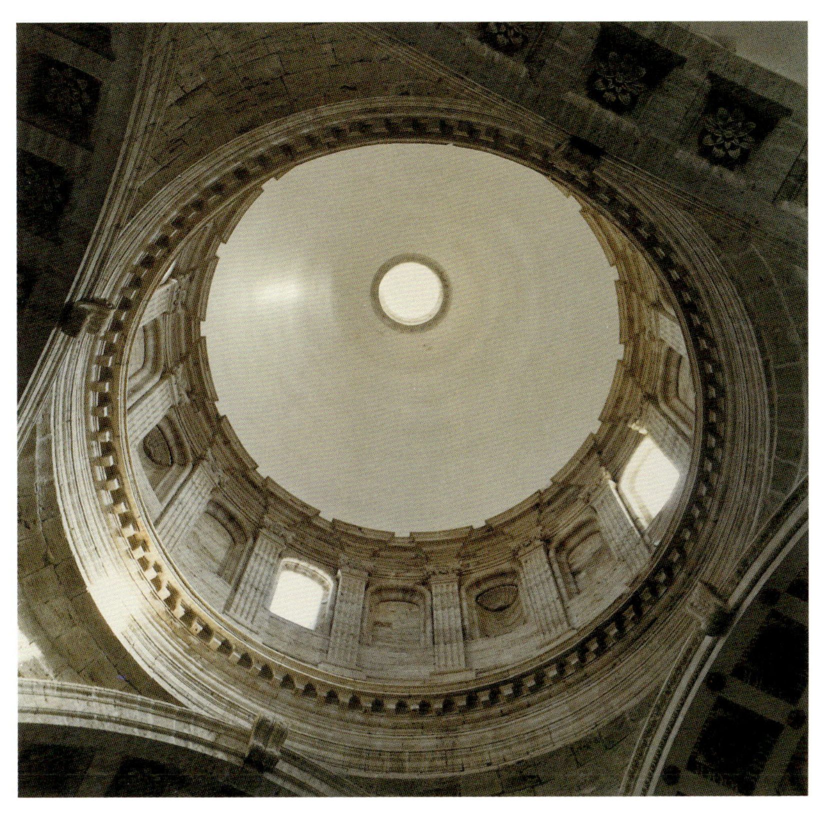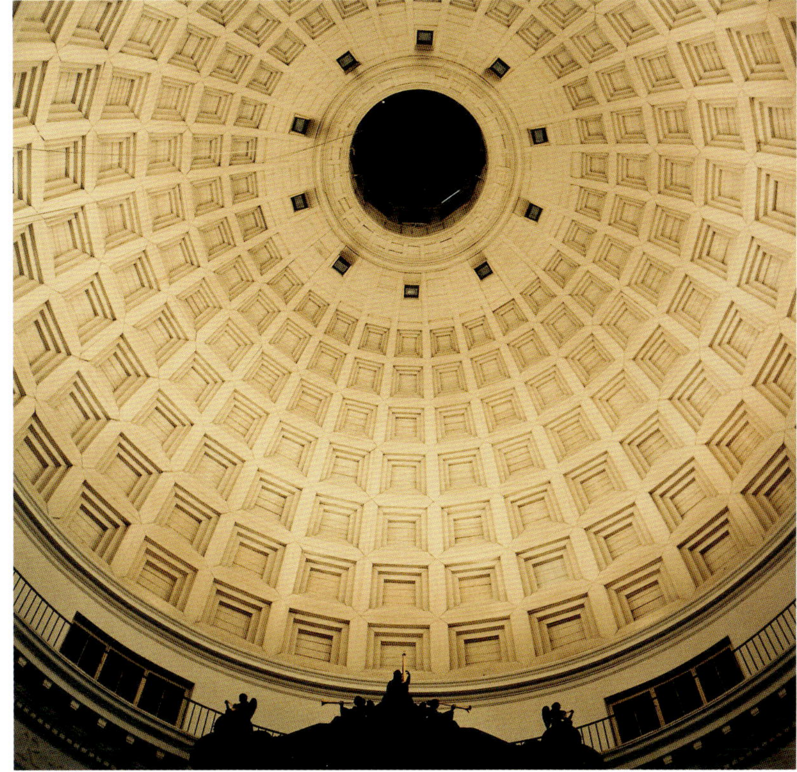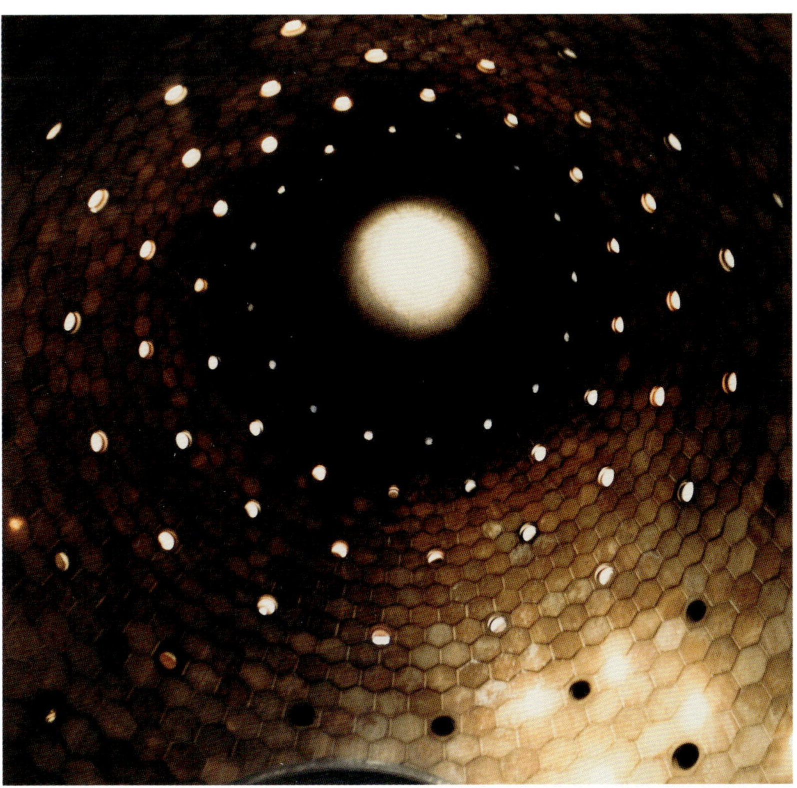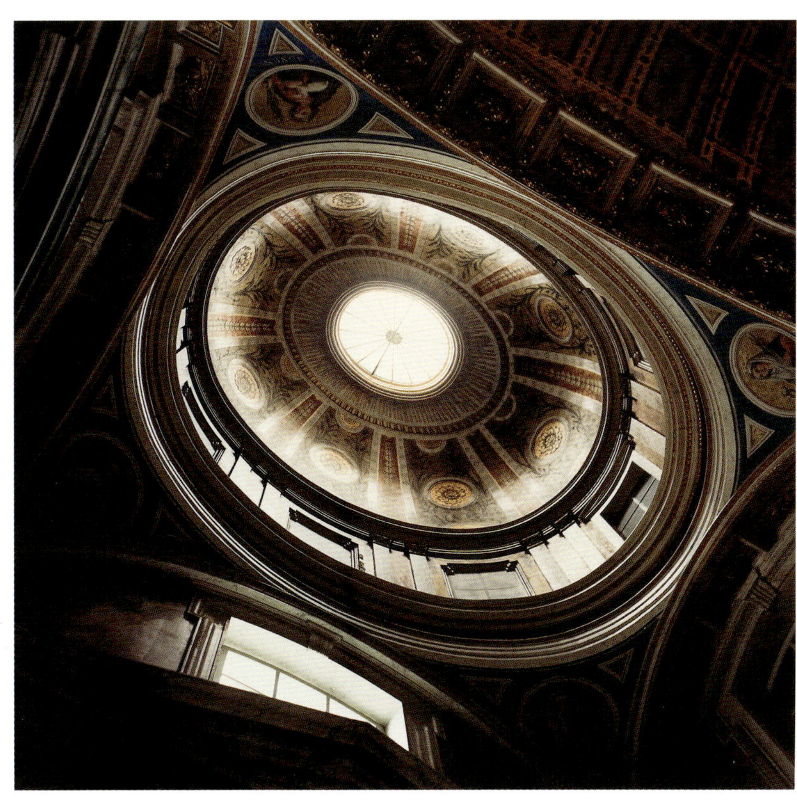

Andy Warhol
American, 1928–1987

Andy Warhol's *Endangered Species* is a series of ten screenprints portraying animals on the verge of extinction that have been named in the official Endangered Species List. The prints are based on photographs taken by noted wildlife photographers. Warhol first enlarged and screenprinted these photographs as black-and-white negatives. He then overprinted the negative images with bold colors and free drawing. The life-affirming beauty of the exotic colorations is countered by an underlying theme of death suggested by the ghost-like forms of the animals. In a related project, Warhol provided illustrations for *Vanishing Animals* (1986), a book copublished with the San Diego Zoo.

Art dealers Ronald and Freda Feldman, longtime environmental activists who shared Warhol's personal concern for the environment, commissioned the *Endangered Species* portfolio. Today the loss of habitat and biodiversity remain important topics as the impact of commercial development reaches critical thresholds.

Since the publication of Warhol's portfolio, five species remain endangered today: Bighorn Ram, Black Rhinoceros, Giant Panda, Orangutan, and Siberian Tiger. Due to successful human intervention, the African Elephant, Grevy's Zebra, and San Francisco Silverspot have been upgraded to the Threatened Species list. The Bald Eagle and Pine Barrens Tree Frog are no longer endangered or threatened.   **RHA**

Endangered Species 1983

African Elephant
Pine Barrens Tree Frog
Giant Panda
Bald Eagle
Siberian Tiger
San Francisco Silverspot
Orangutan
Grevy's Zebra
Black Rhinoceros
Bighorn Ram

Portfolio of ten screenprints on Lenox Museum Board
34 × 34 inches
Edition: 41/150
Published by Ronald Feldman Fine Arts, Inc., New York
Gift of Jim and Mary Nelson in memory of Robert Kellogg Goodwillie
2006.39–48

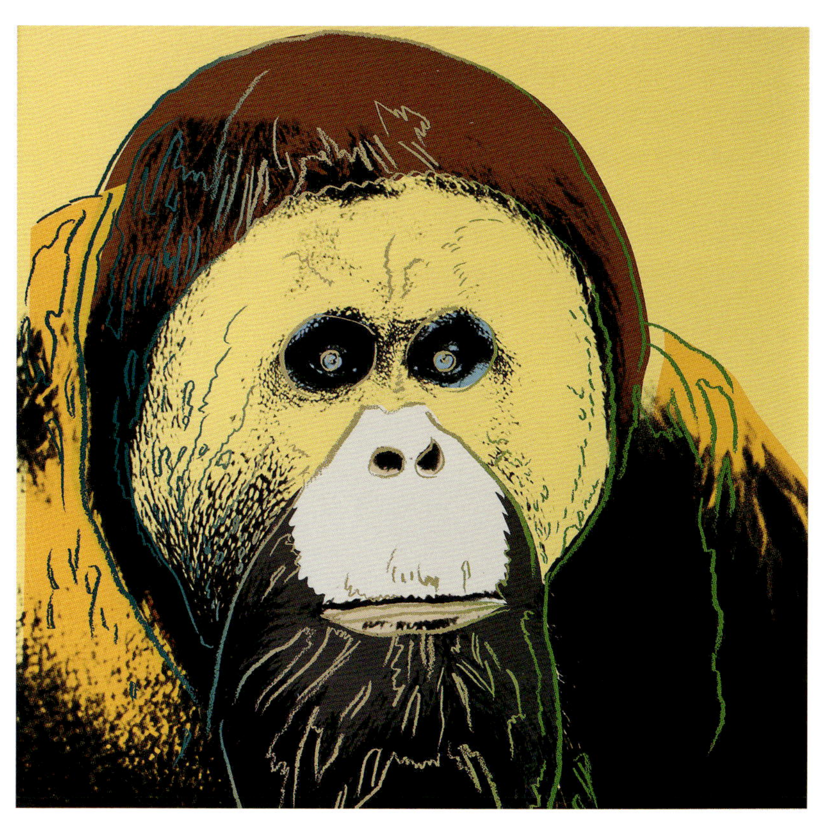
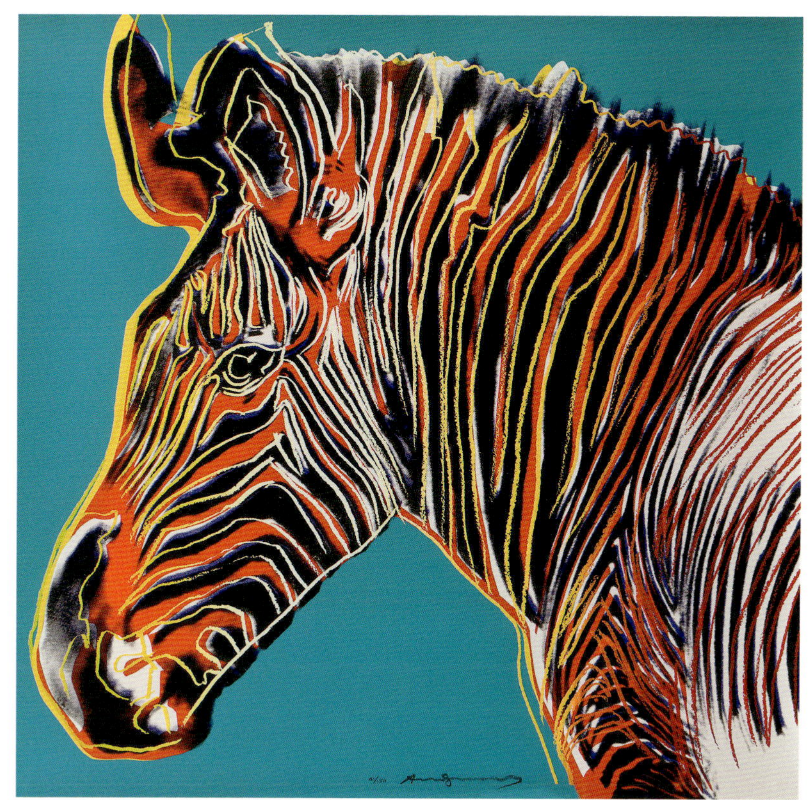
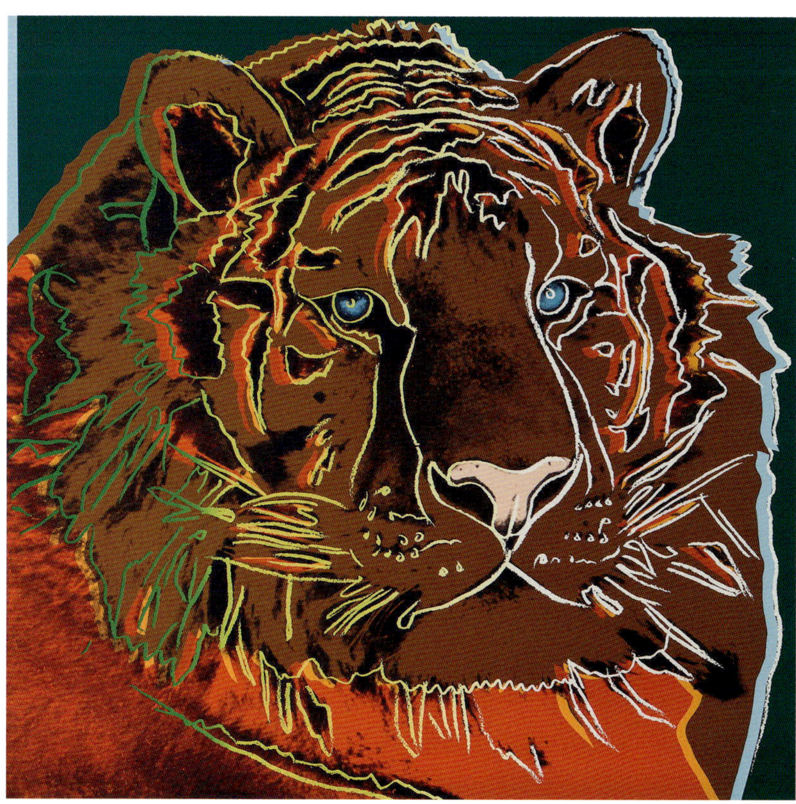
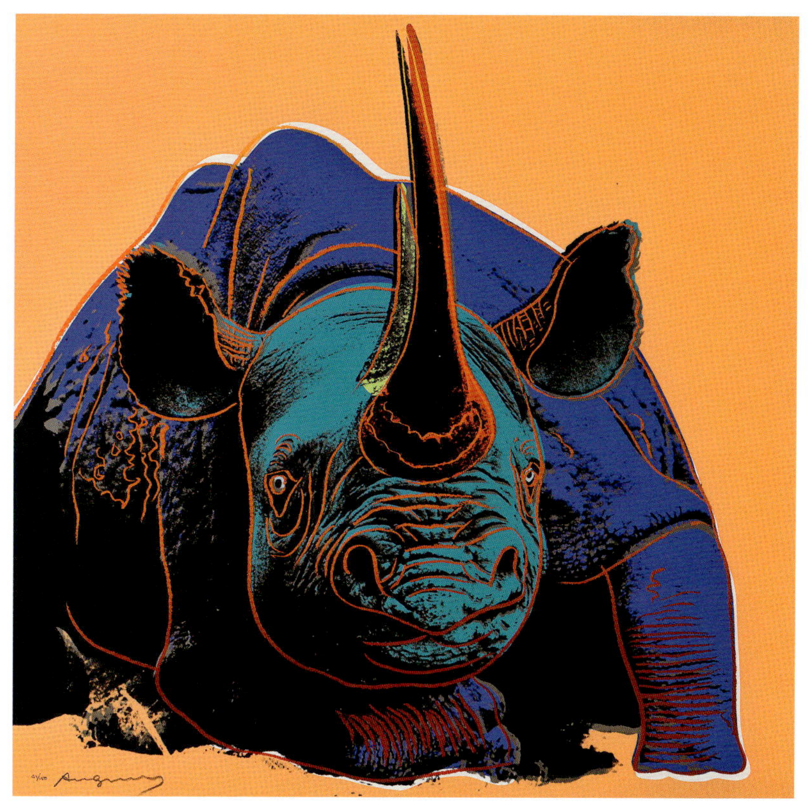

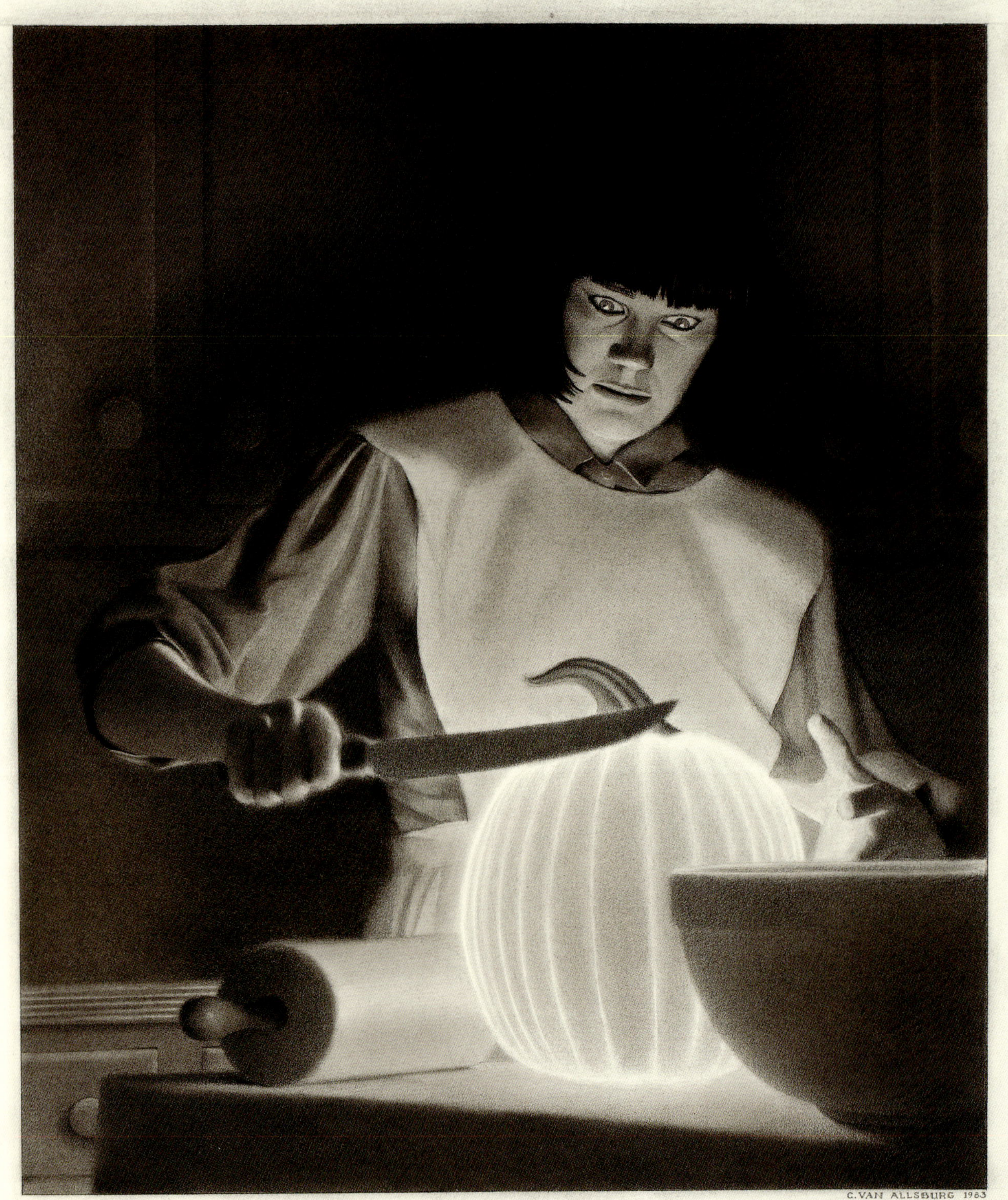

• **Chris van Allsburg**
American, b. 1949

Just Desert 1983

Charcoal on paper
24⅞ × 20⅜ inches
Museum Purchase, Women's Committee
of the Grand Rapids Art Museum
1987.3.1

Chris van Allsburg, born and raised in Grand Rapids, Michigan, is the world's foremost writer and illustrator of children's books. Author of *The Polar Express* and winner of multiple Caldecott medals, he completed this charcoal drawing for his early 1983 work, *The Mysteries of Harris Burdick*. The fourteen illustrations in the book do not present a cohesive storyline; rather, each image was paired with a phrase of text and designed to suggest a narrative independent of other images in the book.

This drawing is accompanied in the book with the caption: "*Just Desert* / 'she lowered the knife and it grew even brighter.'" In the margins of the drawing, Allsburg inscribed another provocative title and phrase in pencil: "*Mrs. Macaulay Makes a Pie—The Real Pumpkin Pie /* 'the room was filled with an eerie glow.'" Allsburg considered each drawing for *The Mysteries of Harris Burdick* a piece of a puzzle that did not reveal a story's meaning. Rather, this was left to the imagination of the reader.

In 2007, the Grand Rapids Art Museum organized a retrospective exhibition of Allsburg's drawings in conjunction with the new museum's opening. For this occasion, the artist lent drawings from each of his publications to present a complete overview of his artistic achievement.   **RHA**

Frank Stella
American, b. 1936

Over a period of twelve years—from 1985 to 1997—Frank Stella produced a major series of works linked to Herman Melville's *Moby Dick*. He made one or more works for each of the novel's 135 chapters. The completed series consists of 266 works: painted and unpainted metal reliefs, monumental sculptures, a mural, collages, and large-scale mixed-media prints that are technically and expressively a milestone in the history of the modern print.

The dominant theme of the *Moby Dick Engravings* is the wave-and-whale shape. It plays about a centered circular element, printed from a separate insert plate, and is intertwined with fragments of Chinese lattices and other wave forms. Stella has a long history in his printmaking of holding back, reworking, and reusing printing elements from previous projects. In addition to newly invented designs, the imagery of the *Moby Dick Engravings* borrows from earlier metal reliefs and print series.

The mixed-media intaglio prints of the *Moby Dick Engravings* are solemn in their black-and-white tonalities yet enlivened with subtle flushes of color. In abstract terms, Stella conveys a dramatic sense of thrashing water, harpoons, and the movements of whales. The expressive gravity of the series is caught in the title reference of *Jonah Historically Regarded* to Chapter 83 of the novel. The Old Testament story of Jonah—who flees God, falls overboard during a storm at sea only to be swallowed by a whale, but lives to tell the tale by submitting to God's will—is a central metaphor in Melville's epic narrative. **RHA**

Moby Dick Engravings 1991

A series of five mixed-media prints variously combining etching, aquatint, relief, drypoint, carborundum, and engraving (from assembled metal plates) printed on TGL handmade paper

Fossil Whale, 74¾ × 54 inches
Museum Purchase
Karl and Patricia Betz
2009.7

Stubb, 73¾ × 53½ inches
Museum Purchase
2009.8

The Cabin, 74¾ × 52½ inches
Museum Purchase
2009.9

Funeral, 78¼ × 59½ inches
Gift of the Artist
2009.12

Jonah Historically Regarded, 74 × 54½ inches
Gift of the Artist in honor of Rick Axsom
2009.23

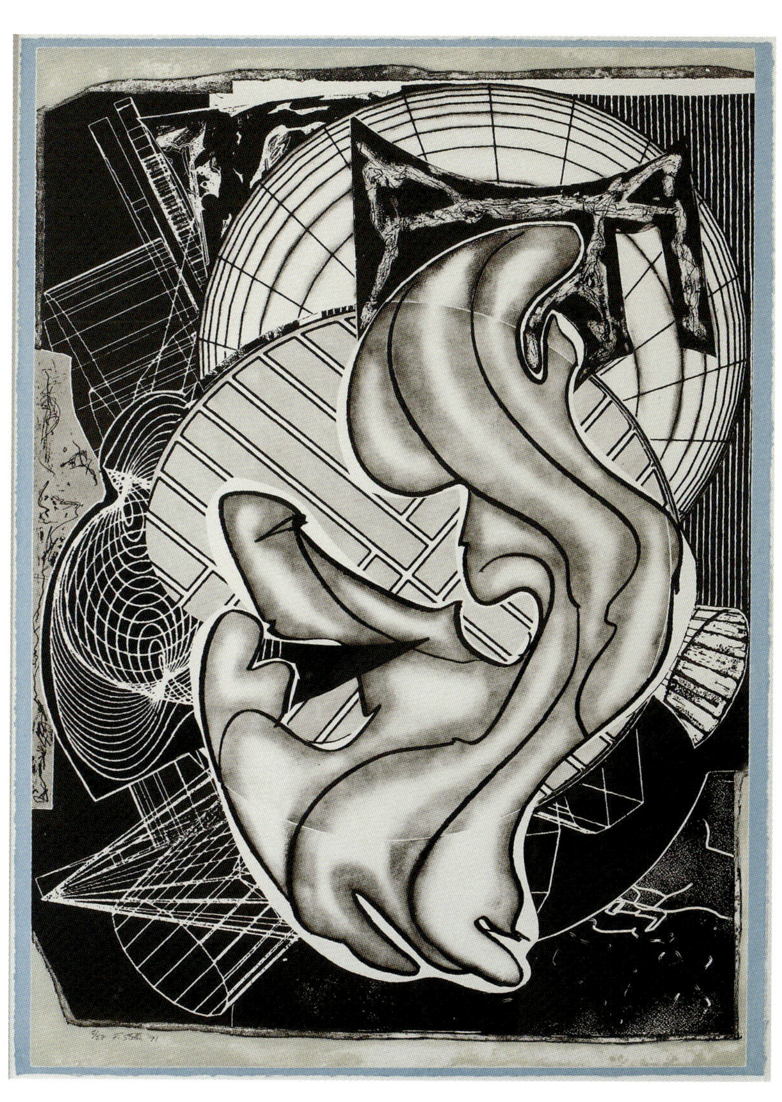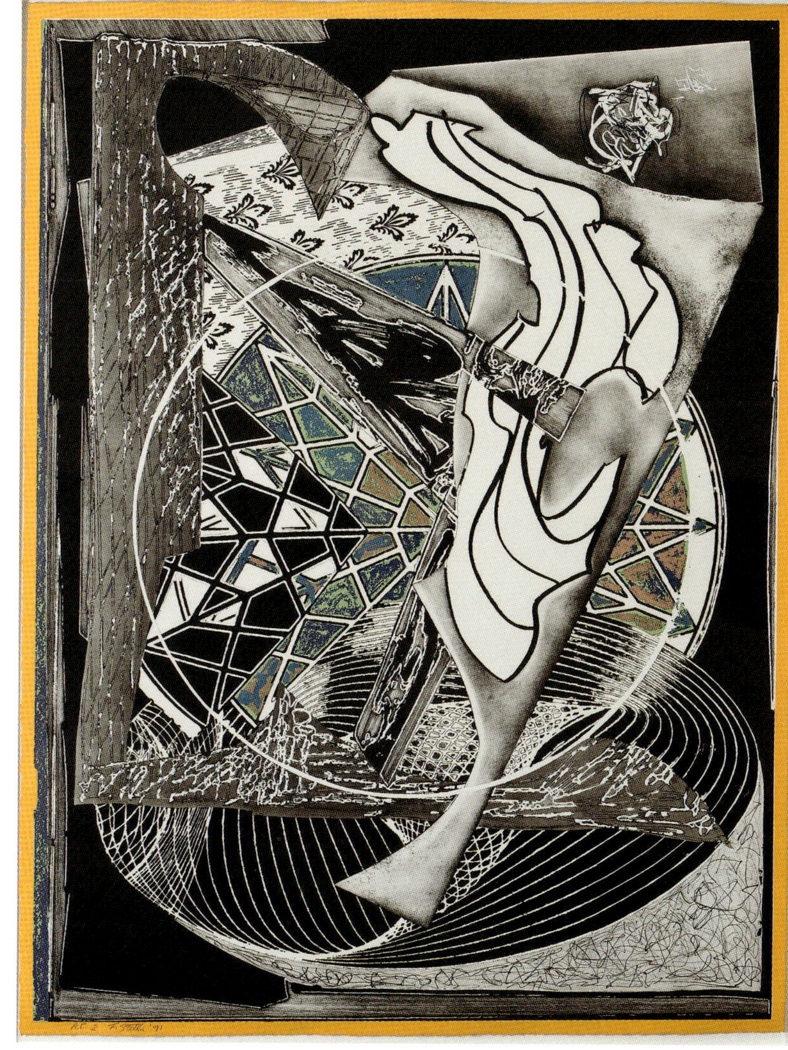

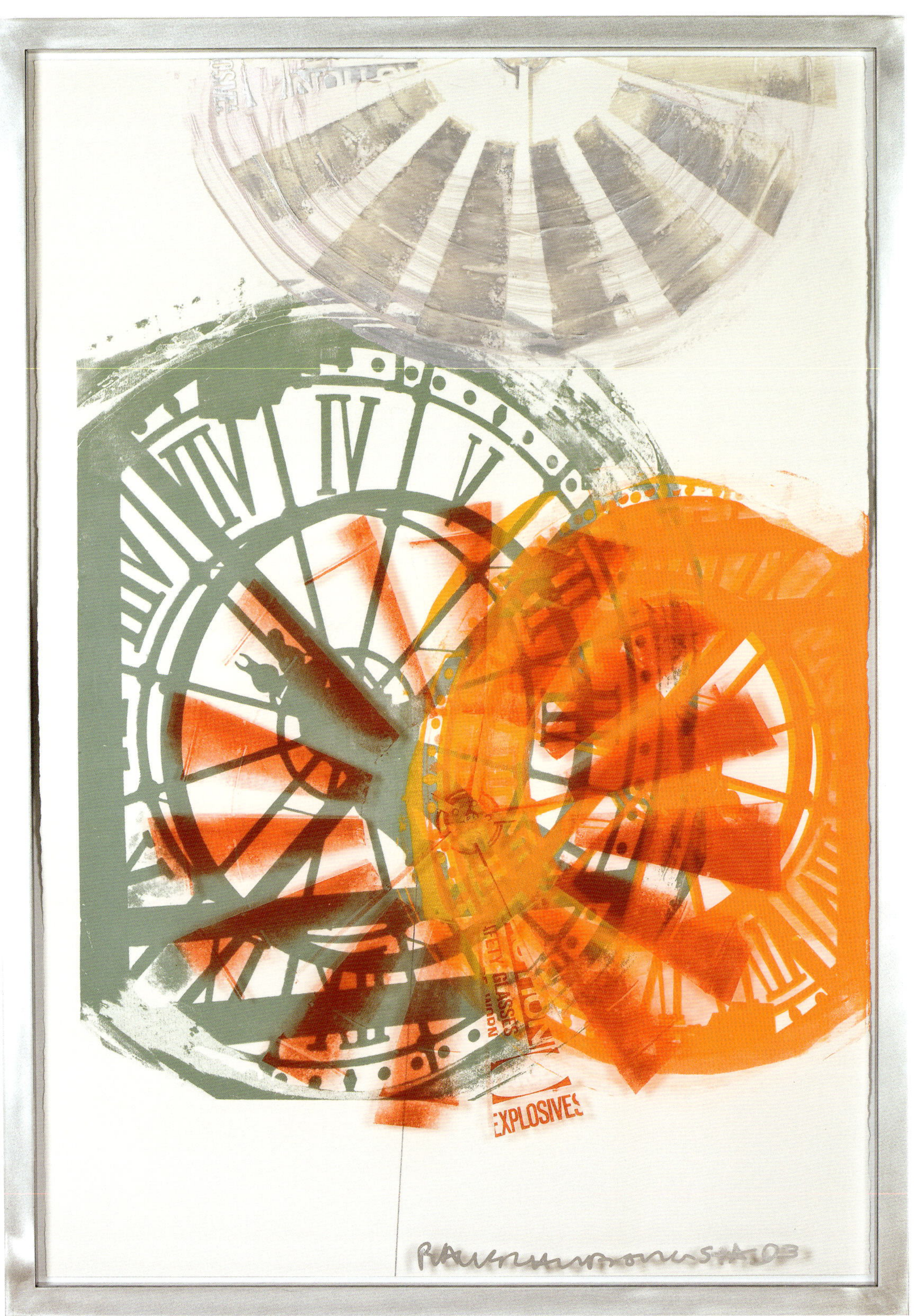
EXPLOSIVES
Rauschenberg

 # Robert Rauschenberg

American, 1925–2008

Sterling/Whirl 1993

Acrylic screenprint, acrylic hand
painting, fire wax and silver pigment
dust on paper with acrylic screenprint
on Lexan in aluminum frame
63½ × 44 inches
One of two printer's proofs
Museum Purchase, Peter M. Wege
2008.18

Robert Rauschenberg was a devoted environmentalist throughout his life. In 1970 he became involved in the first Earth Day environmental teach-in and produced the first Earth Day poster to benefit the American Environment Foundation. At this time, he established his studio and permanent residence in Captiva, Florida, on land that he maintained as a natural habitat and animal preserve.

In 1992–93, Rauschenberg conceived his *Eco-Echo* series in collaboration with Saff Tech Arts in Oxford, Maryland. Working with Donald Saff, innovative director of technical production, Rauschenberg created nine windmill-like structures, each seven feet tall with images silkscreened on the blades. In an interactive exchange, the blades spin when a viewer approaches. The notion of sustainable energy from windmills coincided with Rauschenberg's longtime interest in motion in art. *Sterling/Whirl* was produced immediately following the Eco-Echo series and uses the image of a moving clock face and the spinning windmill to suggest the urgent need for wind-powered technology.   RHA

Jasper Johns
American, b. 1930

A painter who makes prints, Jasper Johns also takes his place along-side Rembrandt van Rijn and Pablo Picasso as one of the great print-makers in the history of western art. Johns assumes such company because of the beauty of his prints, which derives from unmatched craftsmanship, technical innovation, and a richness of imagery.

In three separately printed panels, *Untitled* presents a set of motifs related to making art. In triptych form—lending a reverential tone to the work—stenciled names of the primary colors appear: red, yellow, and blue. Notational arrows point to the lower edge of the print. Their downward emphasis is countered by the upward thrust of the imprinted arm and hand of the artist himself. The sweeping hand in the right panel seems to generate the basic form of a circle—including by suggestion the larger and smaller circles that dominate the work.

Johns' interest in the creative act and issues of meaning generated by shifts of form, color, scale, and medium are evident in the making of *Untitled*. The etched copperplates Johns used to create *Untitled* had been used intermittently over a period of nearly two decades to make six separate prints. In contrast to the earlier prints, which are whimsical, mysterious, or tragic in tone, *Untitled* is unbridled in its freshness, exuberant color, and monumental scale.   RHA

Untitled 1998
Intaglio on hand-torn Hahnemuhle paper
41¾ × 81 inches
Edition: 10/44
Published by Universal Limited Art Editions,
Bay Shore, New York
Museum Purchase
James and Mary Nelson and Peter M. Wege
2010.1

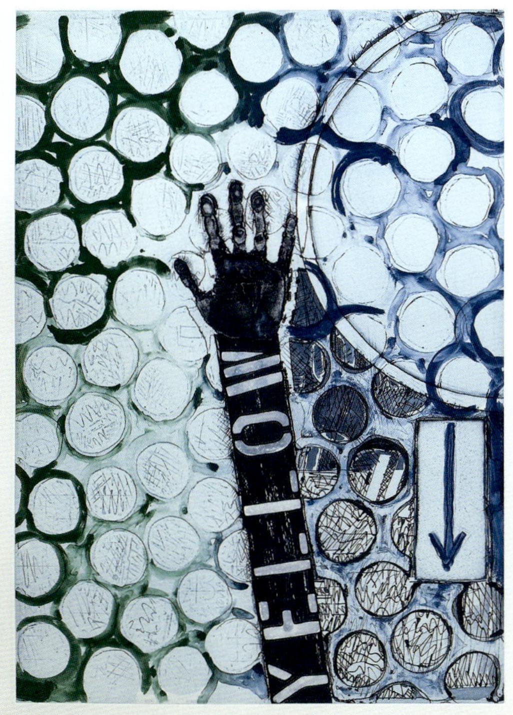
YELLOW
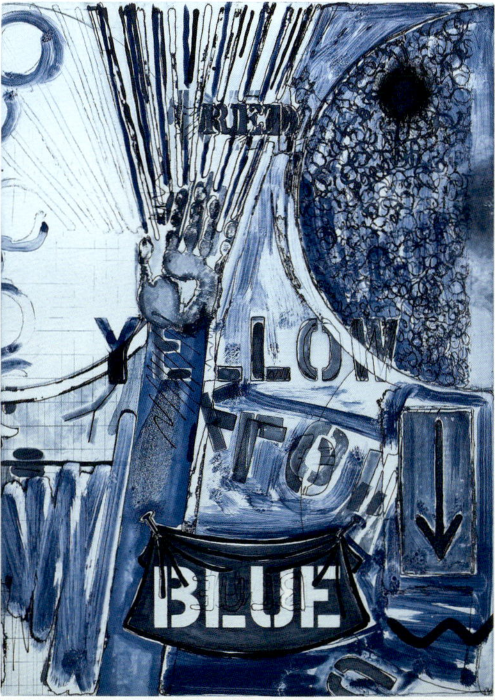
RED
YELLOW
BLUE
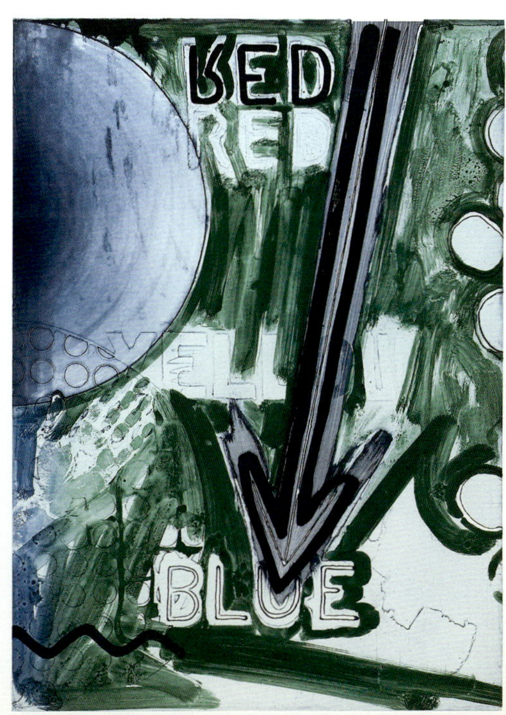
RED
BLUE

. **Jennifer Bartlett**
American, b. 1941

To create *Small House*, Jennifer Bartlett returned to a format and subject that had distinguished her early work. In 1968, she began painting on sixteen-gauge steel plates coated with white enamel and overlaid with a light gray quarter-inch grid. At this time she also introduced the elemental motifs of house, tree, mountain, and ocean that became signature references in her art.

The assembling of separate steel plates in grid fashion was a logical outgrowth of her drawings on graph paper. Composed of myriad dots of six unmixed colors of enamel paints, each dot placed within the grid, paintings in this format were conceived as analytic systems of colors. Like modern-day versions of Georges Seurat's pointillist paintings, they were governed by a system for controlling form and releasing the expressive complexities of color and light.

In *Small House*, the artist places a small schematic image of a house—a square abutted to a triangle—at the center of eighty-one enameled steel plates. Dwarfed by a dynamic landscape of sky blues and earth tones, its diminutive size lends it a gentle poignancy. And yet, the little house asserts itself by its red color and placement at the center of the composition. *Small House* is a shimmering transformation of the world observed and manipulated by the artist.   RHA

Small House 1998–1999
Enamel over silkscreen grid on baked enamel steel plates
116 × 116 inches
Museum Purchase
Peter M. Wege and Jim and Mary Nelson
2007.2

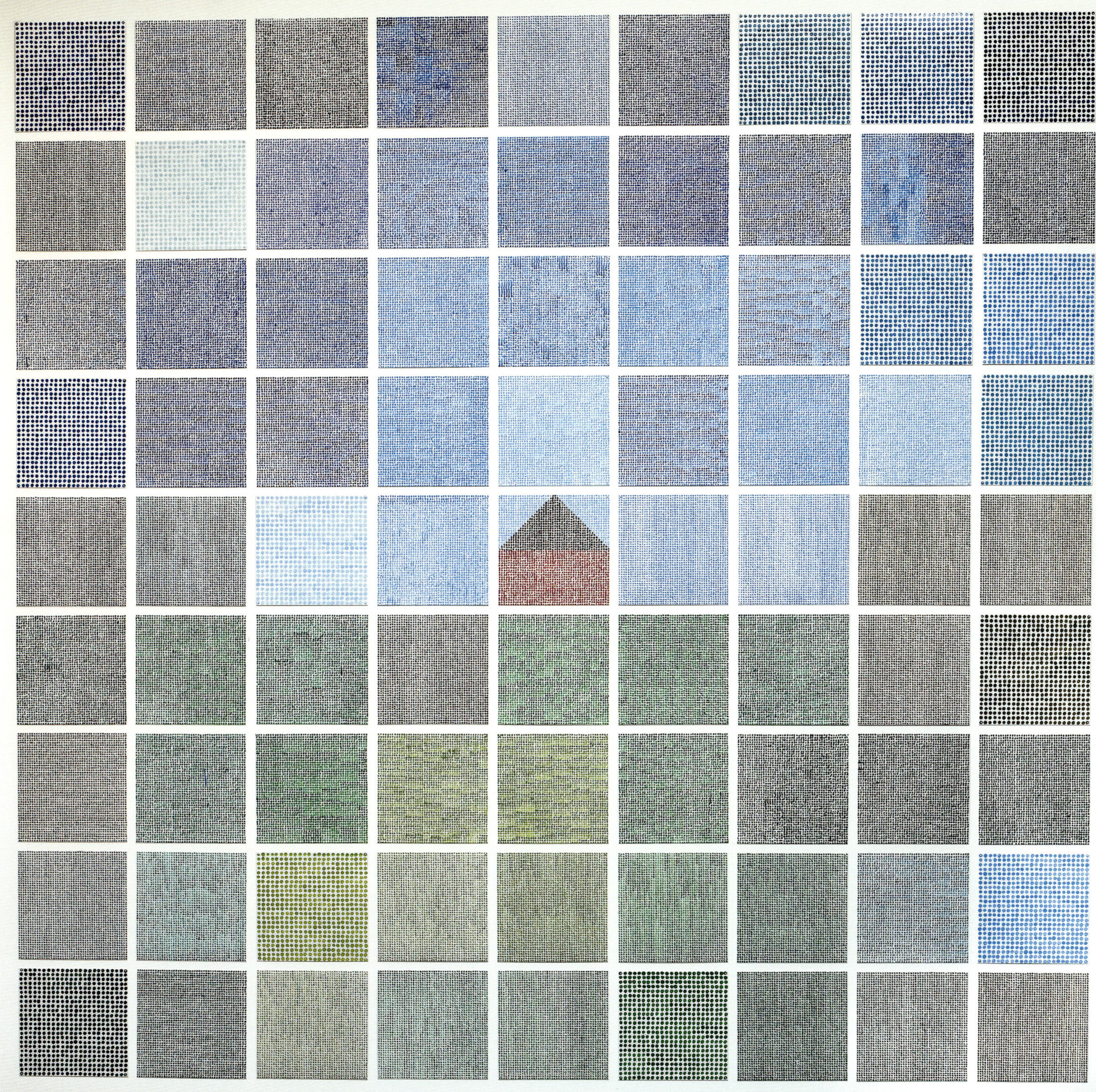

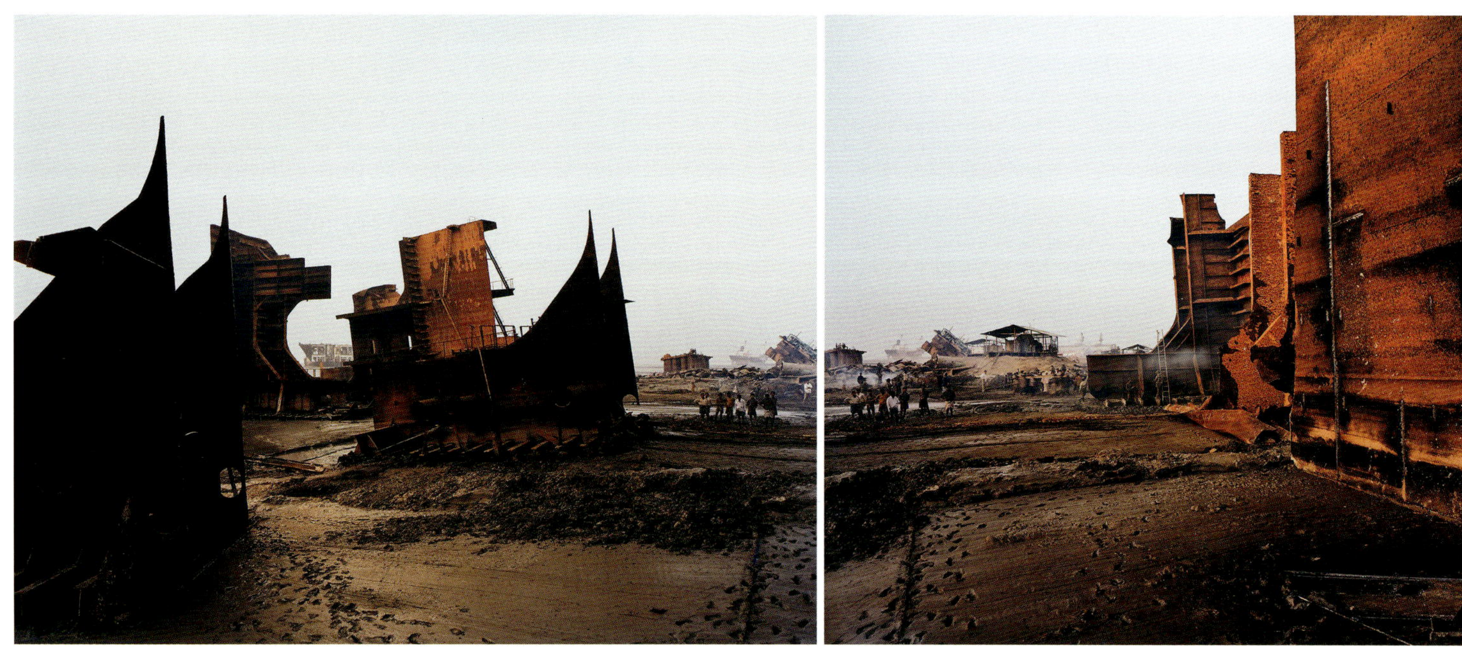

. **Edward Burtynsky**
Canadian, b. 1955

*Shipbreaking #9
(Chittagong, Bangladesh)*

2000
Diptych: dye-coupler prints
52 × 124 inches
Museum Purchase, Jack H. Miller
2004.23a–b

Edward Burtynsky, a major figure in contemporary Canadian photography, is known for his depictions of global industrial landscapes. Nature transformed through industry is the major theme in his work. Combining the raw elements of mining, quarrying, manufacturing, shipping, oil production and recycling, he creates unexpected visions that find beauty and humanity in the most unlikely places.

Shipbreaking #9 presents a primordial landscape that is not easily recognizable. A closer observation reveals a small local crew arduously dismantling the hull of a massive rusted ship. After the devastating Exxon Valdez oil spill off Alaska in 1989, insurance companies refused to cover single-hulled tankers and freighters; these ships were subsequently decommissioned. Many of them were taken to Bangladesh, where they were torn down by manual labor to be recycled into scrap metal and parts. This demolition process transformed the natural seashore into an unearthly scene—a ship graveyard. The joined photographs of *Shipbreaking*—with their large scale, enigmatic subject, and unusual grays and rust colors— assert a strong physical presence. Burtynsky asks the viewer to consider an intersection of nature and industry that results in a new reality—both fascinating and disturbing.   **RHA**

In the wake of the September 11, 2001, attack on the New York World Trade Center, and the subsequent United States invasions of Iraq and Afghanistan, Joan Snyder, a painter of long-held feminist convictions, created this work evoking the suffering of women in times of war. Across a field of broad patches of pale blues and acid yellows, from which paint trickles down in streams of tears, the title words in Latin are repeated. Floral bouquets are evenly strewn over it, suggesting the unmarked graves of war. Snyder's compassion for the suffering of wartime survivors sets the tone for this elegiac work. *Antiquarum Lacrimae* conveys an acquaintance with grief and a celebration of love through beauty of texture and color.

In 2007 Snyder was awarded the John D. and Catherine T. MacArthur Fellowship. Known as the "Genius Award," it recognizes individuals not on the basis of past achievement, but for the promise of continued and enhanced creative work. One of the largest financial grants awarded annually, it is an investment in a person's originality, insight, and potential.   RHA

Antiquarum Lacrimae (The Tears of Ancient Women) 2004
Acrylic and dried flowers on linen
78 × 120 inches
Museum Purchase by exchange with artist
2007.13

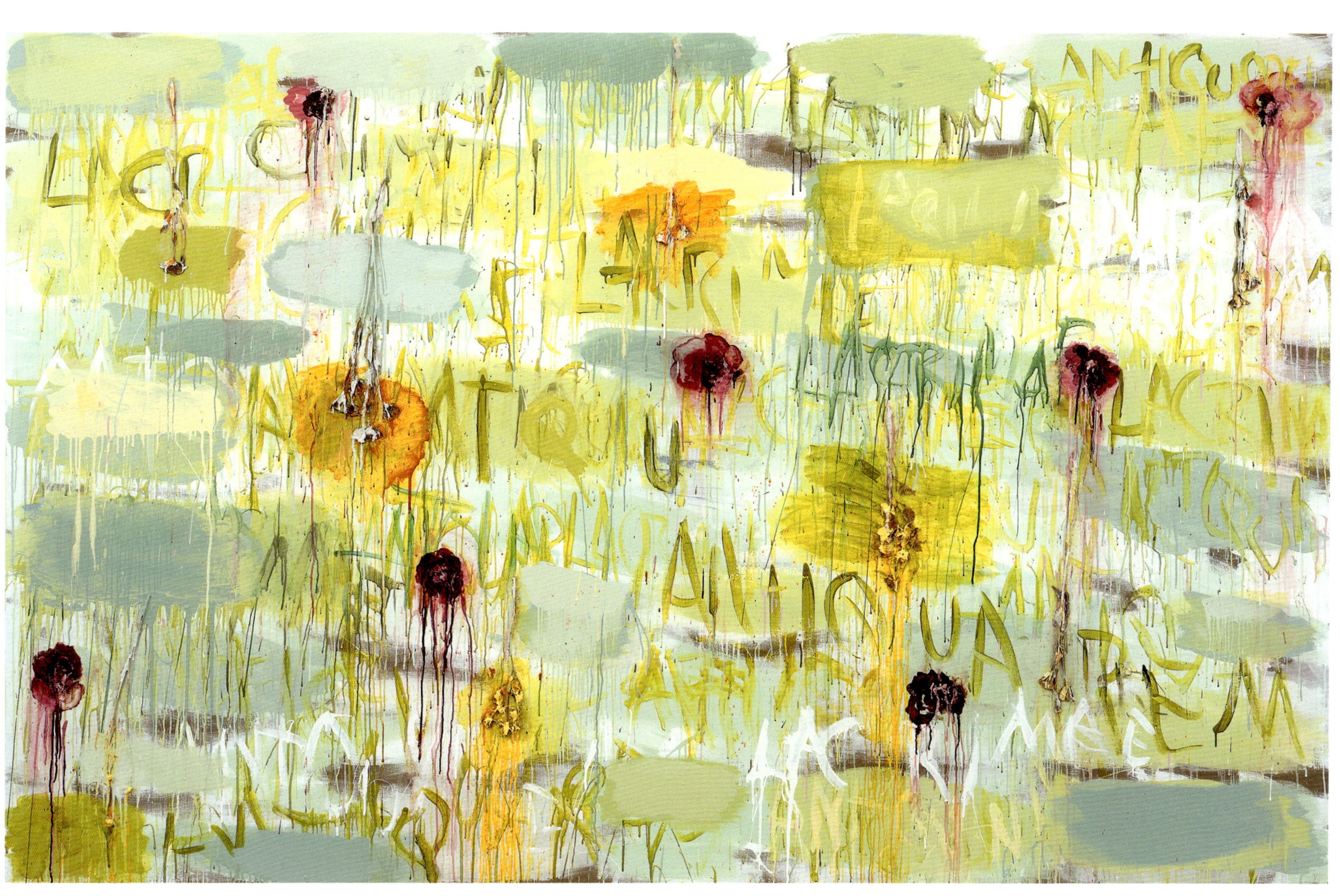

. **Stephen Hannock**
American, b. 1951

Stephen Hannock evokes the pictorial tradition of nineteenth-century American landscape painting in his contemporary mixed-media works. This earlier tradition, initiated by the Hudson River School artists, sought to celebrate American identity in broad expanses of scenic land infused with light. Admiring works by Thomas Cole, Frederic Edwin Church, Albert Bierstadt, and the American Luminists, Hannock has created his own grand American landscapes with a unique painting technique that builds up layers of glazing over pigment and collage. He embeds written texts into the landscape in the manner of a mapmaker's topographical notes, although the phrases are often personal references and reveries.

Luminous Afternoon in Western Michigan is an aerial view of a serene landscape that extends to the rising sand dunes of Lake Michigan in the far distance. Below are open fields demarcated by narrow stands of trees, remnants of once thickly forested woodlands. As the sun begins its slow descent to the western horizon, mists lift from the valley floor. The light at this time of day warms all of nature's colors. Hannock married Bridget Watkins of Grand Rapids in 2000. Bridget died of a brain tumor in 2004 at the age of forty-three. The artist created *Luminous Afternoon in Western Michigan* in her honor.   **RHA**

Luminous Afternoon in Western Michigan: For Bridget 2007
Polished mixed media on canvas
64½ × 96¼ inches
Gift of the Artist
2007.26

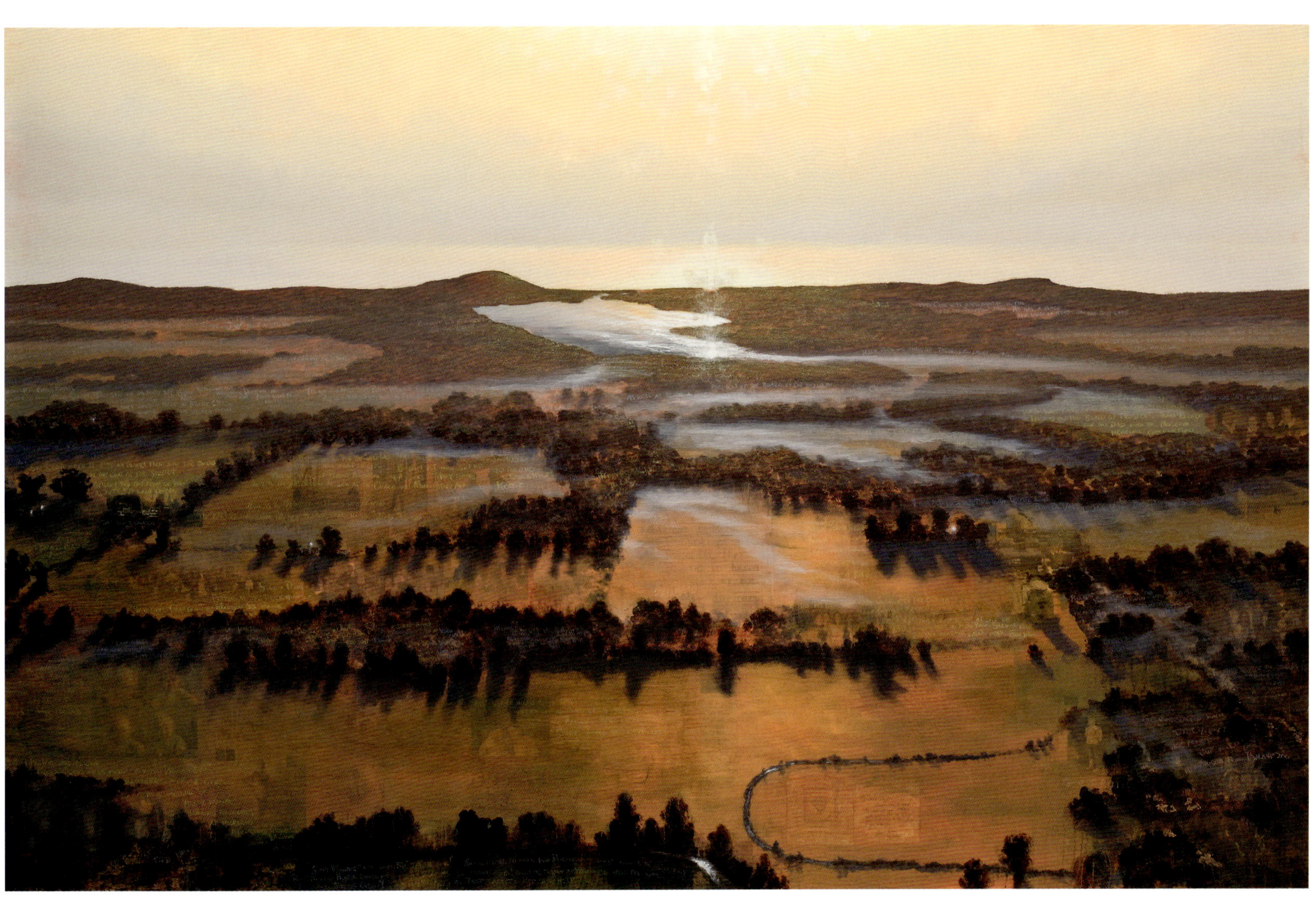

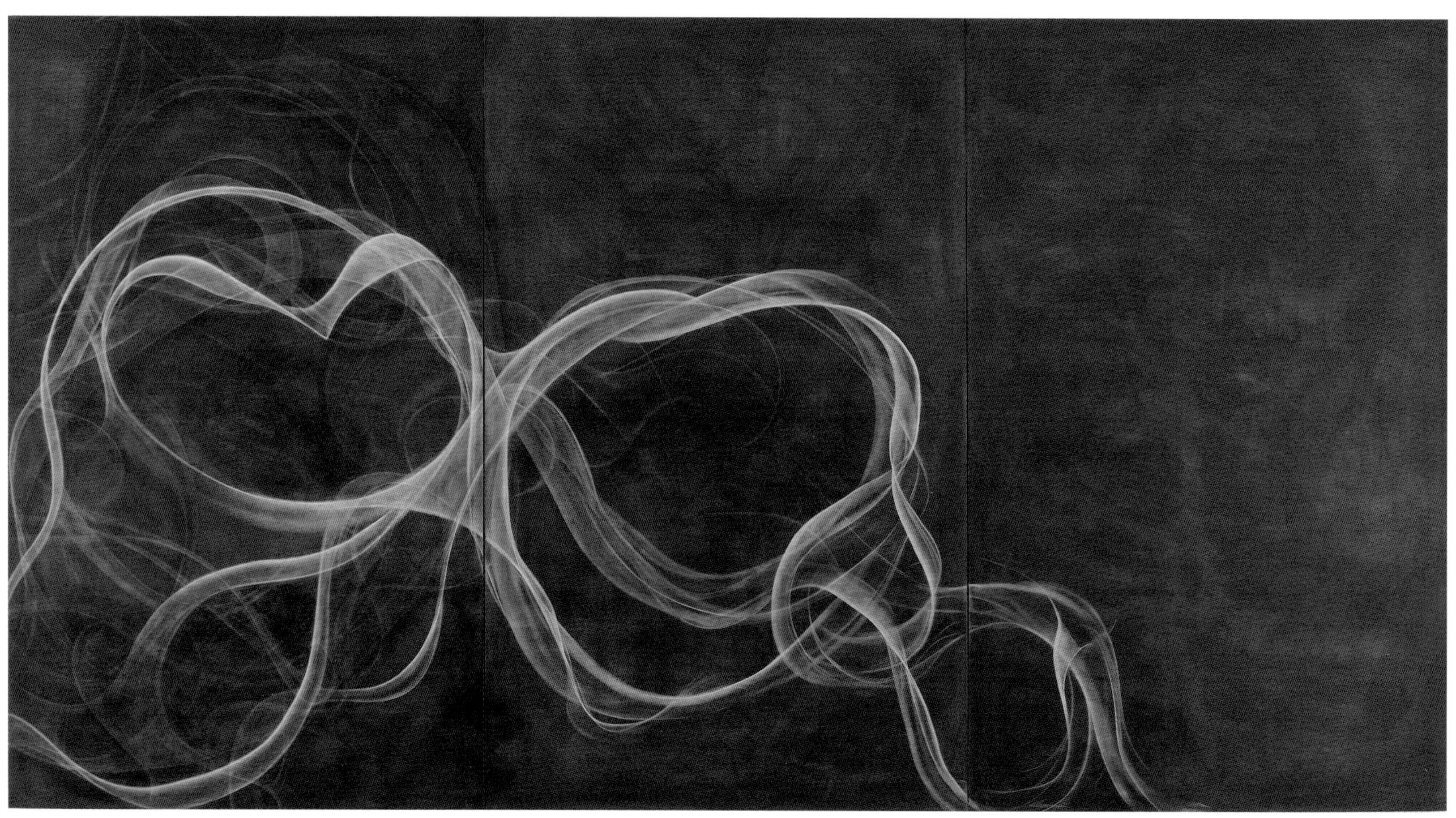

Mark Sheinkman

American, b. 1963

Concourse 2007

Oil, alkyd, and graphite on linen
96 × 174½ inches
Museum Purchase
2008.19

The work of Mark Sheinkman defines itself within the twentieth-century American tradition of linear abstraction. Like Jackson Pollock, Sheinkman explores the process of drawing in space. Unlike Pollock, he employs a process of elimination based on erasing. In both his prints and his paintings, he creates lines by removing a dark overlay to reveal a lighter ground.

Concourse was constructed by initially applying a layer of oil mixed with alkyd to a linen surface. Once a smooth white layer was built up, Sheinkman applied a powdered graphite to the ground with brushes and rags. He then began to erase the graphite, creating a linear structure that seems to emerge mysteriously from depth. The painting is both delicately ephemeral and richly layered.

The result is a lyrical play of line against a greater expanse of void. The lines undulate and glow in contrast to the darkly worked surface areas of the painting. The animated line suggests a scarf floating in space, a dissolving tendril of smoke, or an undulating chalk gesture on a blackboard bearing many layers of erased messages. *Concourse* and other related paintings are named after streets in the neighborhood surrounding his studio in South Bronx, New York.   RHA

. **Ellsworth Kelly**
American, b. 1923

A master of Modernist abstraction, Ellsworth Kelly is also one of the great draftsmen of our time who has produced a significant body of representational drawings. Kelly's "plant lithographs"—a generic term embracing a great variety of flora—are simple line drawings of fruits, flowers, and plants. Kelly's art has always been grounded in nature. His lyrical plant drawings—created with pencil, ink, or lithographic crayon—were initially, in the artist's words, "a bridge to my abstract work in painting and sculpture." In their simplicity of line and shape, they reveal the source of Kelly's art in his observations of the world around him. They provide a critical link to the character of his abstraction.

Over a period of four decades, Kelly has created seventy-two plant lithographs, which fall into five major series and a miscellany of eight individual prints. When examined as a whole, they show a remarkable range of style and expression within the genre of contour drawing. For Kelly, the prints formalize the spontaneity associated with the pencil and ink drawings, in part through the protocols of collaboration and technology necessary for the creation of a print. For the plant lithographs, Kelly draws his subject with crayon on special decal paper or acetate. The finished drawing is then transferred to an aluminum plate. Kelly freely renders each drawing in a matter of minutes with a minimal number of strokes, remarkably never taking his eyes away from the motif until the drawing is complete.

The Grand Rapids Art Museum is the only public institution that holds a complete set of Kelly's seventy-two plant lithographs. **RHA**

The Plant Lithographs 1964–2005

72 lithographs on a variety of papers
Various dimensions
Published at Maeght Editeur, Paris; Gemini G.E.L.,
Los Angeles; Tyler Graphics, Ltd., Mt. Kisco, New York
Museum Purchase and gift of the artist
2004.24–53

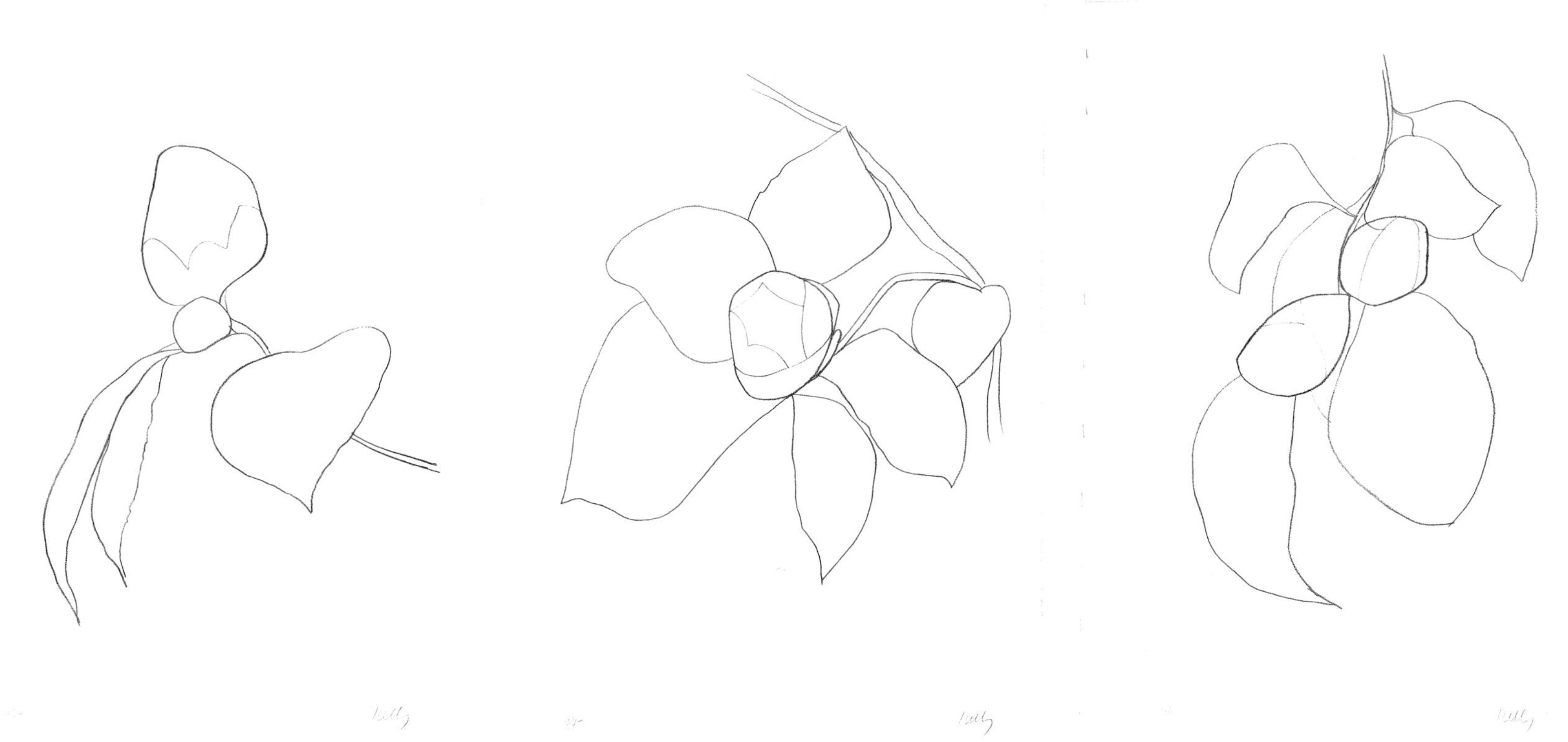
Kelly
Kelly
Kelly

Ellsworth Kelly has been universally acknowledged for the seminal contributions made by his paintings and sculptures that celebrate emphatic shape and pure color. In 1968, he began to experiment with shaped canvases that extended the traditional rectilinear format of western painting. One of the shaped canvases of that year was the bisected parallelogram or "angled banner" as nicknamed by the artist. Kelly felt that this format engaged the eye because the shapes and colors created a dynamic equilibrium. Producing at the time three paintings and one lithograph that utilized this shape, Kelly returned to it nearly four decades later to create the monumental *Blue White*—his fourth and final variation on the "angled banner" theme. This work was commissioned by the Grand Rapids Art Museum for the opening of the new museum in 2007.

Kelly orchestrates the shapes and colors in *Blue White* so that they are held in suspension. He adjusts the blue and white in tone and saturation so that neither dominates the other. The colors and angle of the conjoined shapes allow the work to float, without being bottom- or top-heavy. Any movement suggested by the forward thrust of the work to the right is held in check by the angle of the "banner." Although bisected into two separate color panels, *Blue White* is also read as a single shape. The declarative shape of its basic but deceptive geometry creates a dynamic equilibrium that engages the eye.

The artist's exacting placement of *Blue White* on the wall of the museum plays in concert with the wall's horizontal and vertical extension. Kelly has always felt that the walls on which his works are placed are critical to their aesthetic success. As an assertive form that glides like a heeling sailboat through water, *Blue White* buoyantly evokes the colors and movements of nature.   **RHA**

Blue White 2006
Two joined painted aluminum panels
25 × 8 feet
Commissioned by the Grand Rapids
Art Museum
The Meijer Foundation, Richard and
Helen DeVos, and Daniel and Pamella
DeVos
2007.17

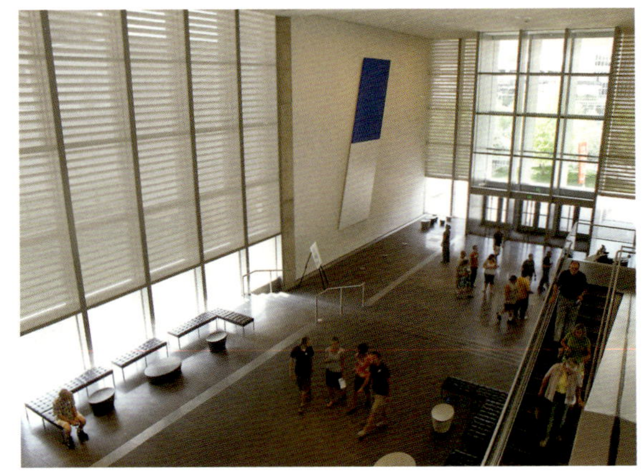

This publication was made possible through generous support from the Wege Foundation.

Library of Congress Cataloging-in-Publication Data
Grand Rapids Art Museum.
     100 years, 100 works of art : introduction to the collection
  of the Grand Rapids Art Museum / {author, Richard H. Axsom}.
        p. cm.
     ISBN 978-0-615-39126-7
     1. Grand Rapids Art Museum—Catalogs. 2. Art—Michigan—Grand Rapids—Catalogs.
  I. Axsom, Richard H., 1943–. II. Title. III. Title: One hundred years, one hundred works of
  art : introduction to the collection of the Grand Rapids Art Museum.
  N570.895.A52 2010
  708.174'56—dc22   2010036283

Published by the Grand Rapids Art Museum
101 Monroe Center
Grand Rapids, MI 49503
www.artmuseumgr.org

Produced by Marquand Books, Inc., Seattle
www.marquand.com

Details:
Frontispiece: Mark Sheinkman, *Concourse,* 2007 (see p. 206)
Page 4: Alexander Calder, *Red: Rudder in the Air,* 1975 (see p. 181)
Page 6: Charles Eames and Ray Eames, *LCW (Low Chair Wood)*, 1945–1946 (see p. 149)

Edited by Celeste M. Adams
Proofread by Carrie Wicks
Designed by Jeff Wincapaw
Photography by Dirk Bakker
Typeset by Marissa Meyer
Color management by iocolor, Seattle
Printed and bound in China by Artron Color Printing Co., Ltd.